# Garfield world-wide

BY: JIM DAVIS

BALLANTINE BOOKS · NEW YORK

Copyright © 1988 by United Feature Syndicate, Inc.
Garfield Comic Strips: © 1986, 1987 by United Feature Syndicate, Inc.

All rights reserved under International and Pan-American Copyright Conventions. Published in the United States by Ballantine Books, a division of Random House, Inc., New York, and simultaneously in Canada by Random House of Canada Limited, Toronto.

Library of Congress Catalog Card Number: 87-91547

ISBN: 0-345-35158-4

Manufactured in the United States of America

First Edition: March 1988

20    19    18    17    16    15

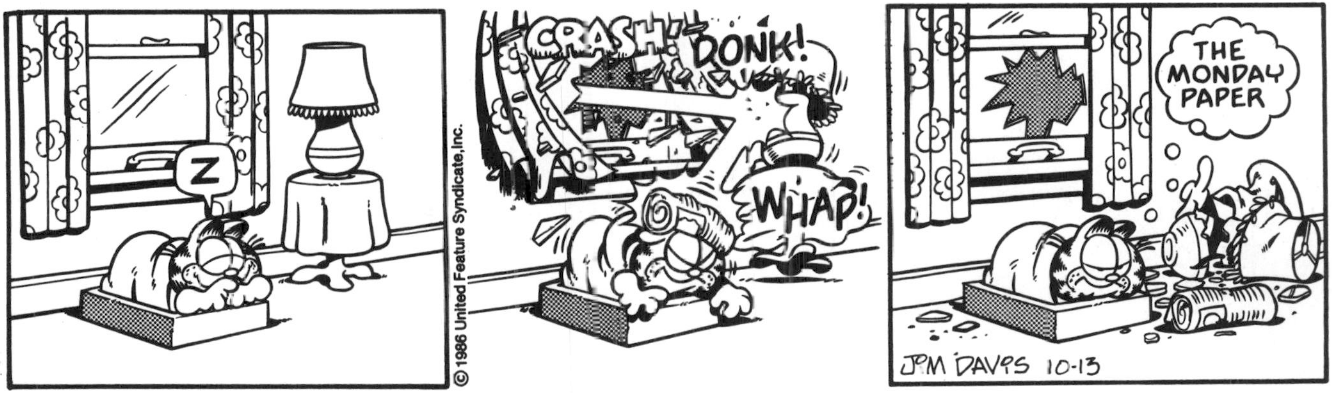
Z
CRASH!
DONK!
WHAP!
THE MONDAY PAPER
© 1986 United Feature Syndicate, Inc.
JIM DAVIS 10-13

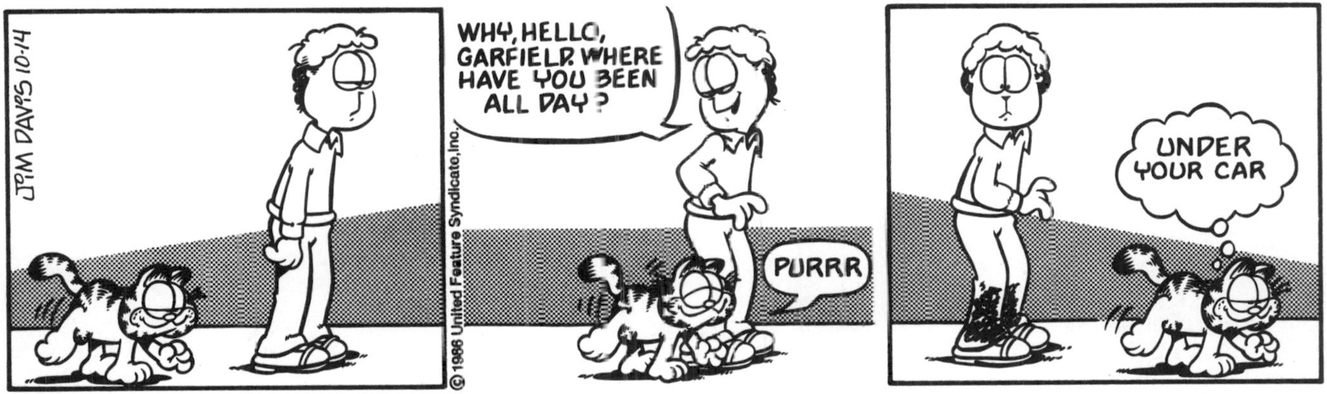
JIM DAVIS 10-14
WHY, HELLO, GARFIELD. WHERE HAVE YOU BEEN ALL DAY?
PURRR
UNDER YOUR CAR
© 1986 United Feature Syndicate, Inc.

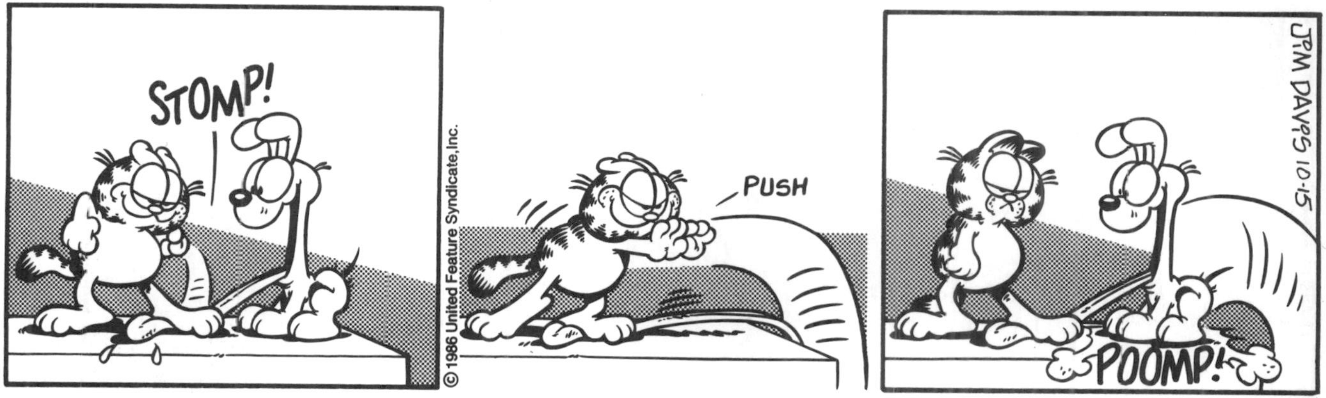
STOMP!
PUSH
POOMP!
JIM DAVIS 10-15


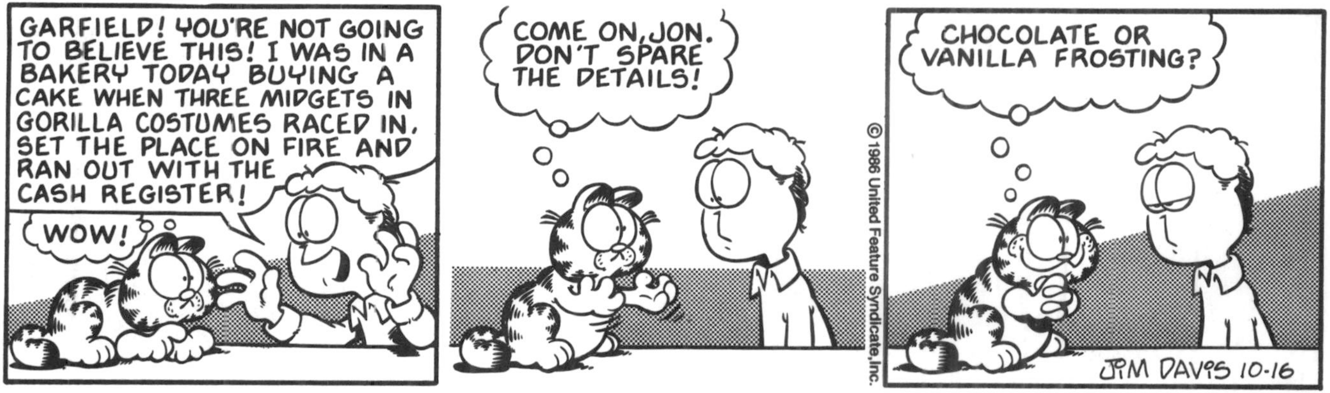
GARFIELD! YOU'RE NOT GOING TO BELIEVE THIS! I WAS IN A BAKERY TODAY BUYING A CAKE WHEN THREE MIDGETS IN GORILLA COSTUMES RACED IN, SET THE PLACE ON FIRE AND RAN OUT WITH THE CASH REGISTER!
WOW!
COME ON, JON. DON'T SPARE THE DETAILS!
CHOCOLATE OR VANILLA FROSTING?
JIM DAVIS 10-16

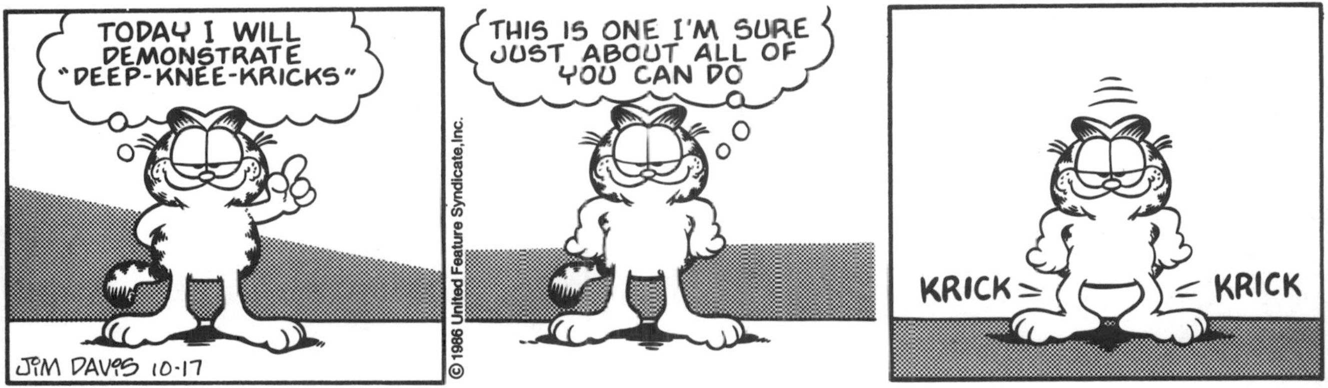
TODAY I WILL DEMONSTRATE "DEEP-KNEE-KRICKS"
JIM DAVIS 10-17
© 1986 United Feature Syndicate, Inc.
THIS IS ONE I'M SURE JUST ABOUT ALL OF YOU CAN DO
KRICK
KRICK

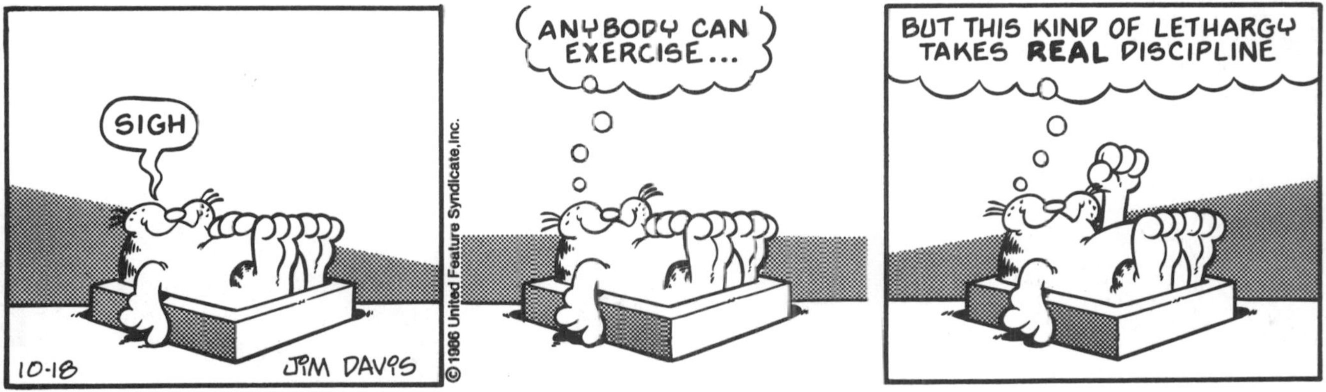
SIGH
10-18
JIM DAVIS
© 1986 United Feature Syndicate, Inc.
ANYBODY CAN EXERCISE...
BUT THIS KIND OF LETHARGY TAKES **REAL** DISCIPLINE

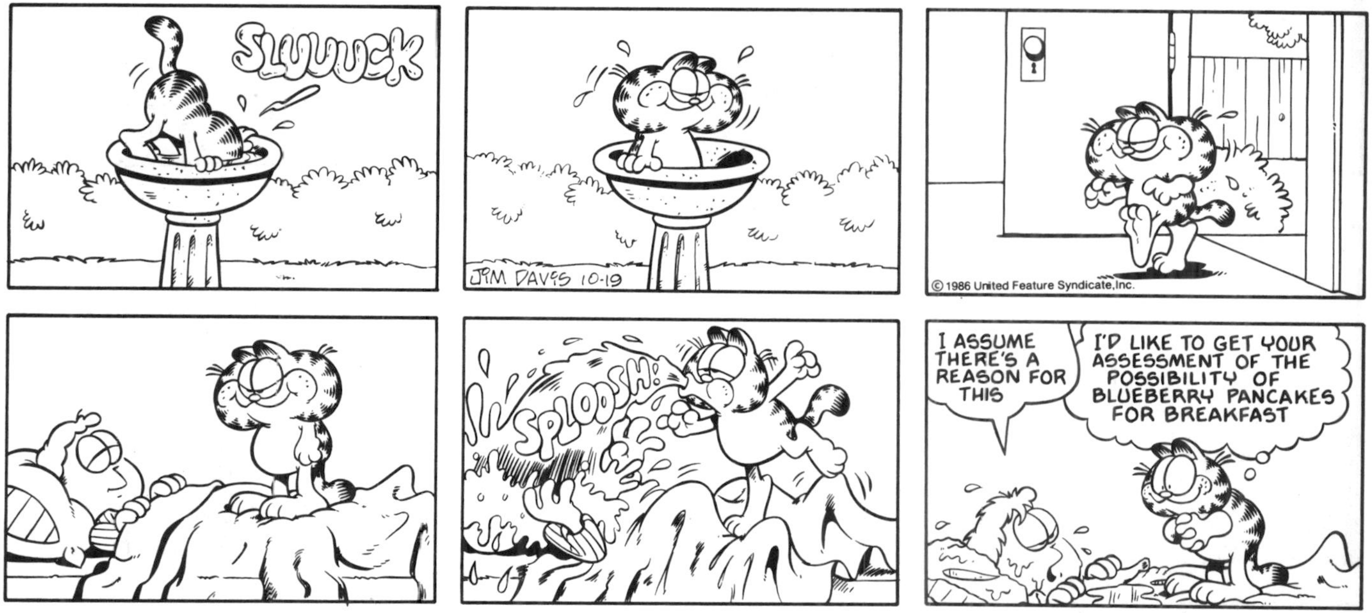
SLUUUCK
JIM DAVIS 10-19
© 1986 United Feature Syndicate, Inc.
SPLOOSH!
I ASSUME THERE'S A REASON FOR THIS
I'D LIKE TO GET YOUR ASSESSMENT OF THE POSSIBILITY OF BLUEBERRY PANCAKES FOR BREAKFAST

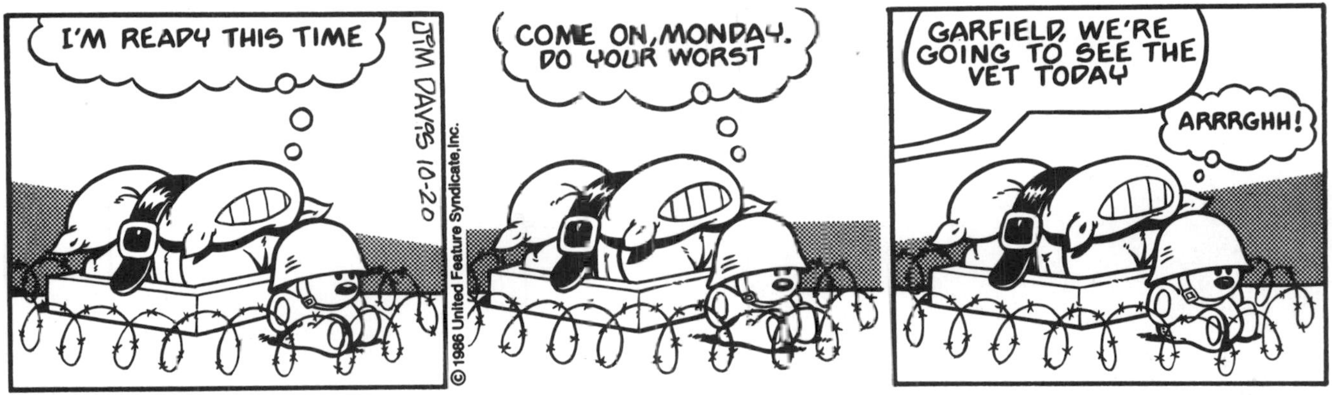
I'M READY THIS TIME
JIM DAVIS 10-20
© 1986 United Feature Syndicate, Inc.
COME ON, MONDAY. DO YOUR WORST
GARFIELD, WE'RE GOING TO SEE THE VET TODAY
ARRRGHH!

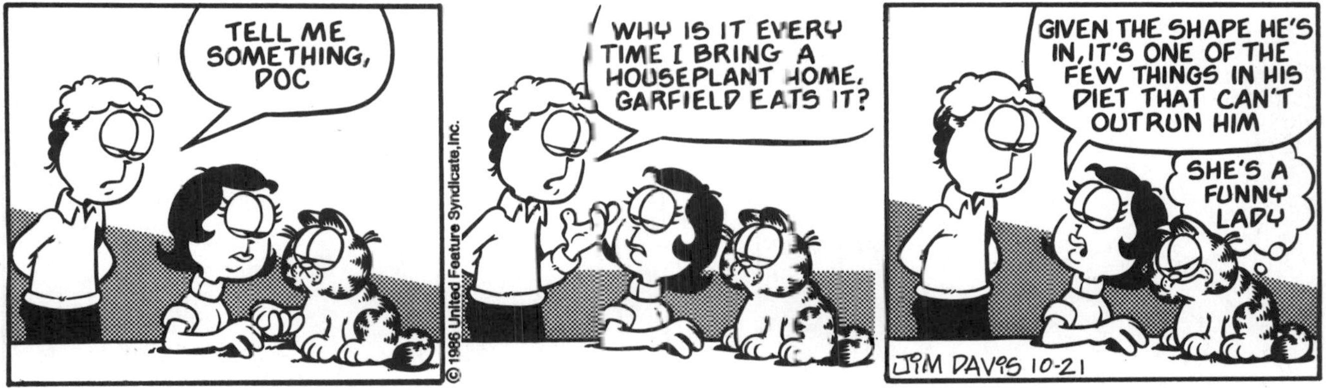
TELL ME SOMETHING, DOC
© 1986 United Feature Syndicate, Inc.
WHY IS IT EVERY TIME I BRING A HOUSEPLANT HOME, GARFIELD EATS IT?
GIVEN THE SHAPE HE'S IN, IT'S ONE OF THE FEW THINGS IN HIS DIET THAT CAN'T OUTRUN HIM
SHE'S A FUNNY LADY
JIM DAVIS 10-21

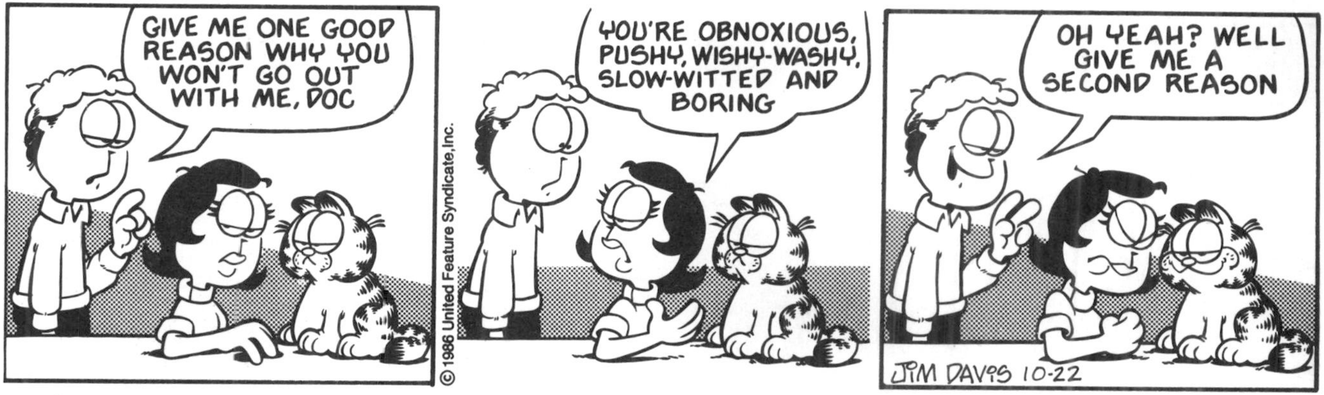
GIVE ME ONE GOOD REASON WHY YOU WON'T GO OUT WITH ME, DOC
© 1986 United Feature Syndicate, Inc.
YOU'RE OBNOXIOUS, PUSHY, WISHY-WASHY, SLOW-WITTED AND BORING
OH YEAH? WELL GIVE ME A SECOND REASON
JIM DAVIS 10-22

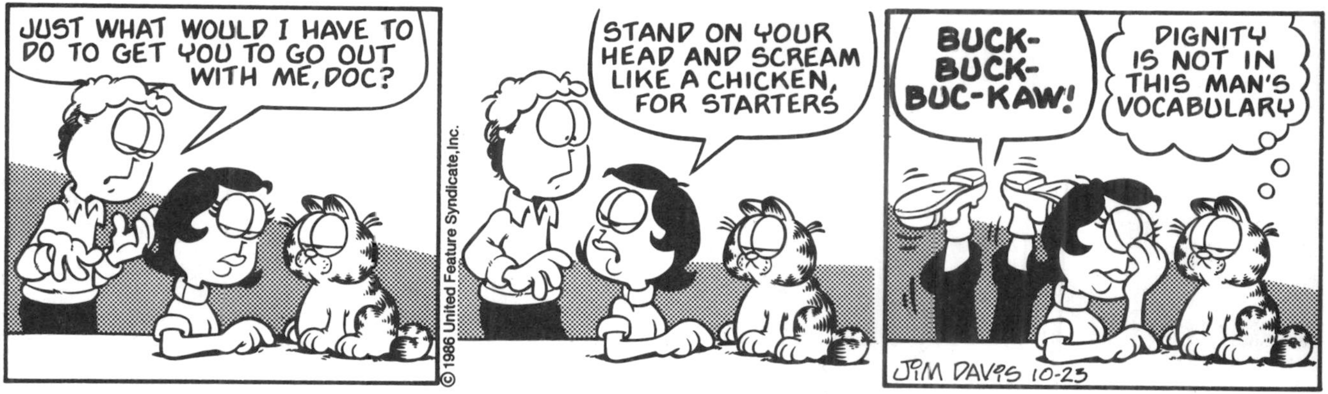
JUST WHAT WOULD I HAVE TO DO TO GET YOU TO GO OUT WITH ME, DOC?
© 1986 United Feature Syndicate, Inc.
STAND ON YOUR HEAD AND SCREAM LIKE A CHICKEN, FOR STARTERS
BUCK-BUCK-BUC-KAW!
DIGNITY IS NOT IN THIS MAN'S VOCABULARY
JIM DAVIS 10-23

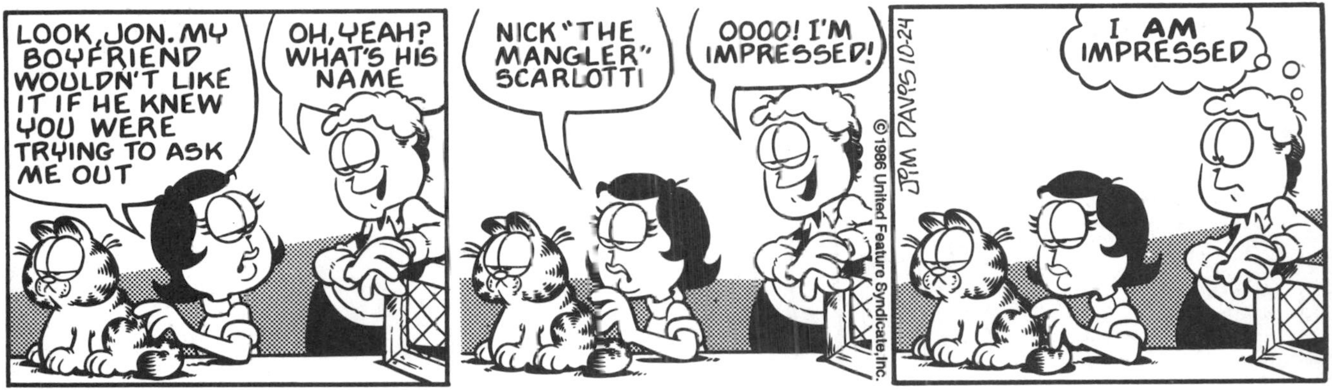
LOOK, JON. MY BOYFRIEND WOULDN'T LIKE IT IF HE KNEW YOU WERE TRYING TO ASK ME OUT
OH, YEAH? WHAT'S HIS NAME
NICK "THE MANGLER" SCARLOTTI
OOOO! I'M IMPRESSED!
© 1986 United Feature Syndicate, Inc.
JIM DAVIS 10-24
I AM IMPRESSED

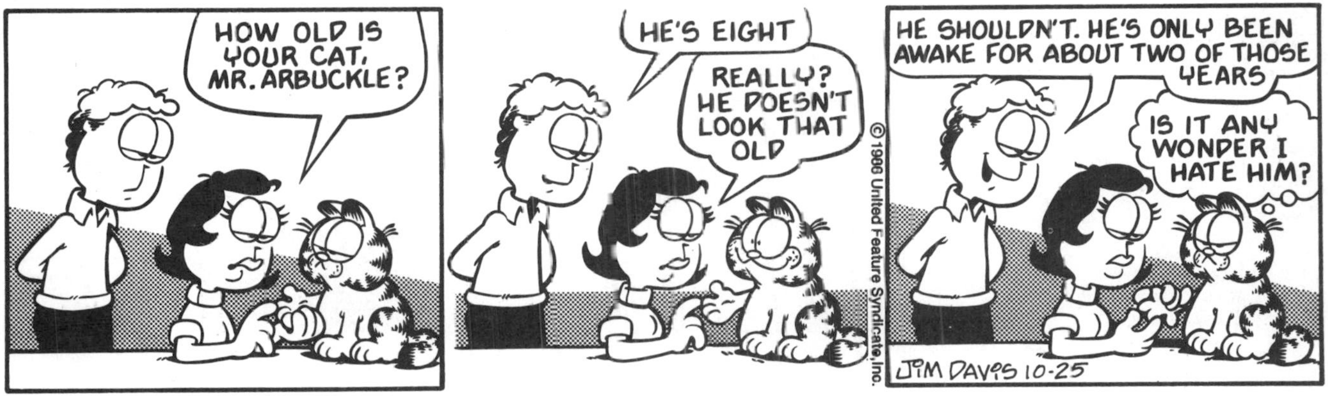
HOW OLD IS YOUR CAT, MR. ARBUCKLE?
HE'S EIGHT
REALLY? HE DOESN'T LOOK THAT OLD
© 1986 United Feature Syndicate, Inc.
HE SHOULDN'T. HE'S ONLY BEEN AWAKE FOR ABOUT TWO OF THOSE YEARS
IS IT ANY WONDER I HATE HIM?
JIM DAVIS 10-25

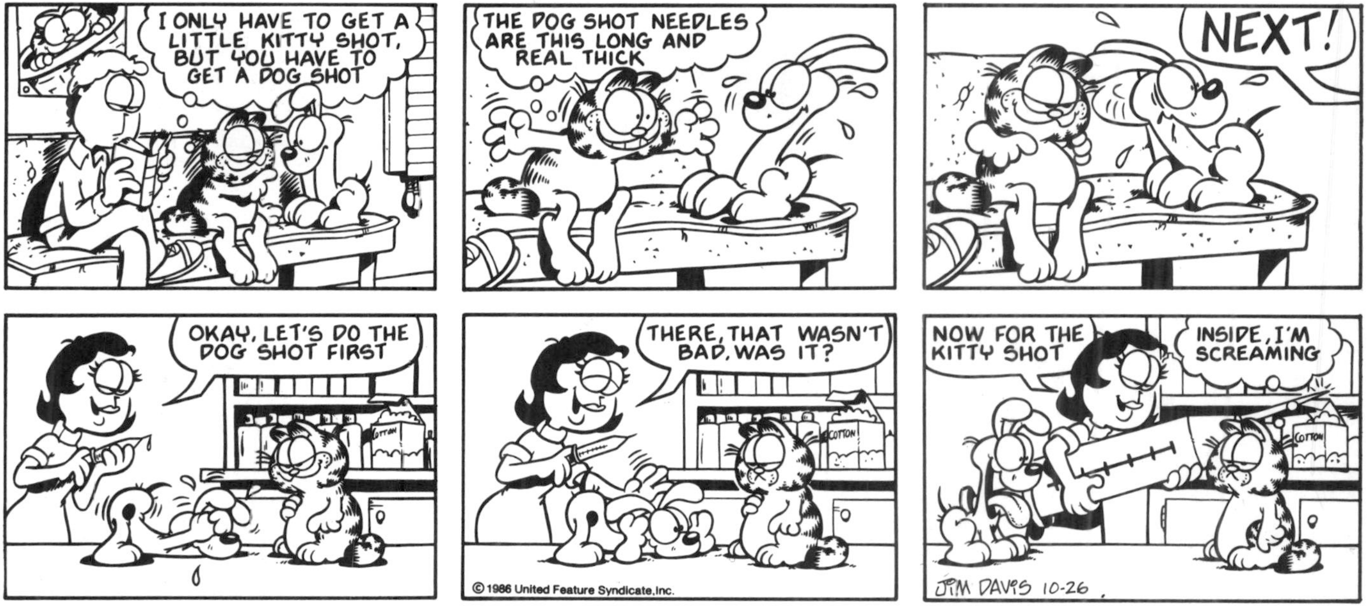
I ONLY HAVE TO GET A LITTLE KITTY SHOT, BUT YOU HAVE TO GET A DOG SHOT
THE DOG SHOT NEEDLES ARE THIS LONG AND REAL THICK
NEXT!
OKAY, LET'S DO THE DOG SHOT FIRST
THERE, THAT WASN'T BAD, WAS IT?
NOW FOR THE KITTY SHOT
INSIDE, I'M SCREAMING
COTTON
© 1986 United Feature Syndicate, Inc.
JIM DAVIS 10-26

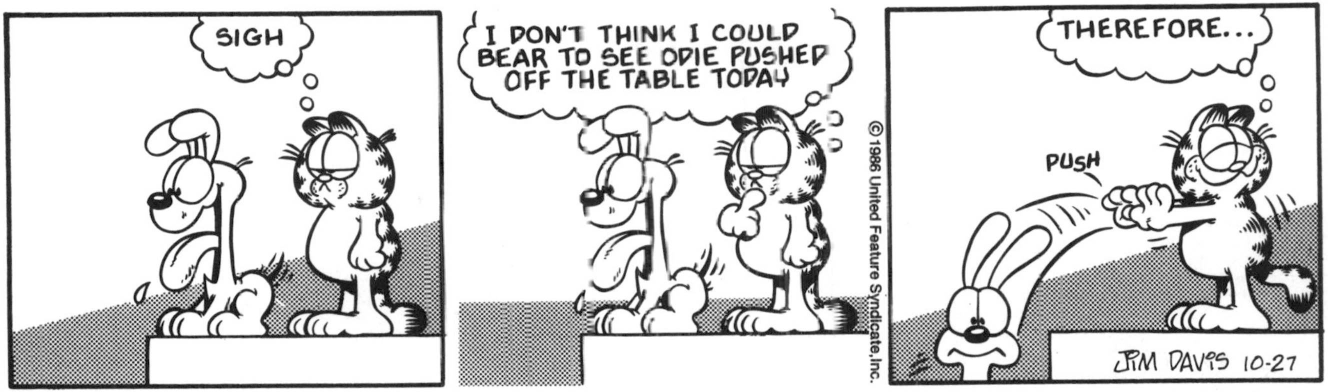
SIGH
I DON'T THINK I COULD BEAR TO SEE ODIE PUSHED OFF THE TABLE TODAY
© 1986 United Feature Syndicate, Inc.
THEREFORE...
PUSH
JIM DAVIS 10-27

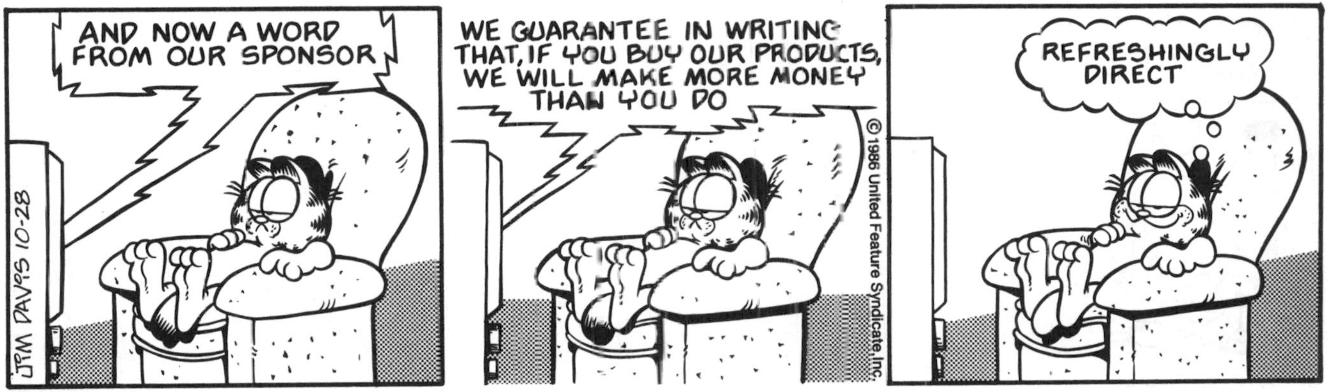
AND NOW A WORD FROM OUR SPONSOR
JIM DAVIS 10-28
WE GUARANTEE IN WRITING THAT, IF YOU BUY OUR PRODUCTS, WE WILL MAKE MORE MONEY THAN YOU DO
© 1986 United Feature Syndicate, Inc.
REFRESHINGLY DIRECT

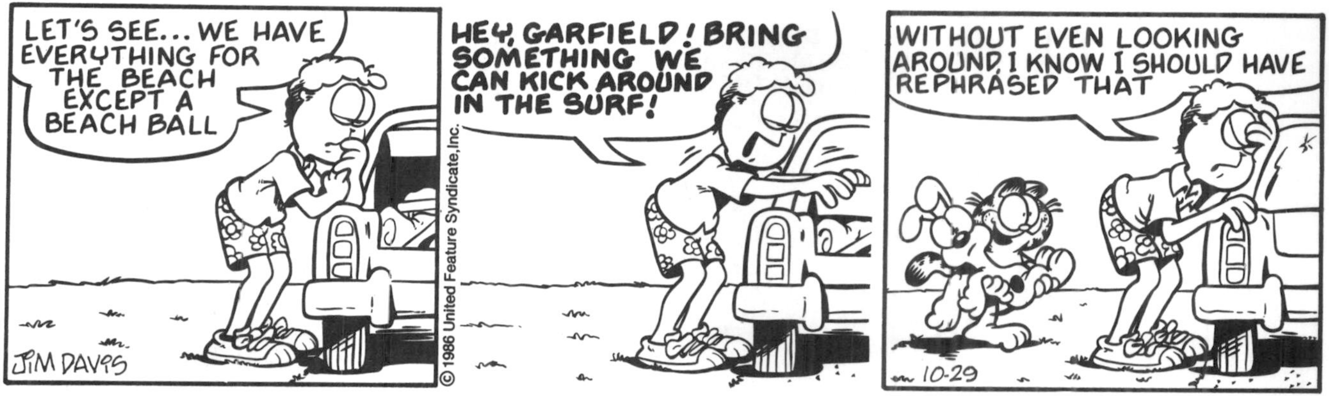
LET'S SEE... WE HAVE EVERYTHING FOR THE BEACH EXCEPT A BEACH BALL
JIM DAVIS
© 1986 United Feature Syndicate, Inc.
HEY, GARFIELD! BRING SOMETHING WE CAN KICK AROUND IN THE SURF!
WITHOUT EVEN LOOKING AROUND, I KNOW I SHOULD HAVE REPHRASED THAT
10-29

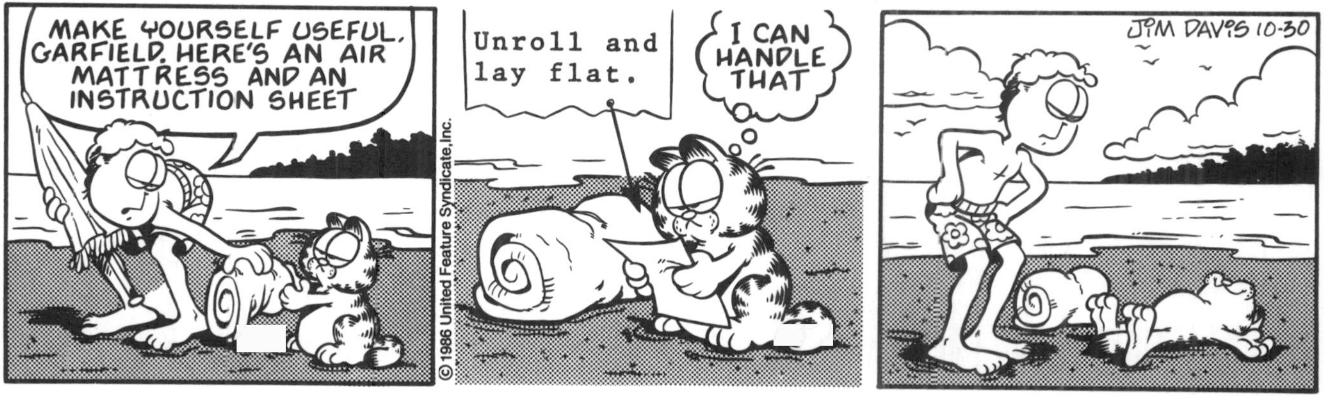
MAKE YOURSELF USEFUL, GARFIELD. HERE'S AN AIR MATTRESS AND AN INSTRUCTION SHEET
© 1986 United Feature Syndicate, Inc.
Unroll and lay flat.
I CAN HANDLE THAT
JIM DAVIS 10-30

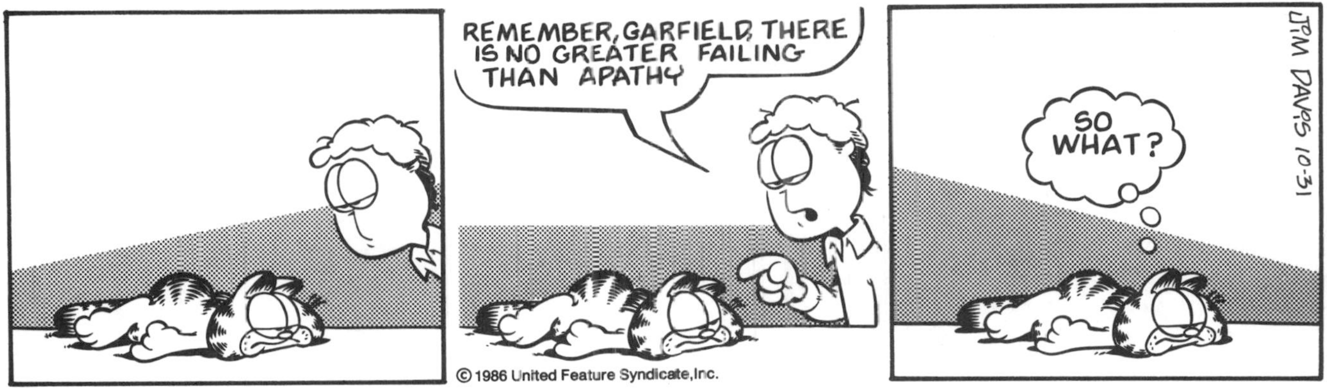
REMEMBER, GARFIELD, THERE IS NO GREATER FAILING THAN APATHY
SO WHAT?
JIM DAVIS 10-31
© 1986 United Feature Syndicate, Inc.

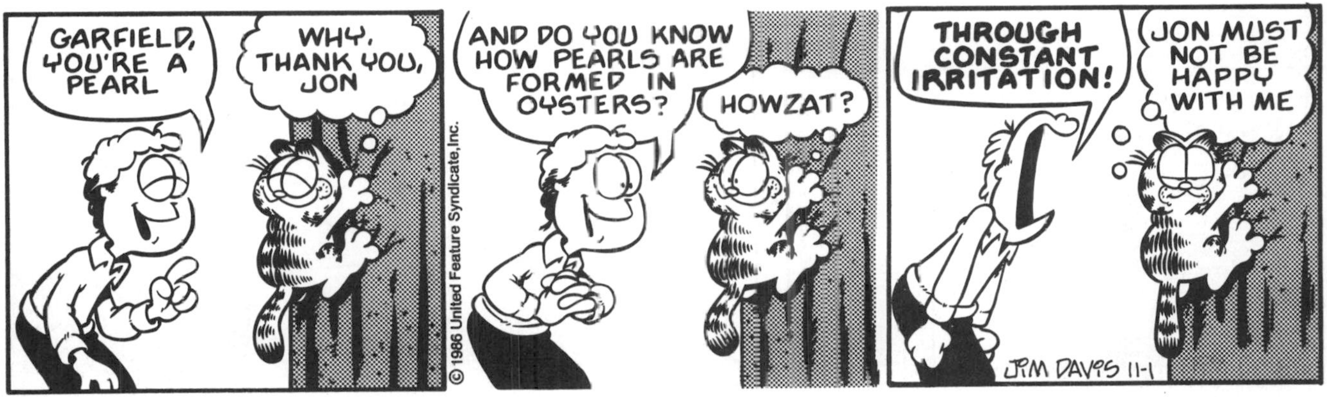
GARFIELD, YOU'RE A PEARL
WHY, THANK YOU, JON
AND DO YOU KNOW HOW PEARLS ARE FORMED IN OYSTERS?
HOWZAT?
THROUGH CONSTANT IRRITATION!
JON MUST NOT BE HAPPY WITH ME
JIM DAVIS 11-1
© 1986 United Feature Syndicate, Inc.

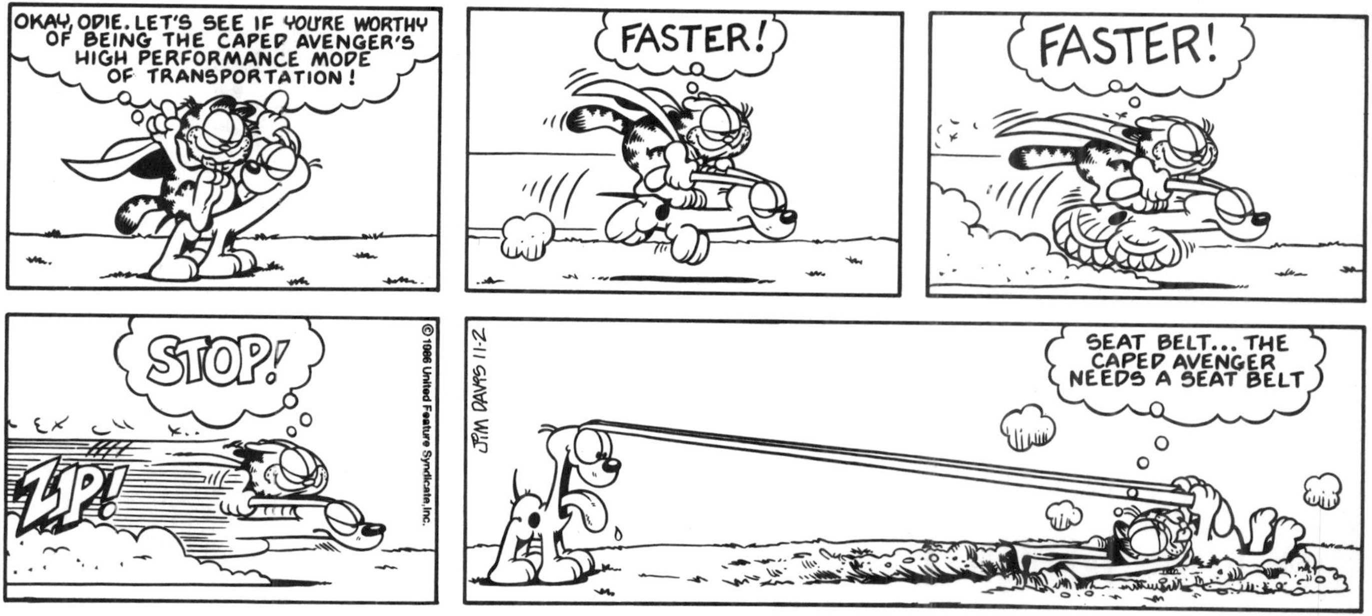

OKAY, ODIE. LET'S SEE IF YOU'RE WORTHY OF BEING THE CAPED AVENGER'S HIGH PERFORMANCE MODE OF TRANSPORTATION!
FASTER!
FASTER!
STOP!
ZIP!
© 1986 United Feature Syndicate, Inc.
JIM DAVIS 11-2
SEAT BELT... THE CAPED AVENGER NEEDS A SEAT BELT

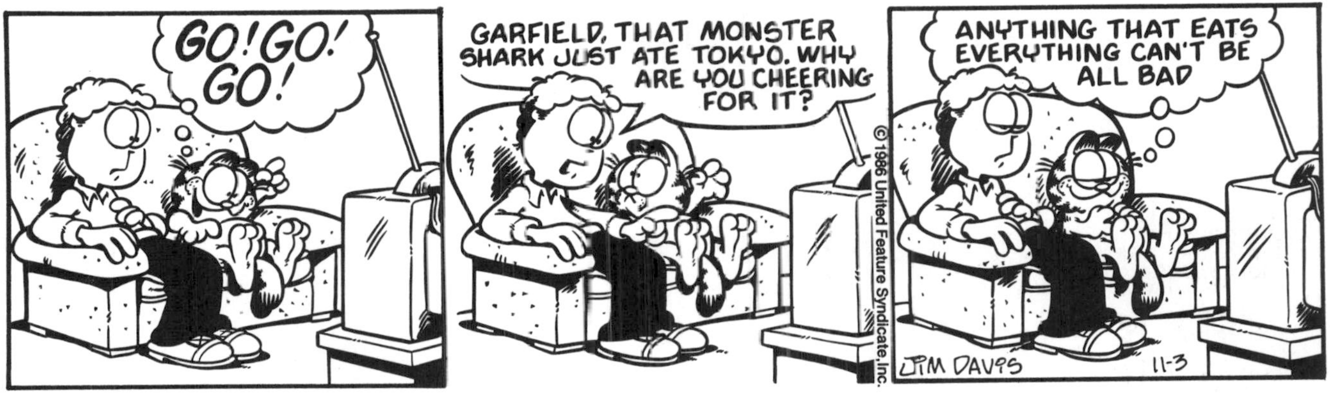
GO! GO! GO!
GARFIELD, THAT MONSTER SHARK JUST ATE TOKYO. WHY ARE YOU CHEERING FOR IT?
ANYTHING THAT EATS EVERYTHING CAN'T BE ALL BAD
© 1986 United Feature Syndicate,Inc.
JIM DAVIS
11-3

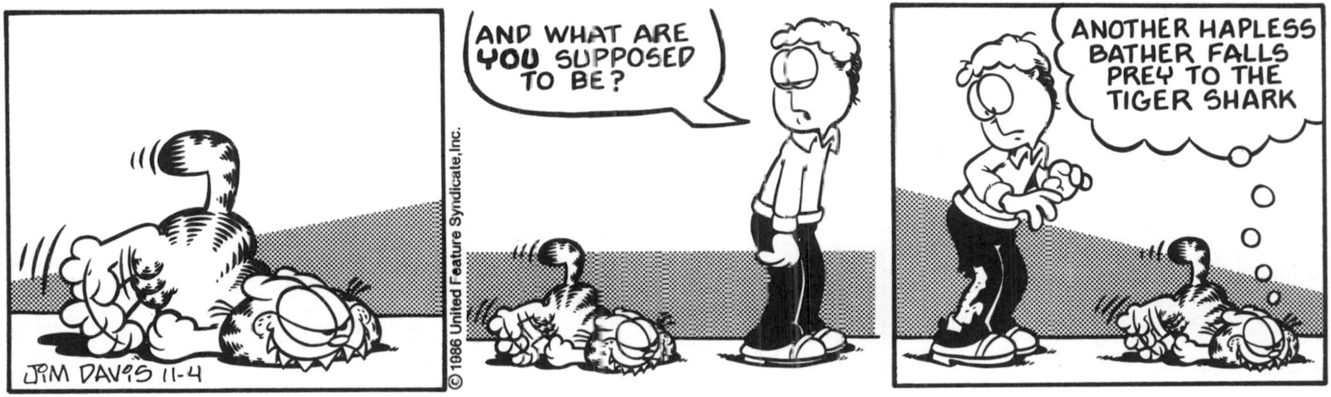
JIM DAVIS 11-4
© 1986 United Feature Syndicate,Inc.
AND WHAT ARE YOU SUPPOSED TO BE?
ANOTHER HAPLESS BATHER FALLS PREY TO THE TIGER SHARK

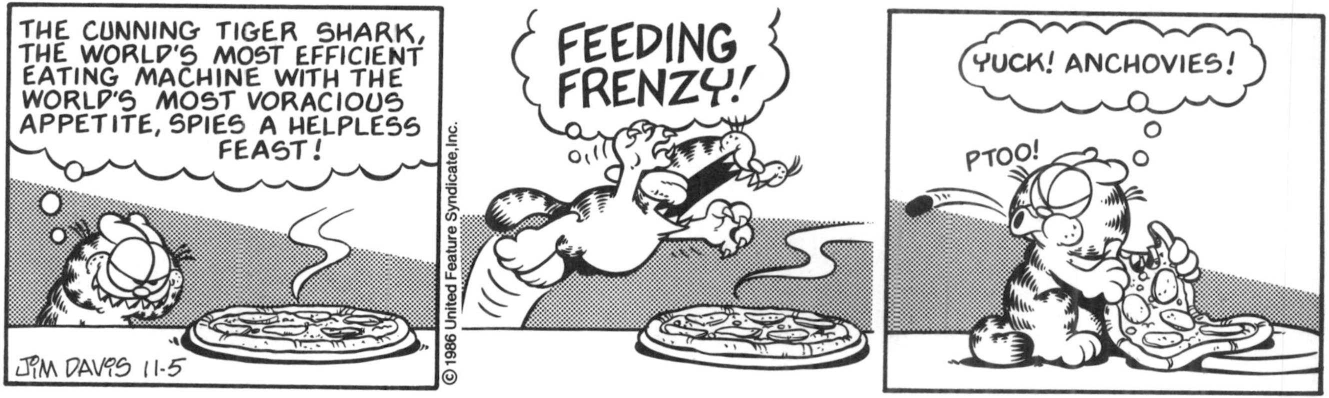
THE CUNNING TIGER SHARK, THE WORLD'S MOST EFFICIENT EATING MACHINE WITH THE WORLD'S MOST VORACIOUS APPETITE, SPIES A HELPLESS FEAST!
JIM DAVIS 11-5
© 1986 United Feature Syndicate, Inc.
FEEDING FRENZY!
YUCK! ANCHOVIES!
PTOO!

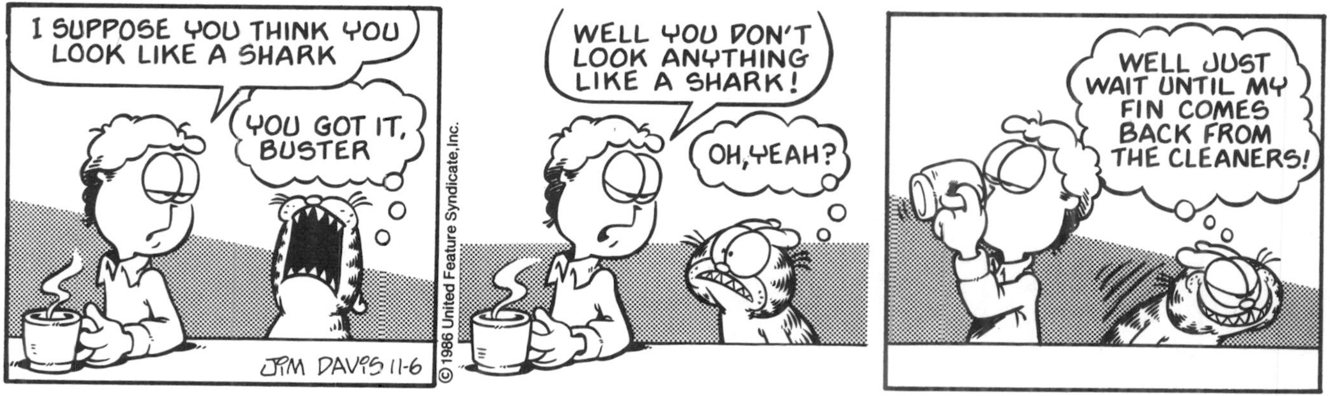
I SUPPOSE YOU THINK YOU LOOK LIKE A SHARK
YOU GOT IT, BUSTER
JIM DAVIS 11-6
© 1986 United Feature Syndicate, Inc.
WELL YOU DON'T LOOK ANYTHING LIKE A SHARK!
OH, YEAH?
WELL JUST WAIT UNTIL MY FIN COMES BACK FROM THE CLEANERS!

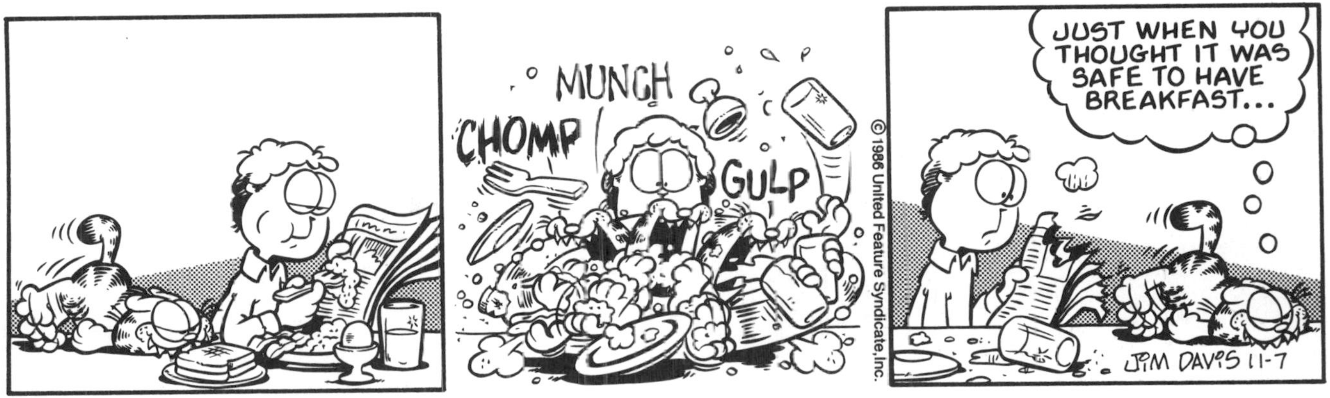
MUNCH
CHOMP
GULP
© 1986 United Feature Syndicate, Inc.
JUST WHEN YOU THOUGHT IT WAS SAFE TO HAVE BREAKFAST...
JIM DAVIS 11-7

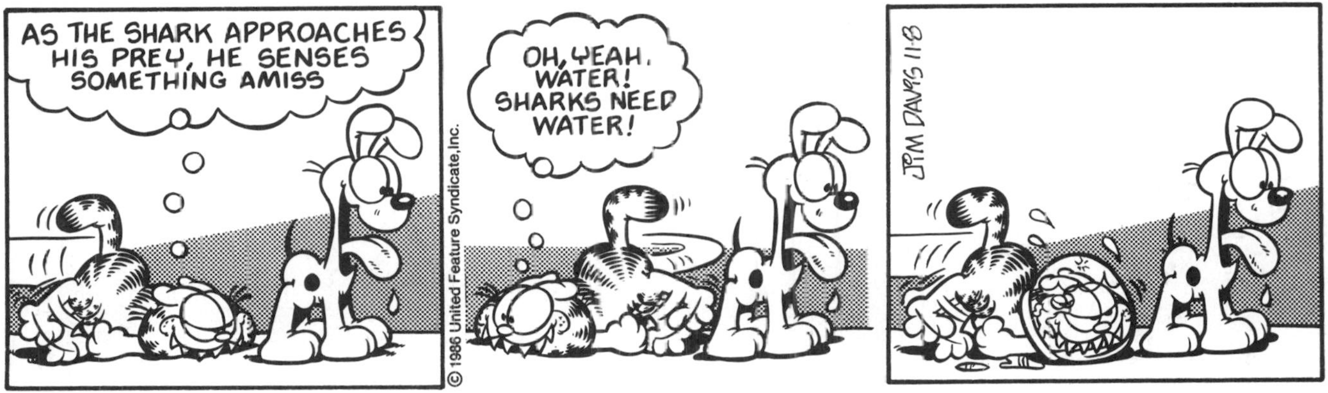
AS THE SHARK APPROACHES HIS PREY, HE SENSES SOMETHING AMISS
© 1986 United Feature Syndicate, Inc.
OH, YEAH. WATER! SHARKS NEED WATER!
JIM DAVIS 11-8

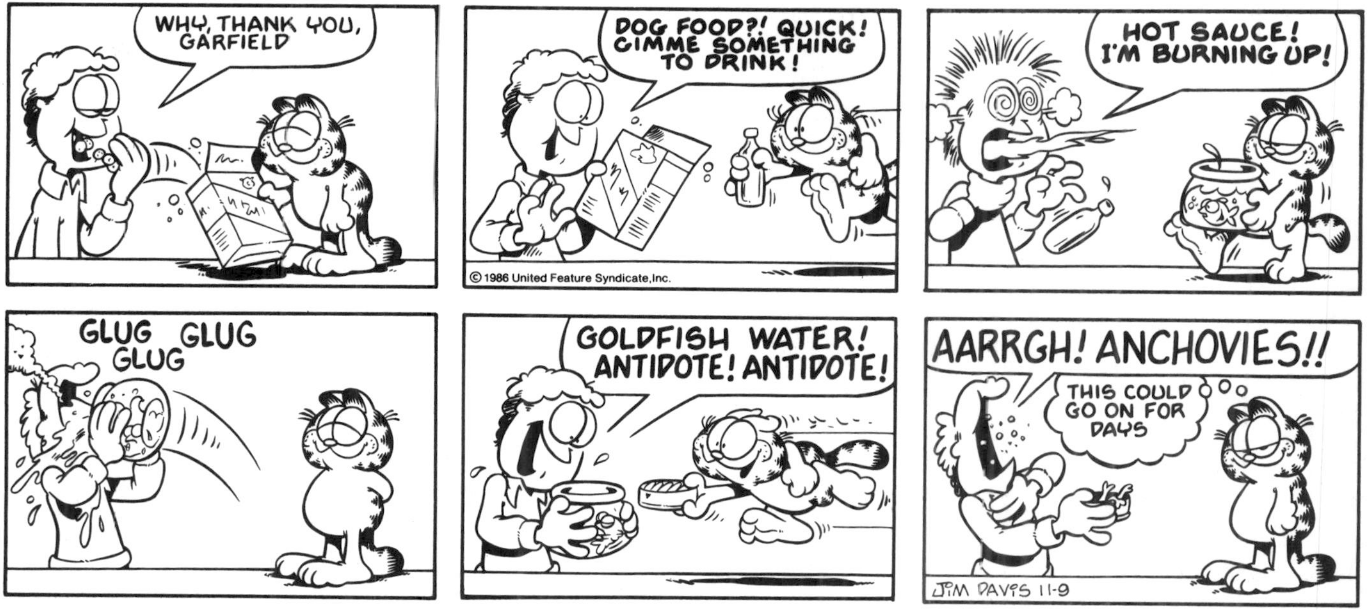
WHY, THANK YOU, GARFIELD
DOG FOOD?! QUICK! GIMME SOMETHING TO DRINK!
© 1986 United Feature Syndicate, Inc.
HOT SAUCE! I'M BURNING UP!
GLUG GLUG GLUG
GOLDFISH WATER! ANTIDOTE! ANTIDOTE!
AARRGH! ANCHOVIES!!
THIS COULD GO ON FOR DAYS
JIM DAVIS 11-9

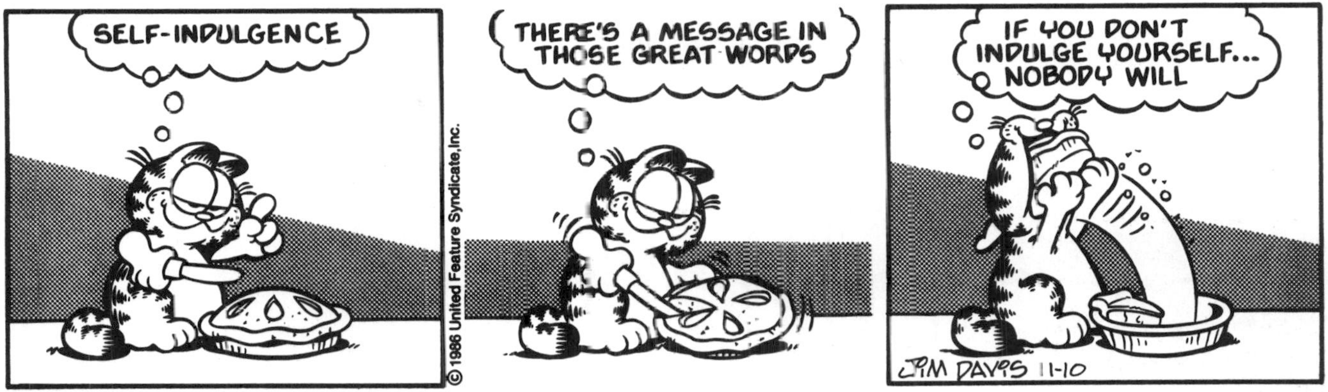
SELF-INDULGENCE
THERE'S A MESSAGE IN THOSE GREAT WORDS
IF YOU DON'T INDULGE YOURSELF... NOBODY WILL
JIM DAVIS 11-10


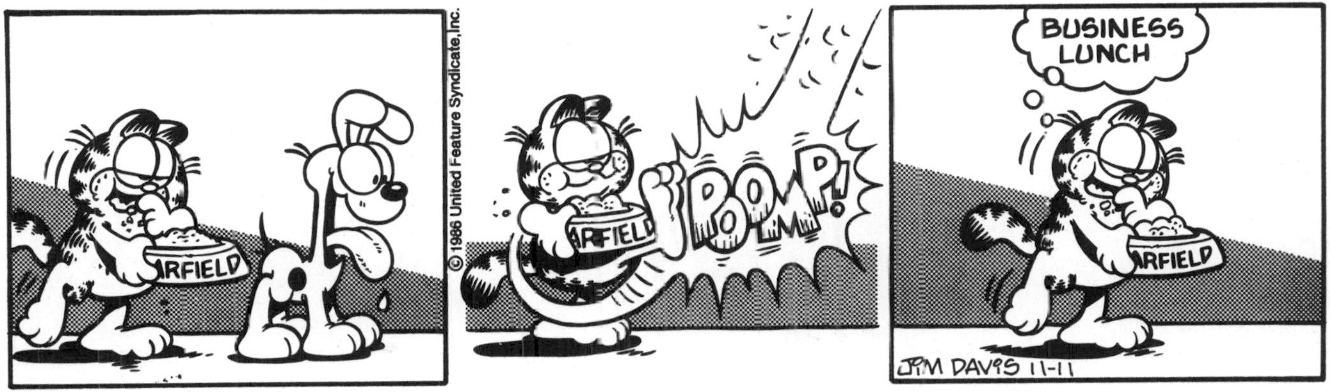
ARFIELD
ARFIELD
BOOMP!
BUSINESS LUNCH
ARFIELD
JIM DAVIS 11-11

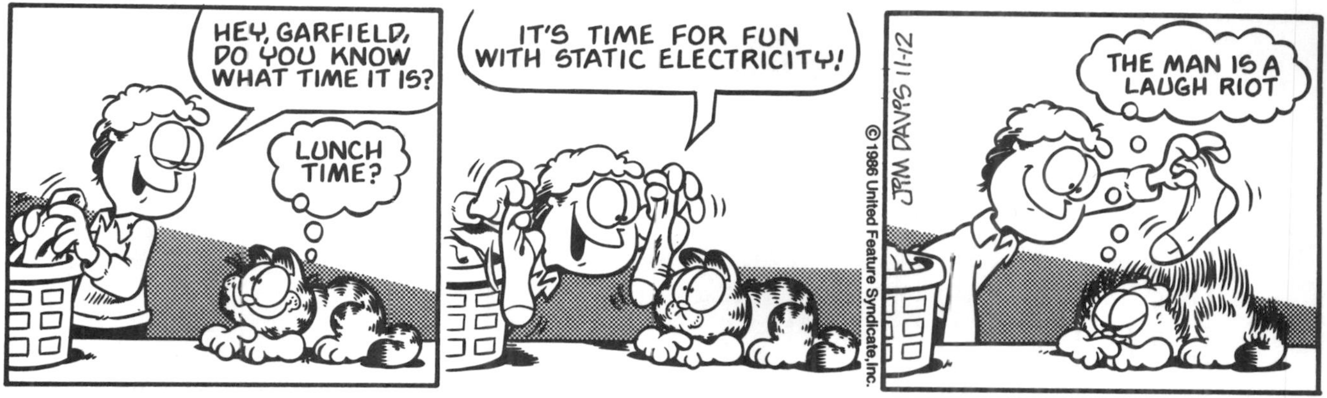
HEY, GARFIELD, DO YOU KNOW WHAT TIME IT IS?
LUNCH TIME?
IT'S TIME FOR FUN WITH STATIC ELECTRICITY!
JIM DAVIS 11-12
© 1986 United Feature Syndicate, Inc.
THE MAN IS A LAUGH RIOT

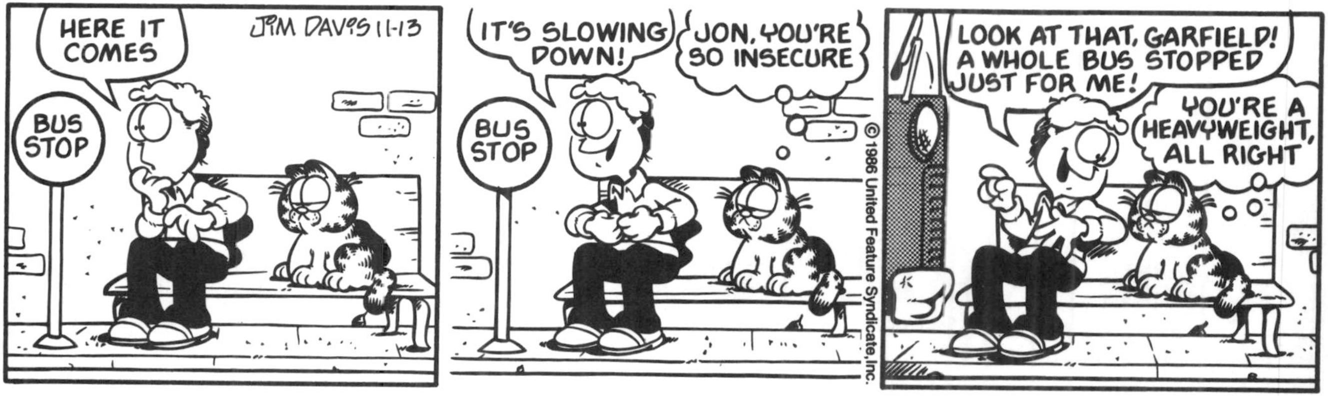
HERE IT COMES
JIM DAVIS 11-13
BUS STOP
IT'S SLOWING DOWN!
JON, YOU'RE SO INSECURE
BUS STOP
© 1986 United Feature Syndicate, Inc.
LOOK AT THAT, GARFIELD! A WHOLE BUS STOPPED JUST FOR ME!
YOU'RE A HEAVYWEIGHT, ALL RIGHT

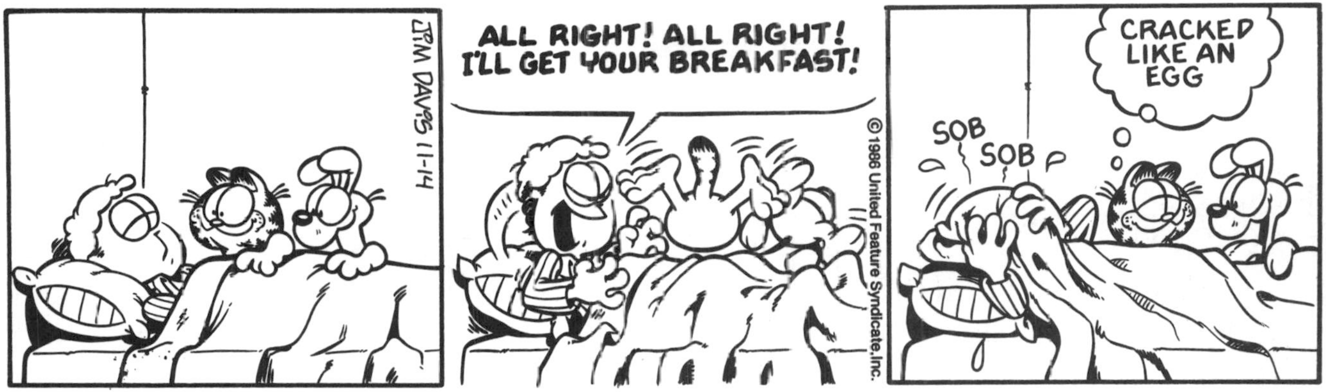
JIM DAVIS 11-14
ALL RIGHT! ALL RIGHT! I'LL GET YOUR BREAKFAST!
© 1986 United Feature Syndicate, Inc.
SOB SOB
CRACKED LIKE AN EGG

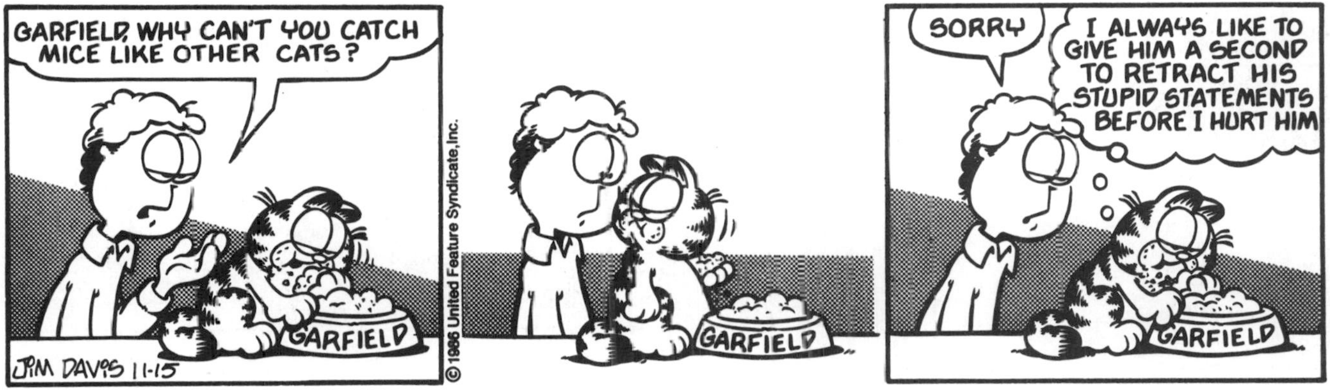
GARFIELD, WHY CAN'T YOU CATCH MICE LIKE OTHER CATS?
GARFIELD
JIM DAVIS 11-15
© 1986 United Feature Syndicate, Inc.
GARFIELD
SORRY
I ALWAYS LIKE TO GIVE HIM A SECOND TO RETRACT HIS STUPID STATEMENTS BEFORE I HURT HIM
GARFIELD

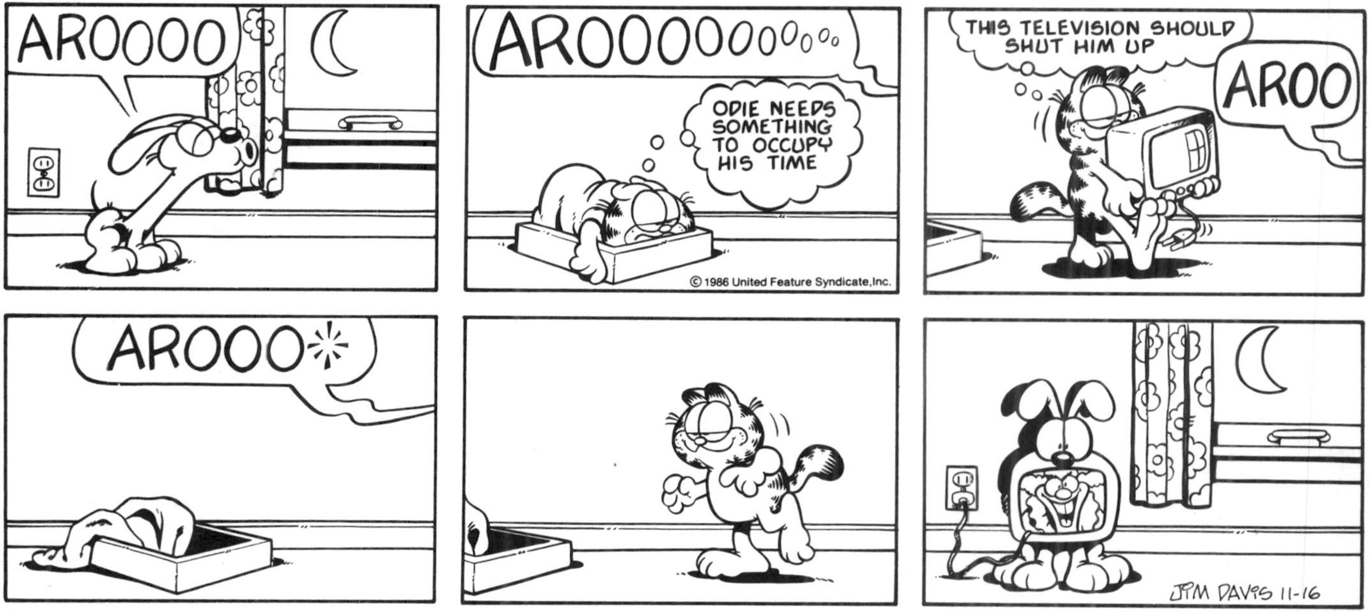
AROOOO
AROOOOOOOOOo
ODIE NEEDS SOMETHING TO OCCUPY HIS TIME
© 1986 United Feature Syndicate, Inc.
THIS TELEVISION SHOULD SHUT HIM UP
AROO
AROOO*
JIM DAVIS 11-16

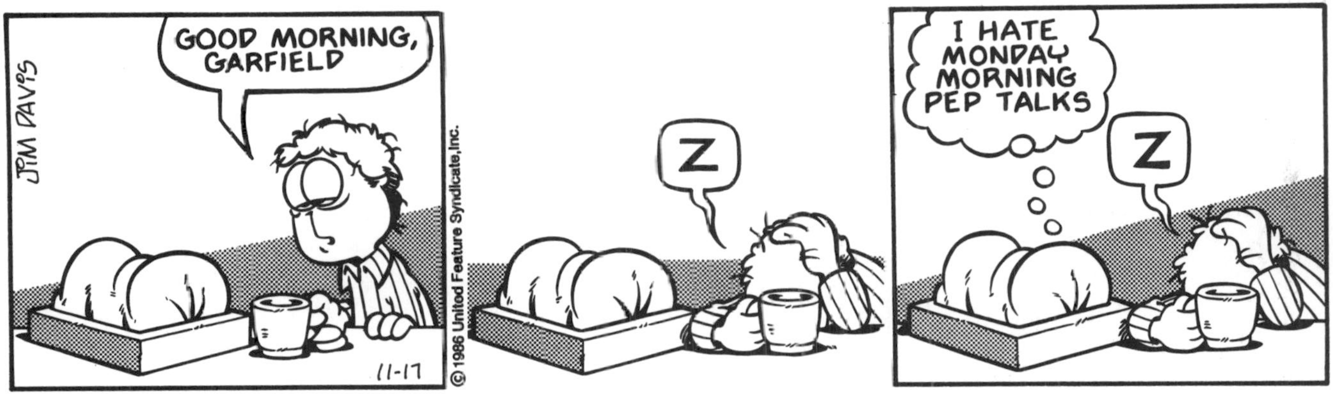
JIM DAVIS
GOOD MORNING, GARFIELD
11-17
© 1986 United Feature Syndicate, Inc.
Z
I HATE MONDAY MORNING PEP TALKS
Z

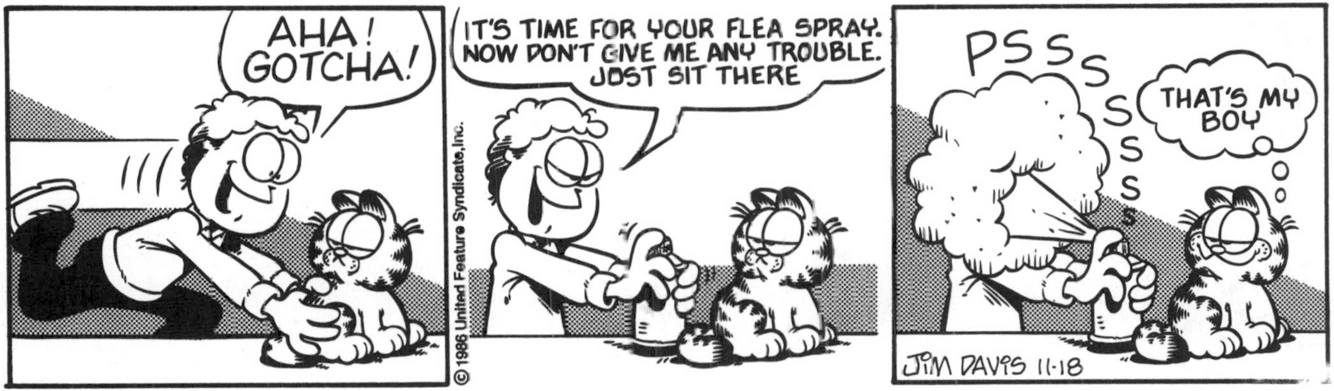
AHA! GOTCHA!
© 1986 United Feature Syndicate, Inc.
IT'S TIME FOR YOUR FLEA SPRAY. NOW DON'T GIVE ME ANY TROUBLE. JUST SIT THERE
PSSSSSSSS
THAT'S MY BOY
JIM DAVIS 11-18

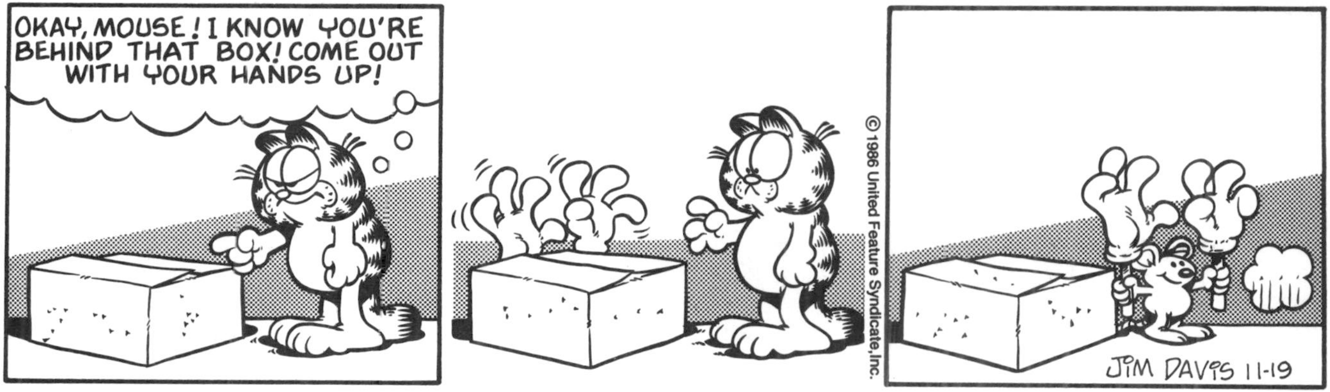
OKAY, MOUSE! I KNOW YOU'RE BEHIND THAT BOX! COME OUT WITH YOUR HANDS UP!
© 1986 United Feature Syndicate, Inc.
JIM DAVIS 11-19

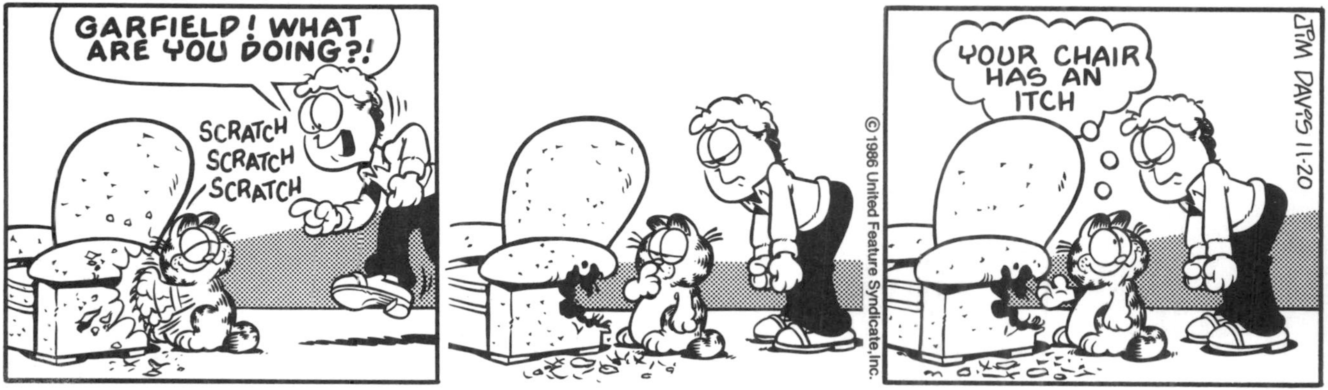
GARFIELD! WHAT ARE YOU DOING?!
SCRATCH
SCRATCH
SCRATCH
© 1986 United Feature Syndicate, Inc.
YOUR CHAIR HAS AN ITCH
JIM DAVIS 11-20

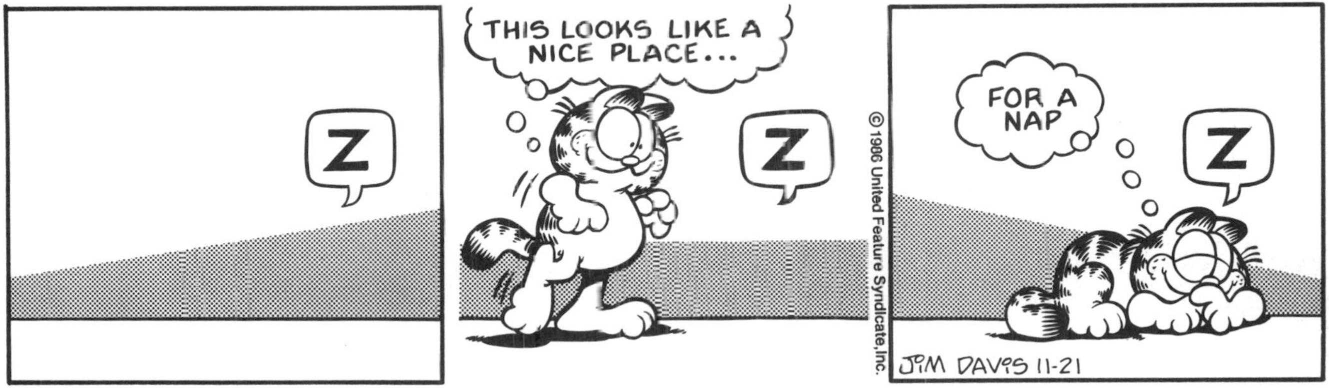
Z
THIS LOOKS LIKE A NICE PLACE...
Z
FOR A NAP
Z
© 1986 United Feature Syndicate, Inc.
JIM DAVIS 11-21

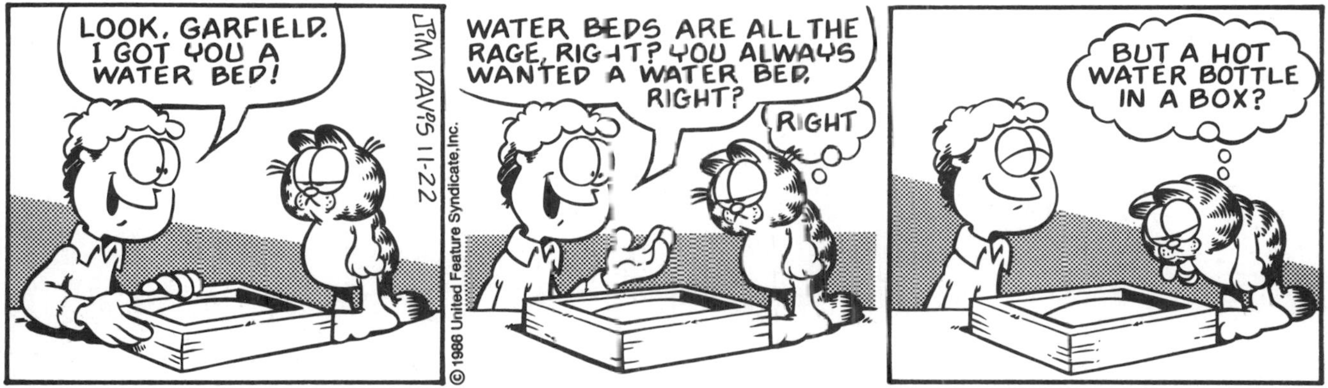
LOOK, GARFIELD. I GOT YOU A WATER BED!
JIM DAVIS 11-22
© 1986 United Feature Syndicate, Inc.
WATER BEDS ARE ALL THE RAGE, RIGHT? YOU ALWAYS WANTED A WATER BED, RIGHT?
RIGHT
BUT A HOT WATER BOTTLE IN A BOX?

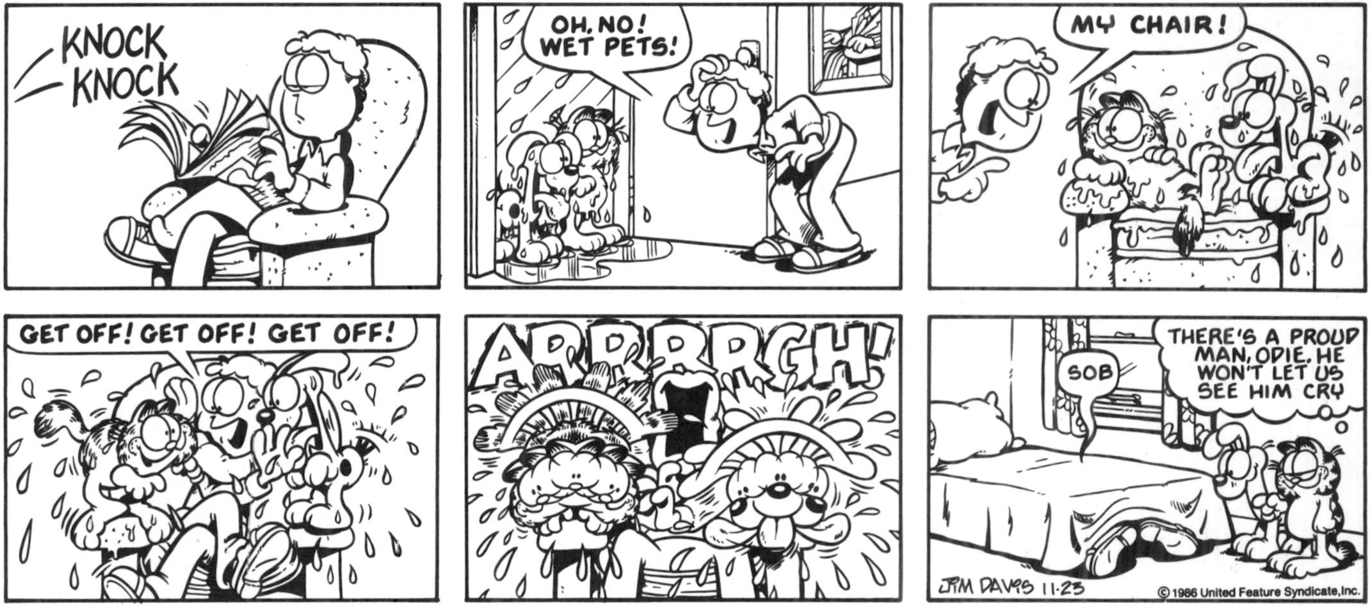
KNOCK
KNOCK
OH, NO! WET PETS!
MY CHAIR!
GET OFF! GET OFF! GET OFF!
ARRRRGH!
SOB
THERE'S A PROUD MAN, ODIE. HE WON'T LET US SEE HIM CRY
JIM DAVIS 11-23
© 1986 United Feature Syndicate, Inc.

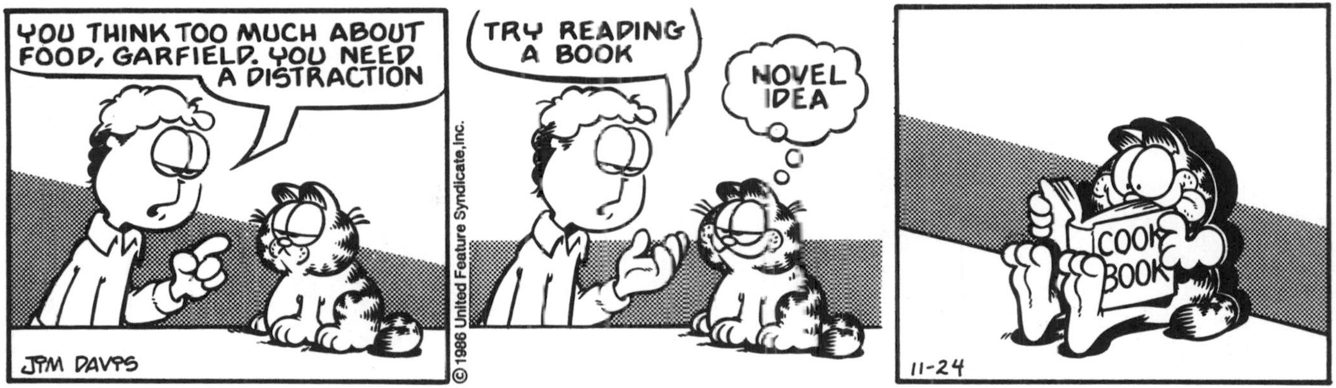
YOU THINK TOO MUCH ABOUT FOOD, GARFIELD. YOU NEED A DISTRACTION
JIM DAVIS
© 1986 United Feature Syndicate, Inc.
TRY READING A BOOK
NOVEL IDEA
COOK BOOK
11-24

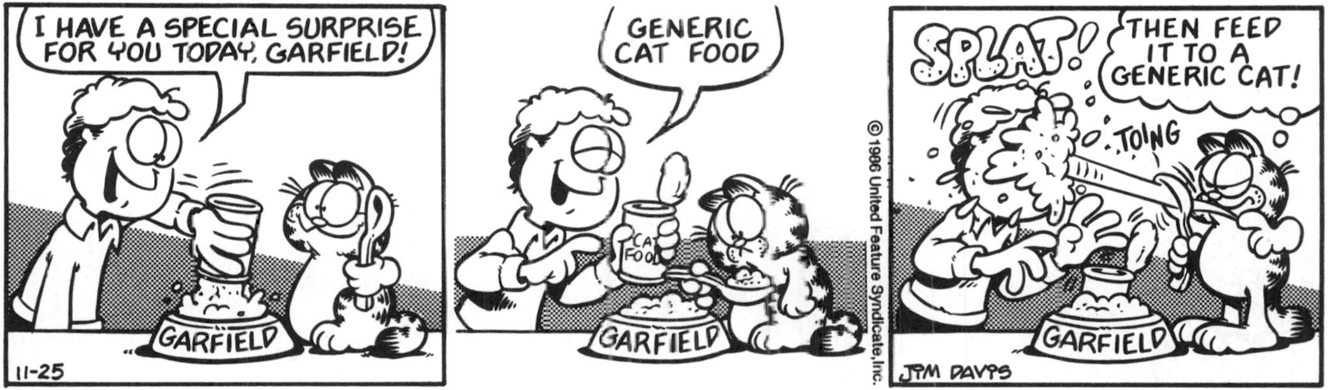
I HAVE A SPECIAL SURPRISE FOR YOU TODAY, GARFIELD!
GARFIELD
11-25
GENERIC CAT FOOD
CAT FOOD
GARFIELD
© 1986 United Feature Syndicate, Inc.
SPLAT!
THEN FEED IT TO A GENERIC CAT!
TOING
GARFIELD
JIM DAVIS

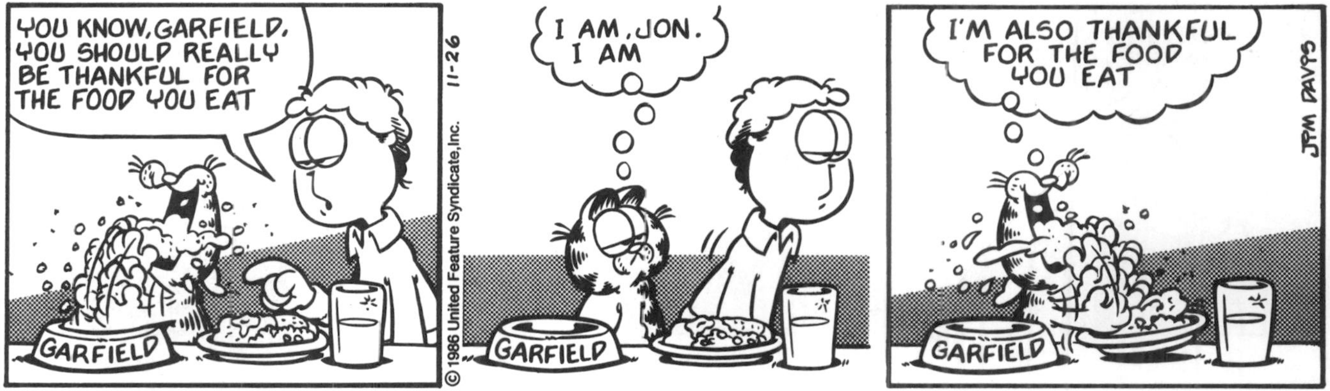
YOU KNOW, GARFIELD, YOU SHOULD REALLY BE THANKFUL FOR THE FOOD YOU EAT
GARFIELD
11-26
© 1986 United Feature Syndicate, Inc.
I AM, JON. I AM
GARFIELD
I'M ALSO THANKFUL FOR THE FOOD YOU EAT
GARFIELD
JPM DAVPS

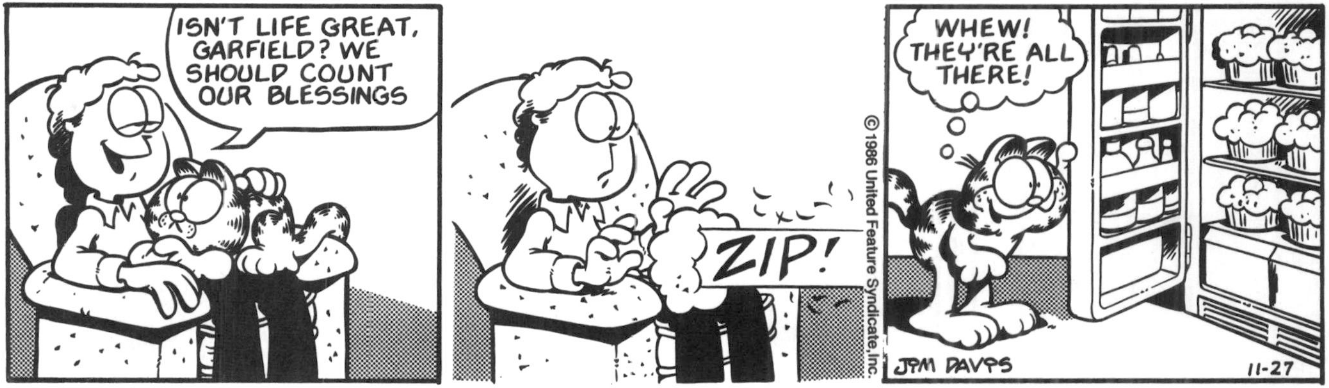
ISN'T LIFE GREAT, GARFIELD? WE SHOULD COUNT OUR BLESSINGS
ZIP!
© 1986 United Feature Syndicate, Inc.
WHEW! THEY'RE ALL THERE!
JPM DAVPS
11-27

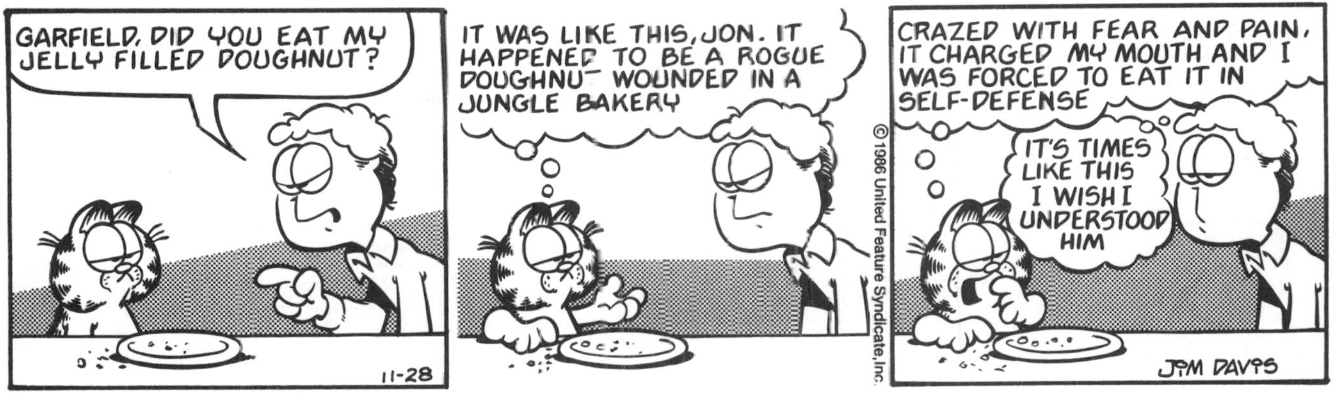
GARFIELD, DID YOU EAT MY JELLY FILLED DOUGHNUT?
11-28
IT WAS LIKE THIS, JON. IT HAPPENED TO BE A ROGUE DOUGHNUT WOUNDED IN A JUNGLE BAKERY
© 1986 United Feature Syndicate, Inc.
CRAZED WITH FEAR AND PAIN, IT CHARGED MY MOUTH AND I WAS FORCED TO EAT IT IN SELF-DEFENSE
IT'S TIMES LIKE THIS I WISH I UNDERSTOOD HIM
JIM DAVIS

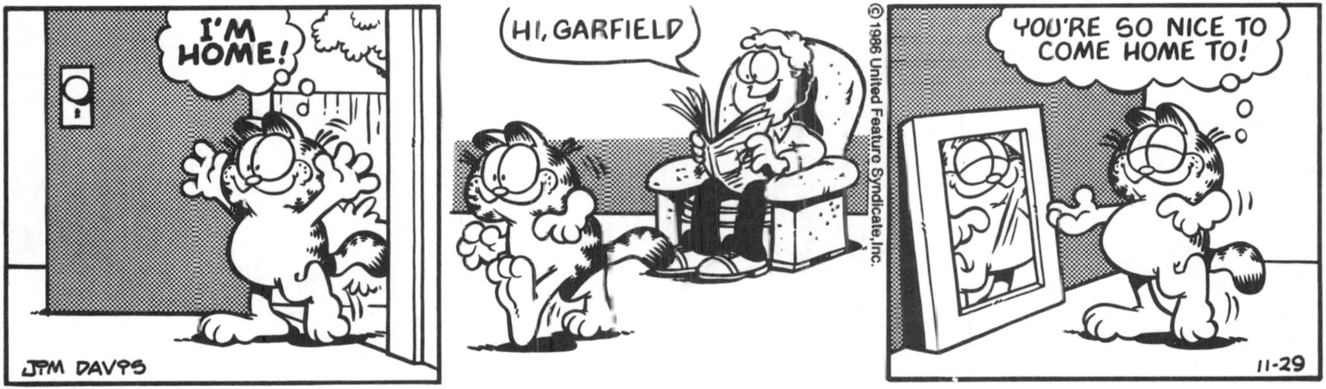
I'M HOME!
JIM DAVIS
HI, GARFIELD
© 1986 United Feature Syndicate, Inc.
YOU'RE SO NICE TO COME HOME TO!
11-29

SCREEEE
GULP
GARFIELD
© 1986 United Feature Syndicate, Inc.
GARFIELD, YOU CAN'T STILL BE HUNGRY
YOU HAVE TO LOSE WEIGHT. NO MORE FOOD UNTIL BREAKFAST
DO YOU REALLY WANT THAT, JON? DO YOU KNOW WHAT HAPPENS TO SKINNY PEOPLE?
JIM DAVIS 11-30
THEY BECOME MIMES, JON. IS THAT WHAT YOU WANT?!! A MIME?!

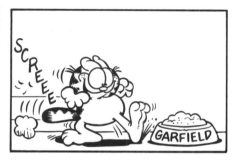

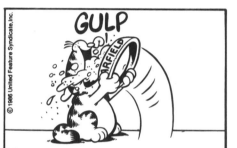

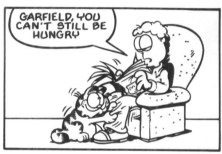

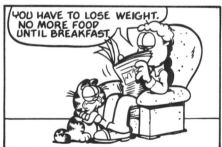

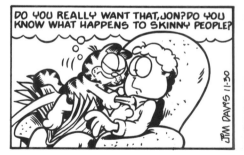

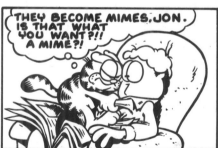

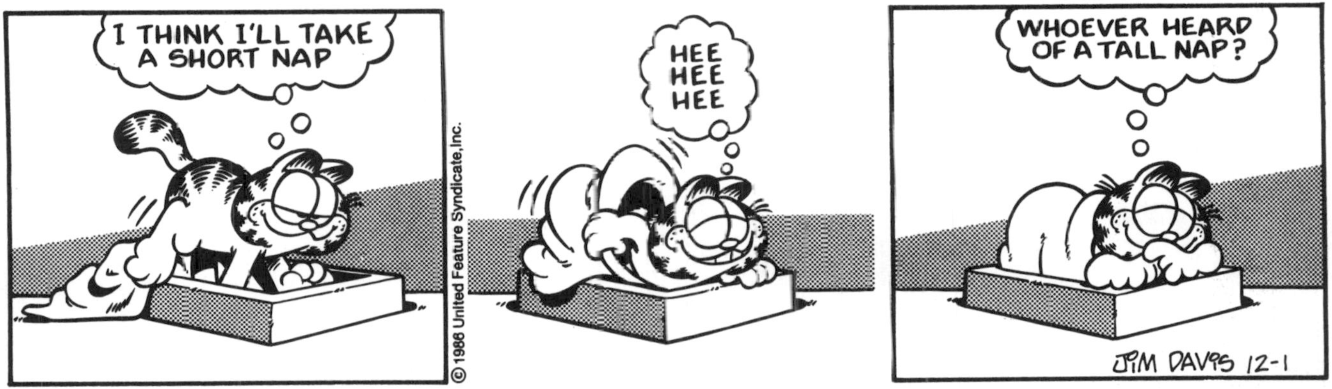
I THINK I'LL TAKE A SHORT NAP
© 1986 United Feature Syndicate, Inc.
HEE HEE HEE
WHOEVER HEARD OF A TALL NAP?
JIM DAVIS 12-1

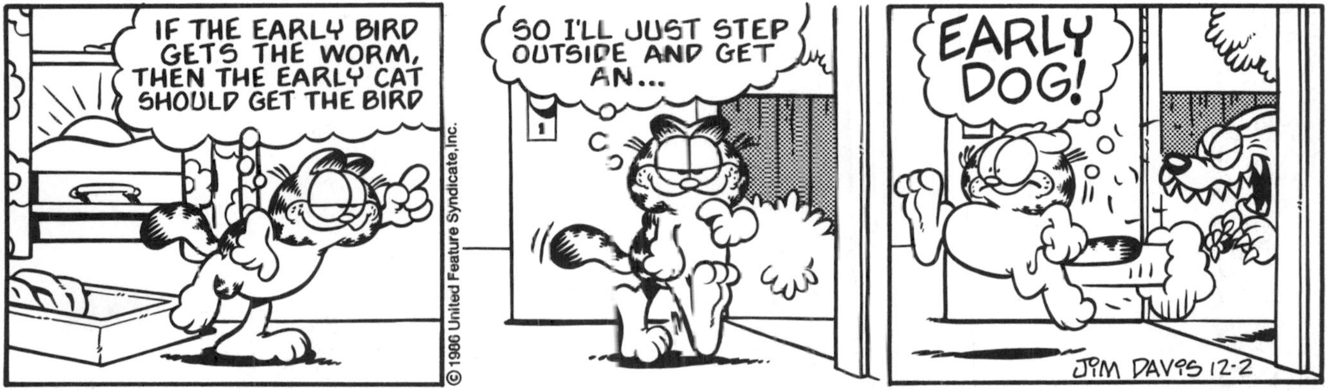
IF THE EARLY BIRD GETS THE WORM, THEN THE EARLY CAT SHOULD GET THE BIRD
© 1986 United Feature Syndicate, Inc.
SO I'LL JUST STEP OUTSIDE AND GET AN...
EARLY DOG!
JIM DAVIS 12-2

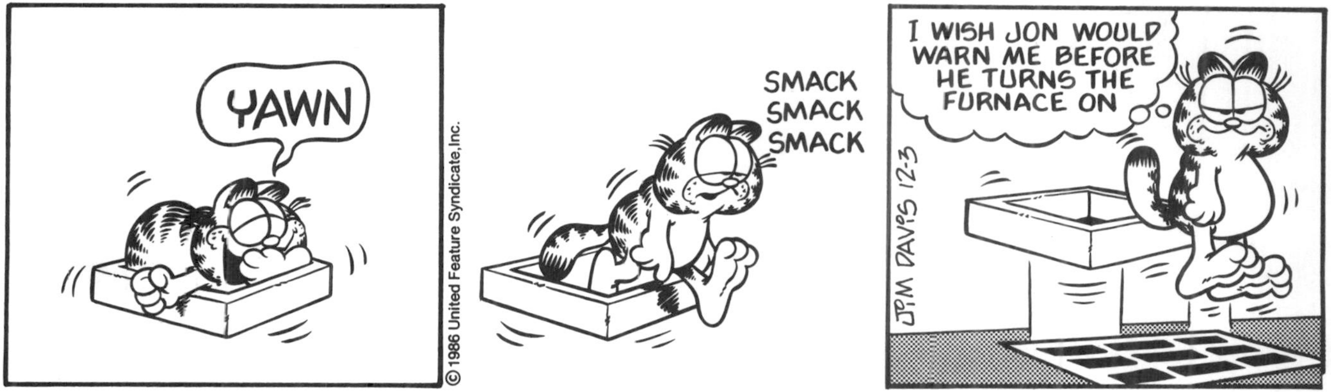
YAWN
SMACK SMACK SMACK
I WISH JON WOULD WARN ME BEFORE HE TURNS THE FURNACE ON
© 1986 United Feature Syndicate, Inc.
JIM DAVIS 12-3

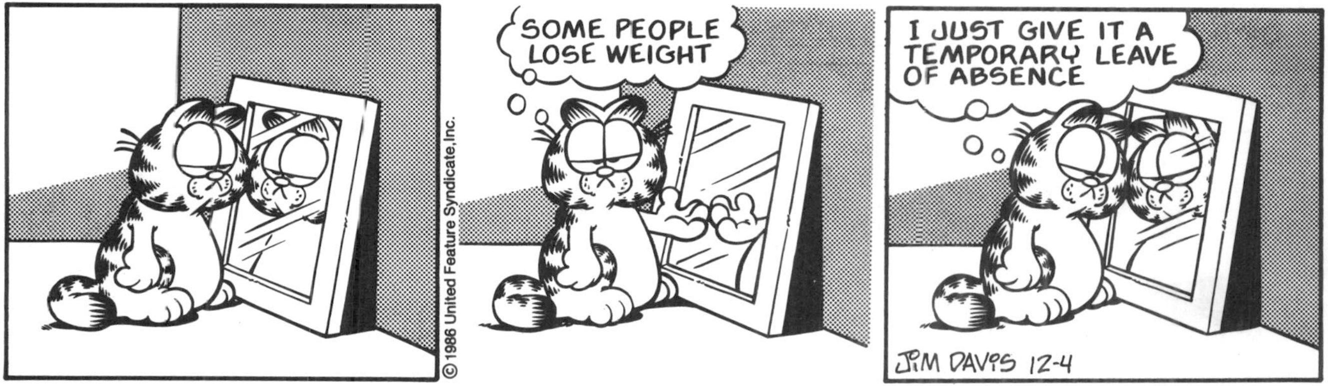
SOME PEOPLE LOSE WEIGHT
I JUST GIVE IT A TEMPORARY LEAVE OF ABSENCE
© 1986 United Feature Syndicate, Inc.
JIM DAVIS 12-4

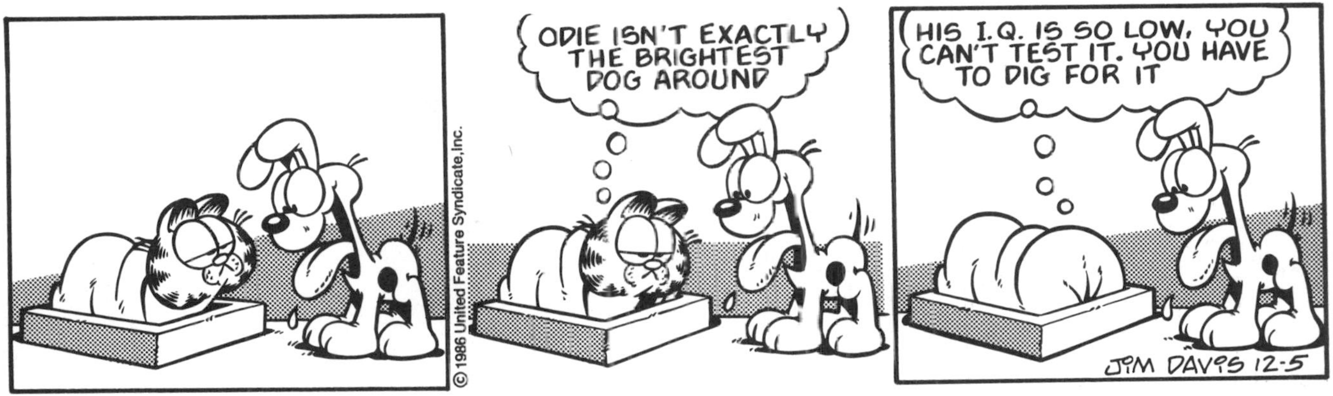

© 1986 United Feature Syndicate, Inc.
ODIE ISN'T EXACTLY THE BRIGHTEST DOG AROUND
HIS I.Q. IS SO LOW, YOU CAN'T TEST IT. YOU HAVE TO DIG FOR IT
JIM DAVIS 12-5


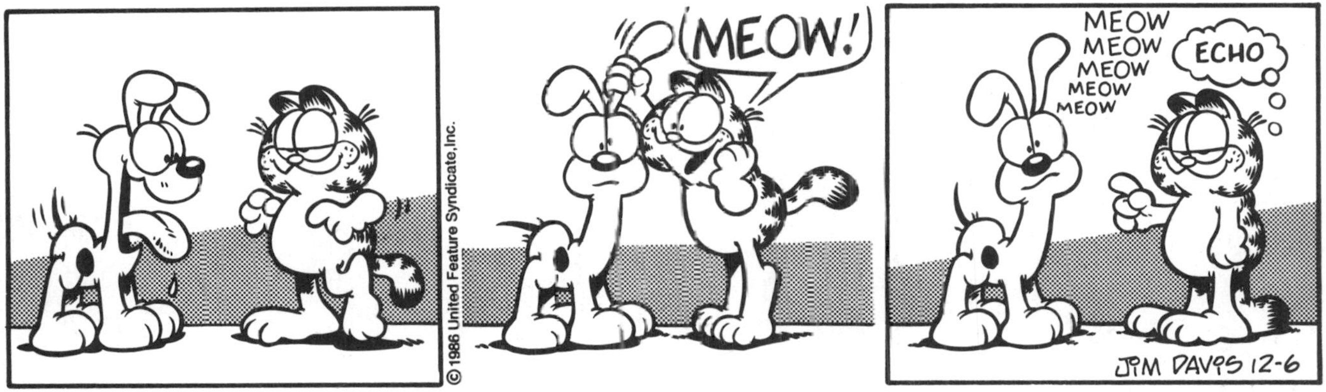

© 1986 United Feature Syndicate, Inc.
MEOW!
MEOW MEOW MEOW MEOW MEOW
ECHO
JIM DAVIS 12-6

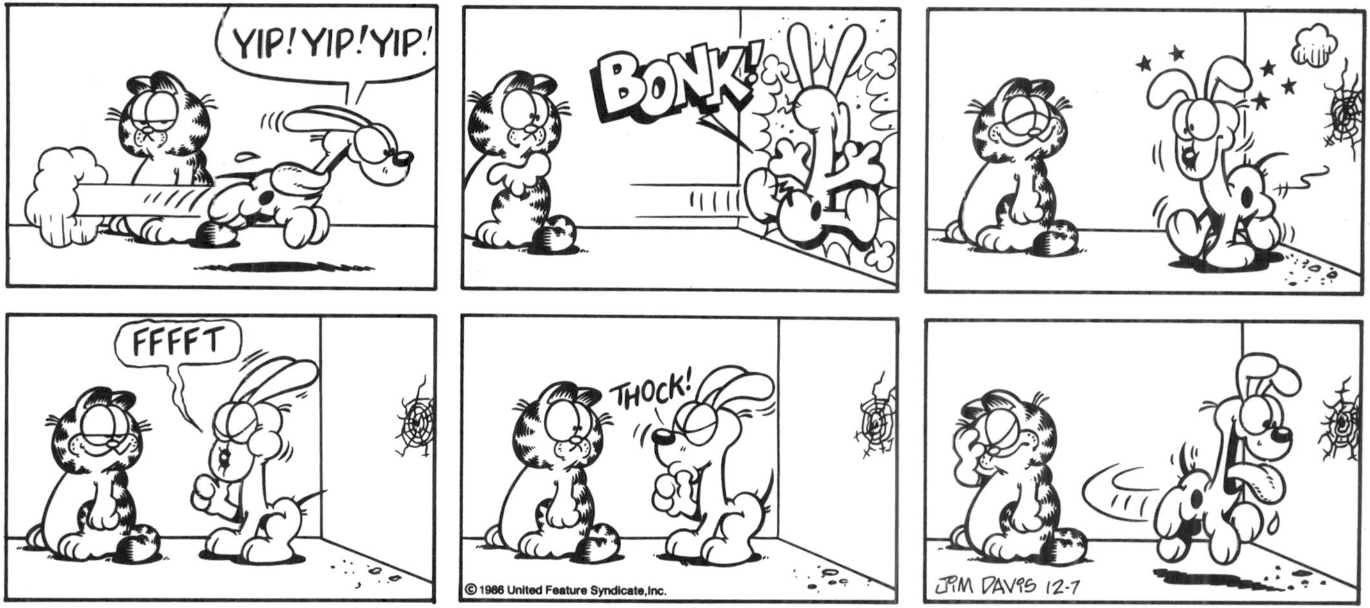

YIP! YIP! YIP!
BONK!
FFFFT
THOCK!
© 1986 United Feature Syndicate, Inc.
JIM DAVIS 12-7

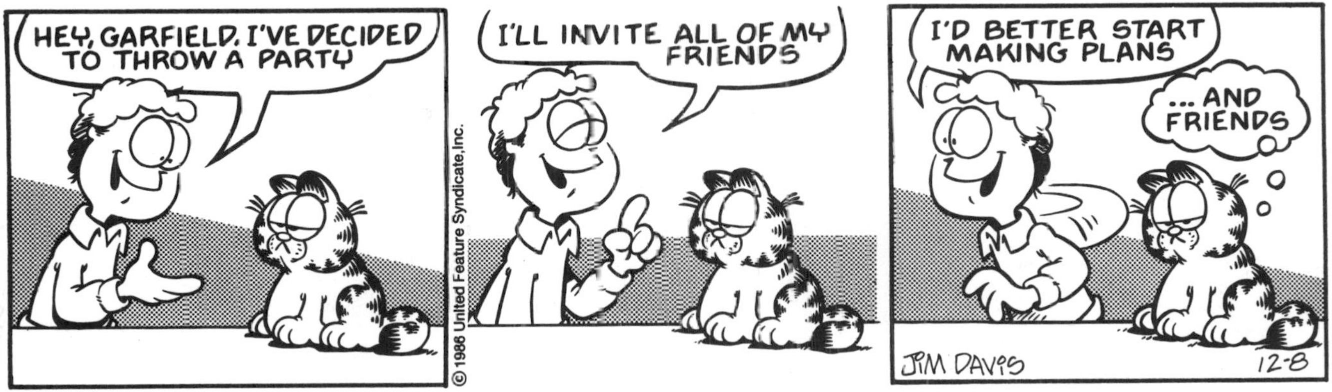
HEY, GARFIELD. I'VE DECIDED TO THROW A PARTY
I'LL INVITE ALL OF MY FRIENDS
I'D BETTER START MAKING PLANS
... AND FRIENDS
JIM DAVIS
12-8
© 1986 United Feature Syndicate, Inc.

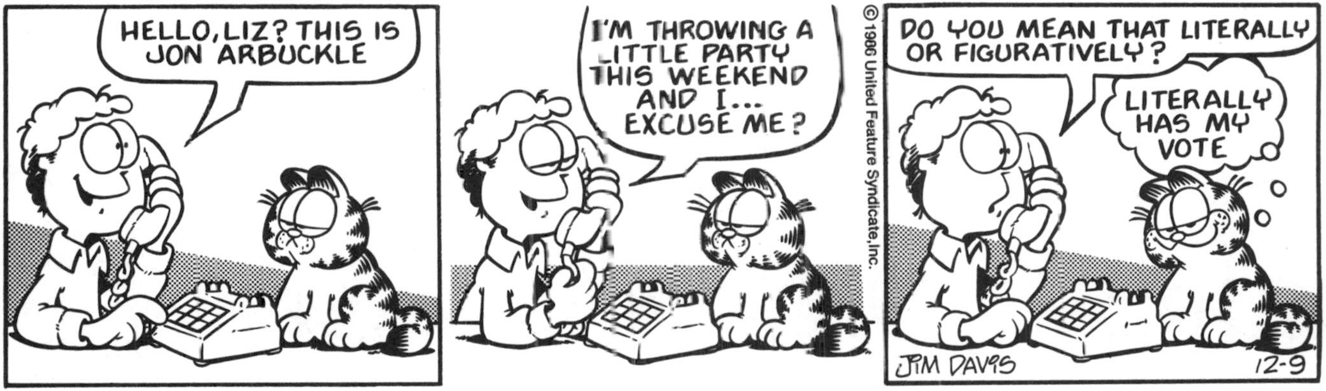
HELLO, LIZ? THIS IS JON ARBUCKLE
I'M THROWING A LITTLE PARTY THIS WEEKEND AND I... EXCUSE ME?
DO YOU MEAN THAT LITERALLY OR FIGURATIVELY?
LITERALLY HAS MY VOTE
JIM DAVIS
12-9
© 1986 United Feature Syndicate, Inc.

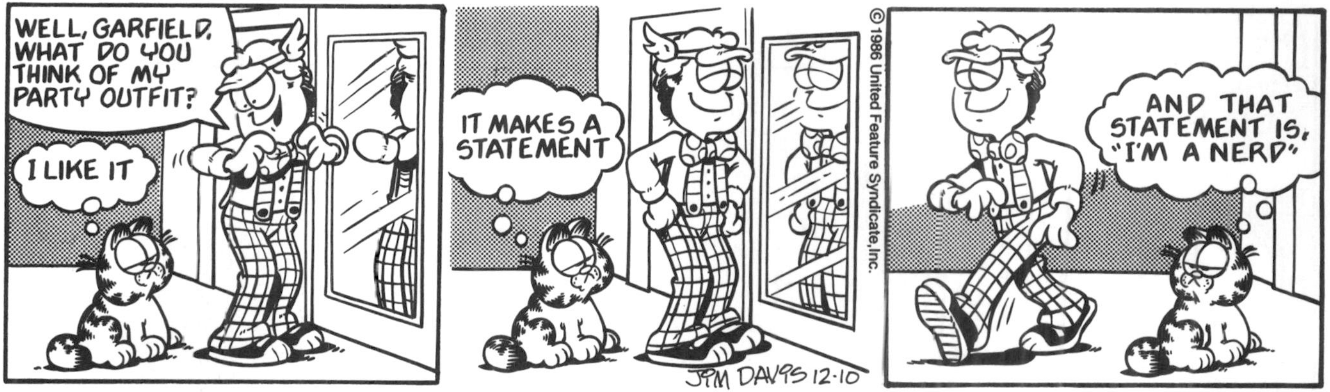
WELL, GARFIELD. WHAT DO YOU THINK OF MY PARTY OUTFIT?
I LIKE IT
IT MAKES A STATEMENT
AND THAT STATEMENT IS, "I'M A NERD"
JIM DAVIS 12-10
© 1986 United Feature Syndicate, Inc.

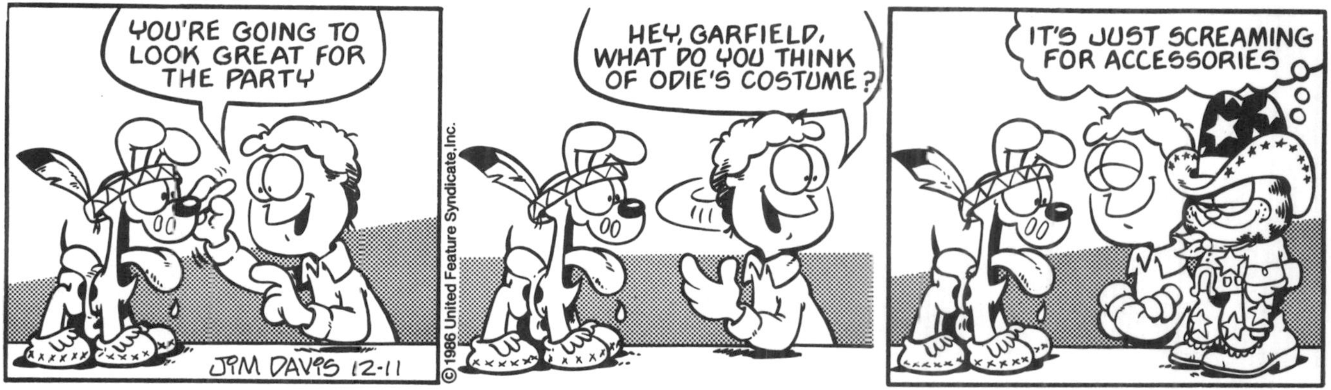
YOU'RE GOING TO LOOK GREAT FOR THE PARTY
JIM DAVIS 12-11
© 1986 United Feature Syndicate, Inc.
HEY, GARFIELD, WHAT DO YOU THINK OF ODIE'S COSTUME?
IT'S JUST SCREAMING FOR ACCESSORIES

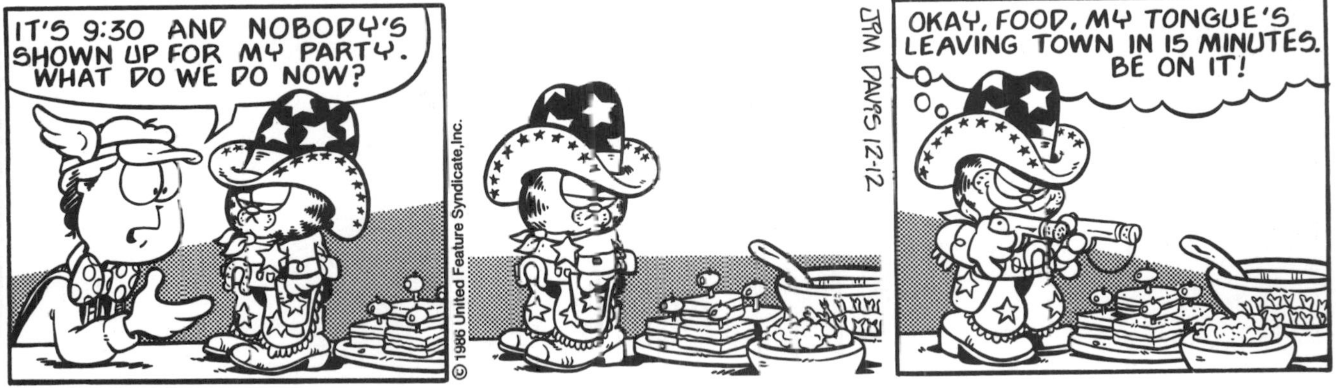
IT'S 9:30 AND NOBODY'S SHOWN UP FOR MY PARTY. WHAT DO WE DO NOW?
© 1986 United Feature Syndicate, Inc.
JIM DAVIS 12-12
OKAY, FOOD, MY TONGUE'S LEAVING TOWN IN 15 MINUTES. BE ON IT!

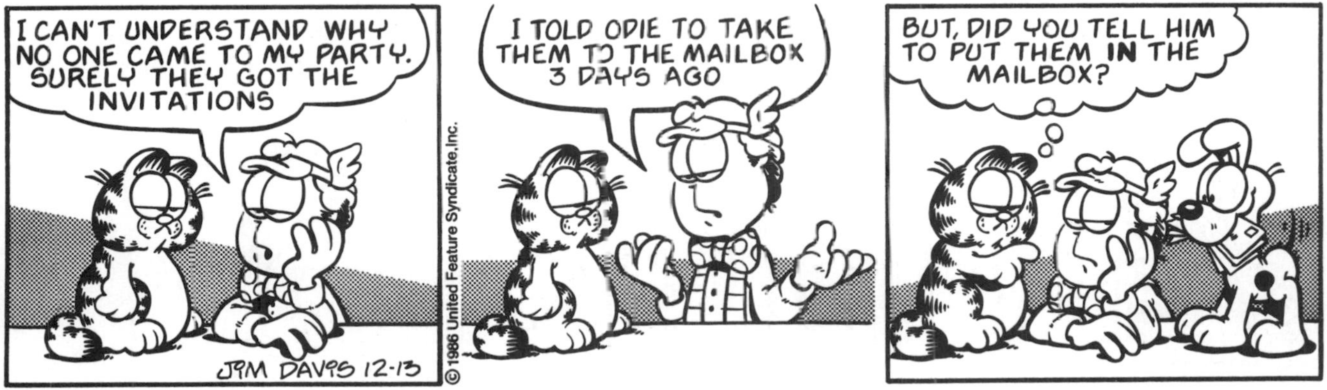
I CAN'T UNDERSTAND WHY NO ONE CAME TO MY PARTY. SURELY THEY GOT THE INVITATIONS
JIM DAVIS 12-13
© 1986 United Feature Syndicate, Inc.
I TOLD ODIE TO TAKE THEM TO THE MAILBOX 3 DAYS AGO
BUT, DID YOU TELL HIM TO PUT THEM **IN** THE MAILBOX?

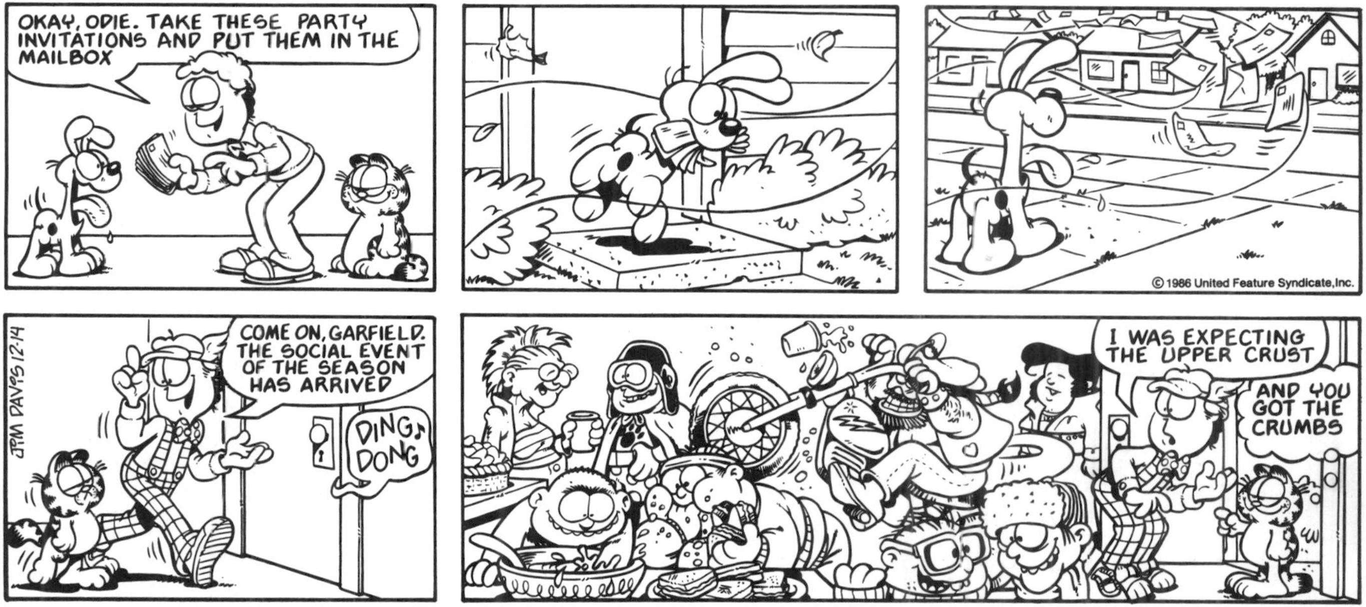
OKAY, ODIE. TAKE THESE PARTY INVITATIONS AND PUT THEM IN THE MAILBOX
© 1986 United Feature Syndicate, Inc.
JIM DAVIS 12·14
COME ON, GARFIELD. THE SOCIAL EVENT OF THE SEASON HAS ARRIVED
DING DONG
I WAS EXPECTING THE UPPER CRUST
AND YOU GOT THE CRUMBS

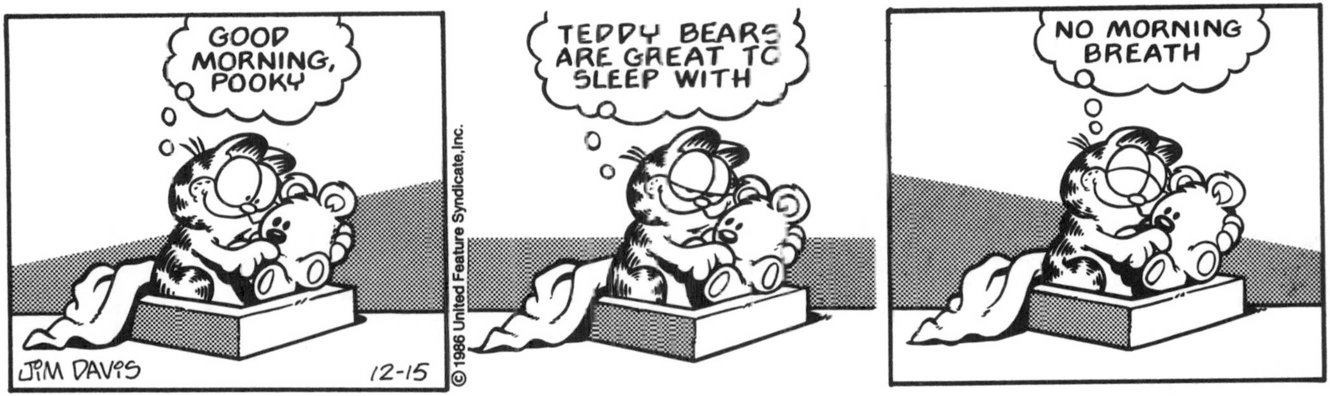
GOOD MORNING, POOKY
JIM DAVIS
12-15
© 1986 United Feature Syndicate, Inc.
TEDDY BEARS ARE GREAT TO SLEEP WITH
NO MORNING BREATH

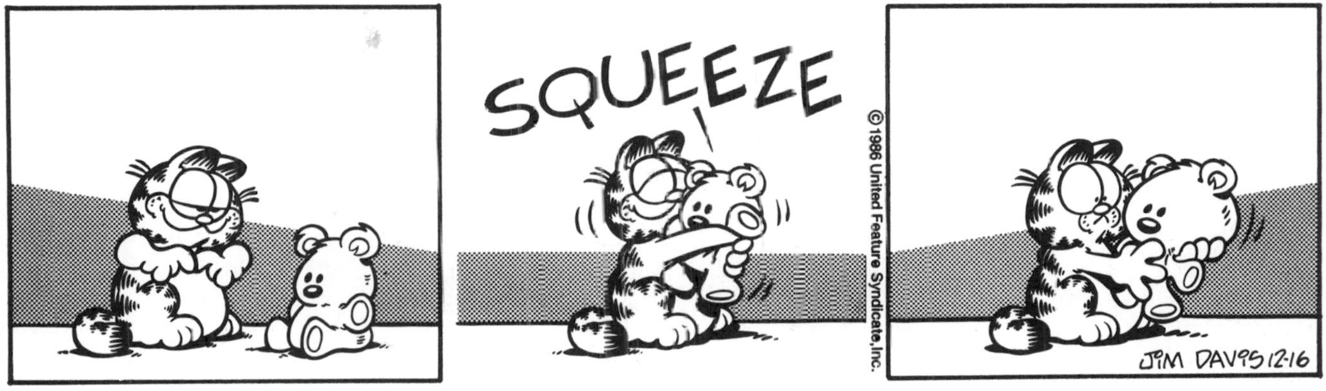
SQUEEZE
© 1986 United Feature Syndicate, Inc.
JIM DAVIS 12-16

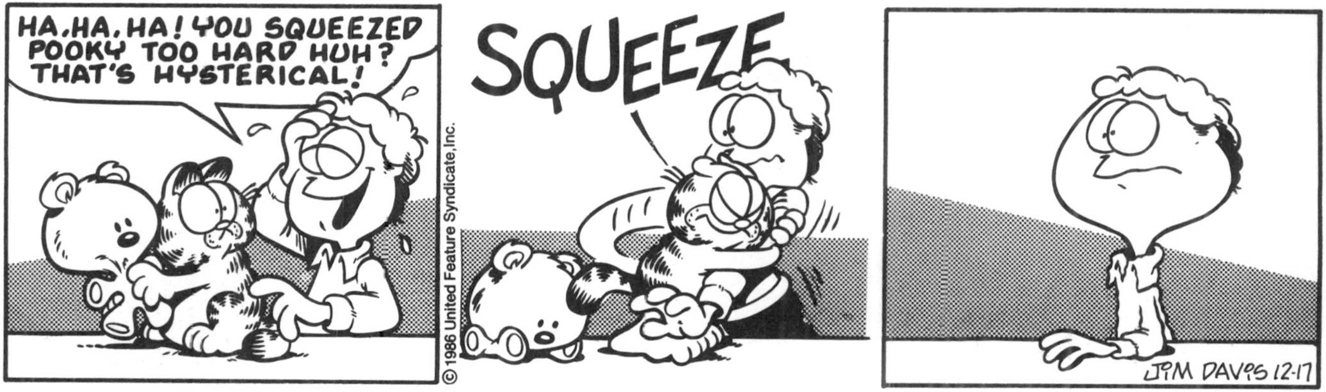
HA, HA, HA! YOU SQUEEZED POOKY TOO HARD HUH? THAT'S HYSTERICAL!
© 1986 United Feature Syndicate, Inc.
SQUEEZE
JIM DAVIS 12-17

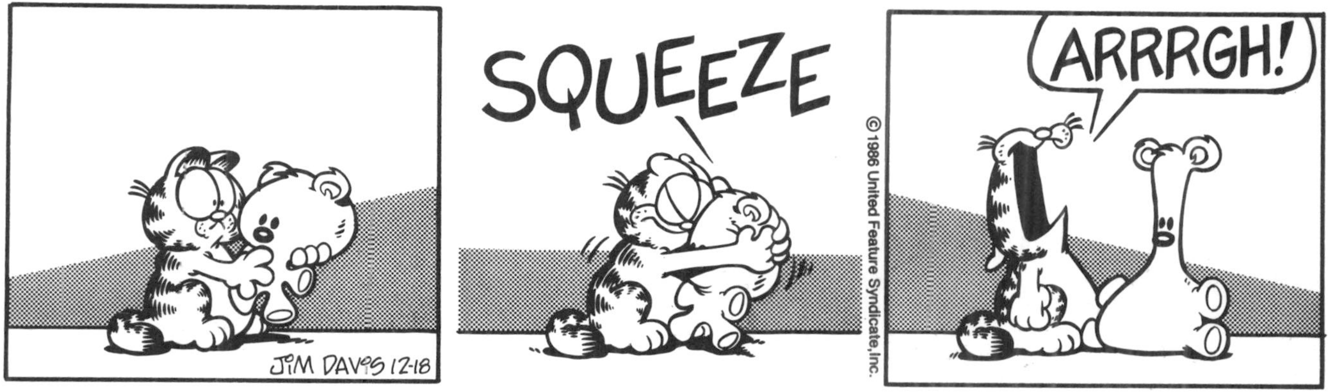
JIM DAVIS 12-18
SQUEEZE
© 1986 United Feature Syndicate, Inc.
ARRRGH!

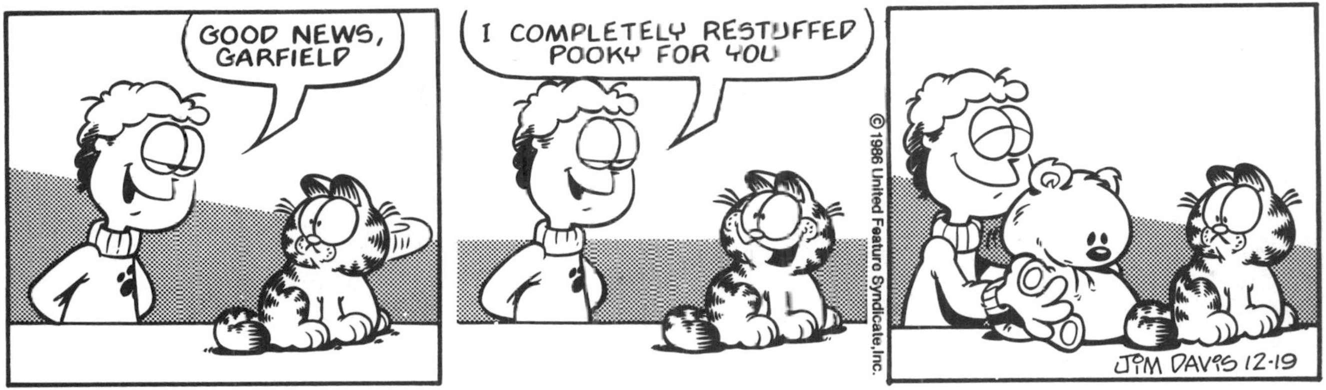
GOOD NEWS, GARFIELD
I COMPLETELY RESTUFFED POOKY FOR YOU
JIM DAVIS 12-19


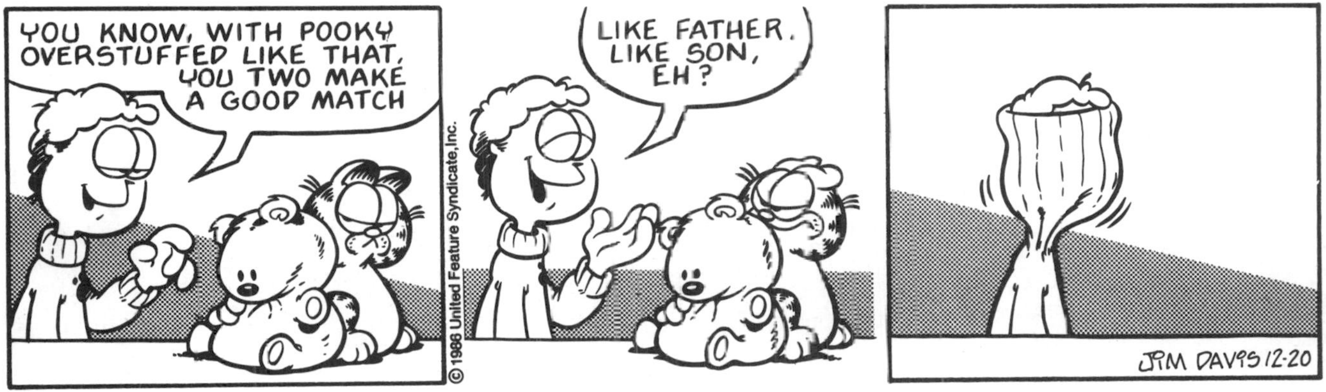
YOU KNOW, WITH POOKY OVERSTUFFED LIKE THAT, YOU TWO MAKE A GOOD MATCH
LIKE FATHER, LIKE SON, EH?
JIM DAVIS 12-20

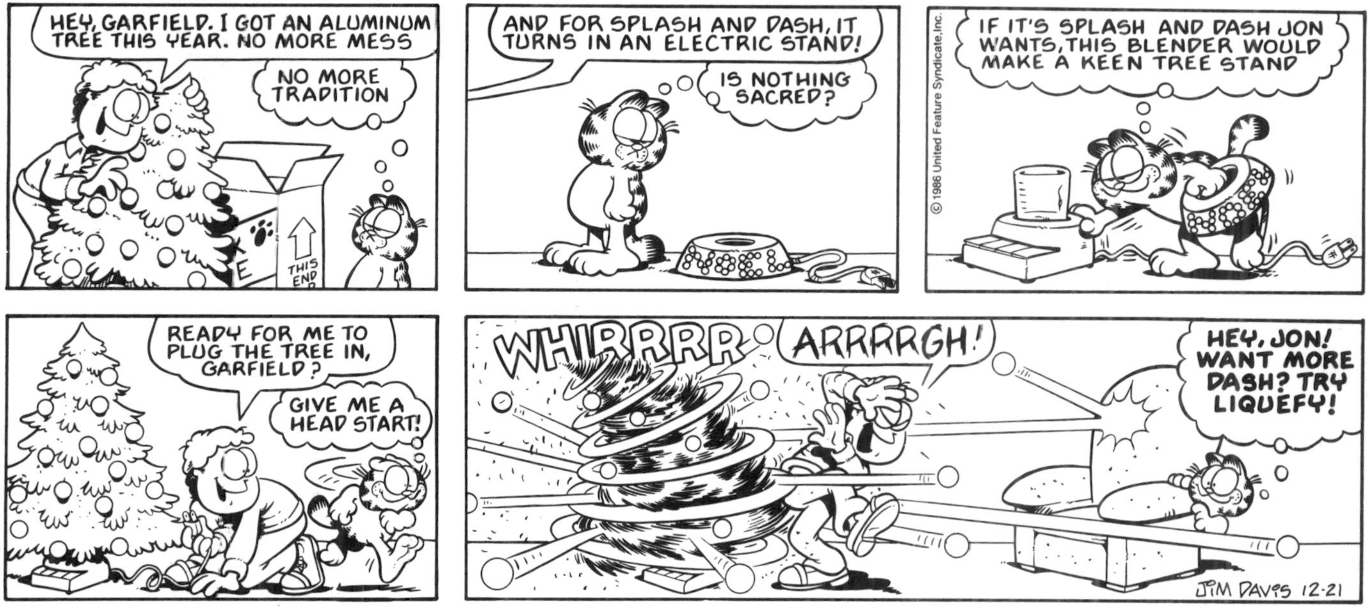
HEY, GARFIELD. I GOT AN ALUMINUM TREE THIS YEAR. NO MORE MESS
NO MORE TRADITION
THIS END
AND FOR SPLASH AND DASH, IT TURNS IN AN ELECTRIC STAND!
IS NOTHING SACRED?
IF IT'S SPLASH AND DASH JON WANTS, THIS BLENDER WOULD MAKE A KEEN TREE STAND
© 1986 United Feature Syndicate, Inc.
READY FOR ME TO PLUG THE TREE IN, GARFIELD?
GIVE ME A HEAD START!
WHIRRRR
ARRRRGH!
HEY, JON! WANT MORE DASH? TRY LIQUEFY!
JIM DAVIS 12-21

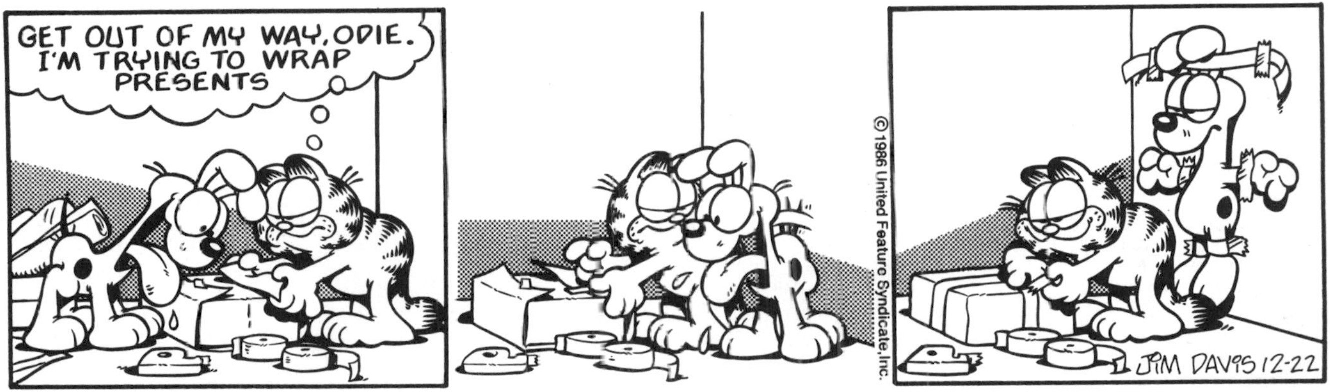
GET OUT OF MY WAY, ODIE. I'M TRYING TO WRAP PRESENTS
© 1986 United Feature Syndicate, Inc.
JIM DAVIS 12-22

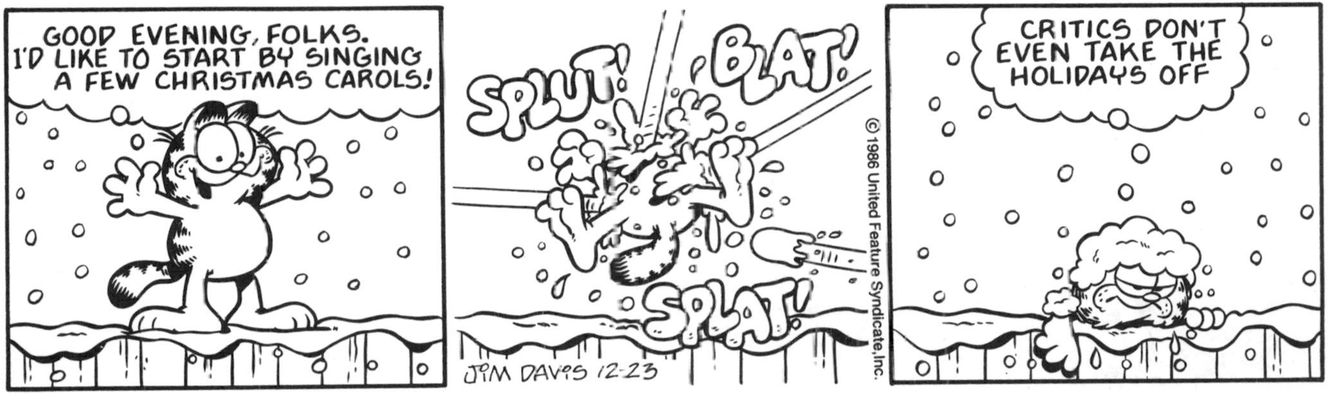
GOOD EVENING, FOLKS. I'D LIKE TO START BY SINGING A FEW CHRISTMAS CAROLS!
SPLUT!
BLAT!
SPLAT!
JIM DAVIS 12-23
© 1986 United Feature Syndicate, Inc.
CRITICS DON'T EVEN TAKE THE HOLIDAYS OFF

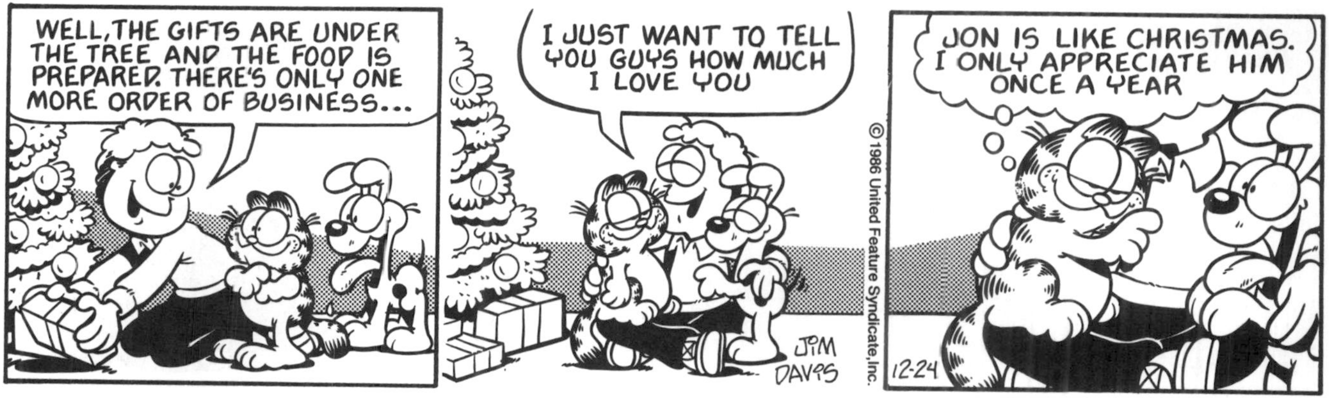
WELL, THE GIFTS ARE UNDER THE TREE AND THE FOOD IS PREPARED. THERE'S ONLY ONE MORE ORDER OF BUSINESS...
I JUST WANT TO TELL YOU GUYS HOW MUCH I LOVE YOU
JIM DAVIS
© 1986 United Feature Syndicate, Inc.
12-24
JON IS LIKE CHRISTMAS. I ONLY APPRECIATE HIM ONCE A YEAR

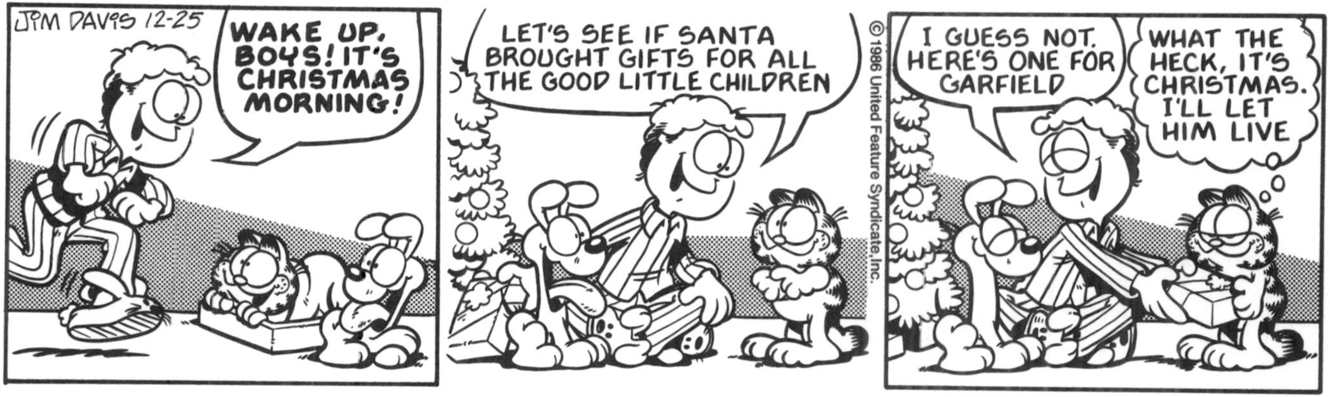
JIM DAVIS 12-25
WAKE UP, BOYS! IT'S CHRISTMAS MORNING!
LET'S SEE IF SANTA BROUGHT GIFTS FOR ALL THE GOOD LITTLE CHILDREN
© 1986 United Feature Syndicate, Inc.
I GUESS NOT. HERE'S ONE FOR GARFIELD
WHAT THE HECK, IT'S CHRISTMAS. I'LL LET HIM LIVE

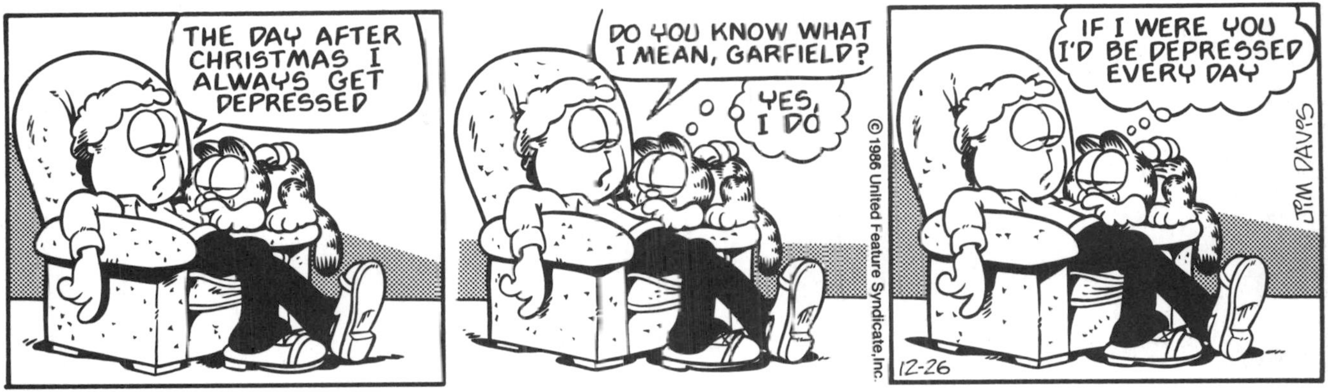
THE DAY AFTER CHRISTMAS I ALWAYS GET DEPRESSED
DO YOU KNOW WHAT I MEAN, GARFIELD?
YES, I DO
© 1986 United Feature Syndicate, Inc.
IF I WERE YOU I'D BE DEPRESSED EVERY DAY
JIM DAVIS
12-26

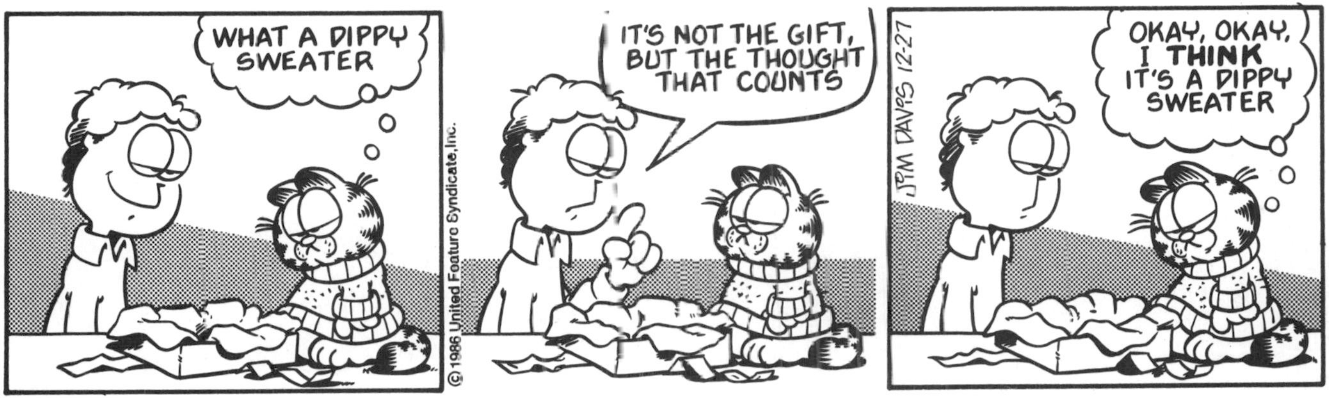
WHAT A DIPPY SWEATER
© 1986 United Feature Syndicate, Inc.
IT'S NOT THE GIFT, BUT THE THOUGHT THAT COUNTS
JIM DAVIS 12-27
OKAY, OKAY, I **THINK** IT'S A DIPPY SWEATER

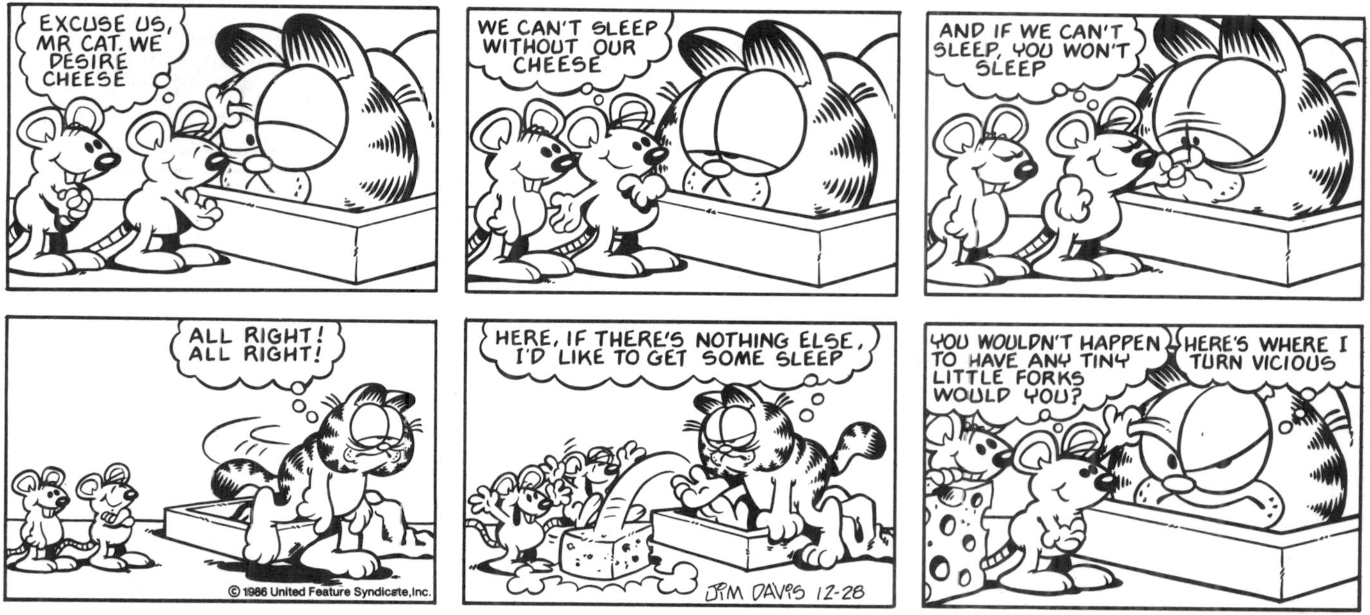
EXCUSE US, MR CAT. WE DESIRE CHEESE
WE CAN'T SLEEP WITHOUT OUR CHEESE
AND IF WE CAN'T SLEEP, YOU WON'T SLEEP
ALL RIGHT! ALL RIGHT!
© 1986 United Feature Syndicate, Inc.
HERE, IF THERE'S NOTHING ELSE, I'D LIKE TO GET SOME SLEEP
JIM DAVIS 12-28
YOU WOULDN'T HAPPEN TO HAVE ANY TINY LITTLE FORKS WOULD YOU?
HERE'S WHERE I TURN VICIOUS

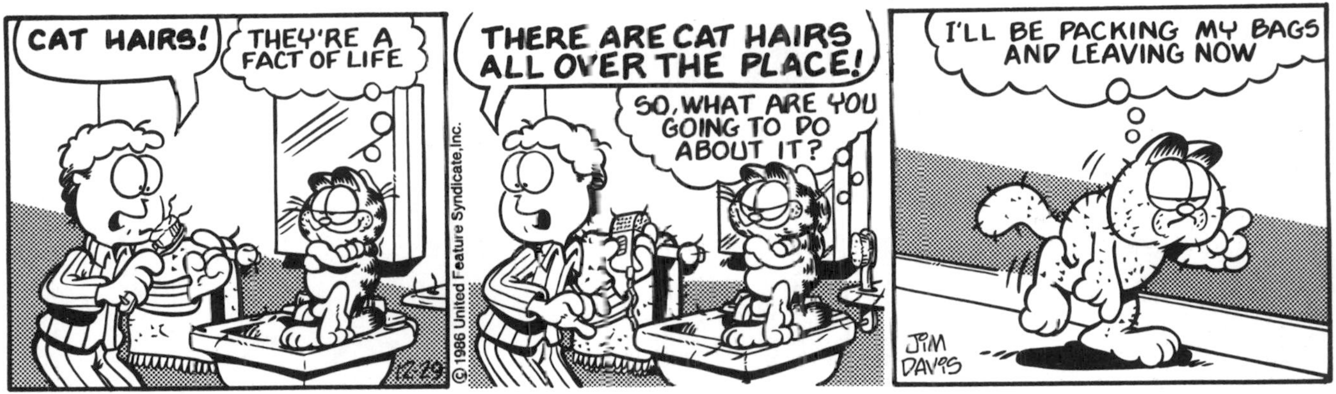
CAT HAIRS!
THEY'RE A FACT OF LIFE
12-29
© 1986 United Feature Syndicate, Inc.
THERE ARE CAT HAIRS ALL OVER THE PLACE!
SO, WHAT ARE YOU GOING TO DO ABOUT IT?
I'LL BE PACKING MY BAGS AND LEAVING NOW
JIM DAVIS

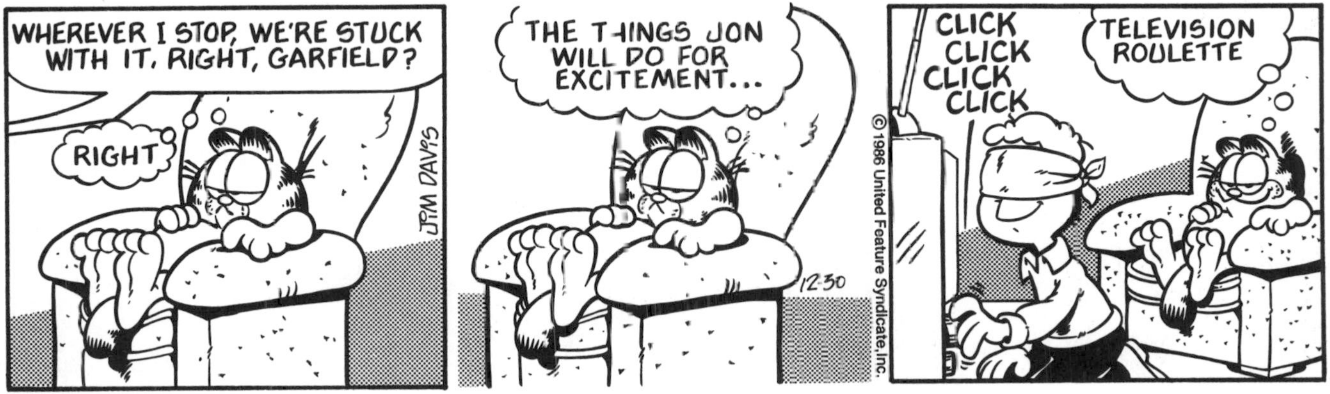
WHEREVER I STOP, WE'RE STUCK WITH IT. RIGHT, GARFIELD?
RIGHT
JIM DAVIS
THE THINGS JON WILL DO FOR EXCITEMENT...
12-30
© 1986 United Feature Syndicate, Inc.
CLICK
CLICK
CLICK
CLICK
TELEVISION ROULETTE

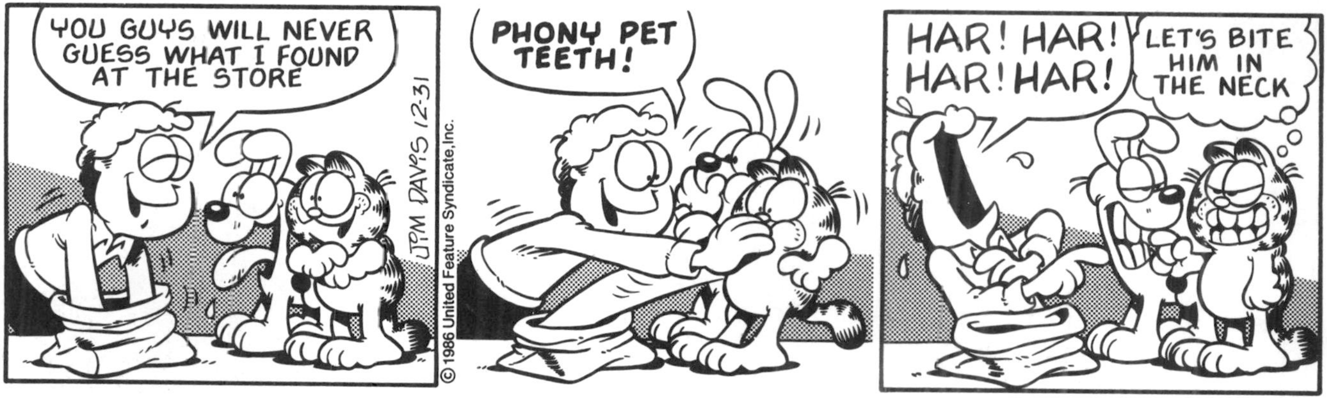
YOU GUYS WILL NEVER GUESS WHAT I FOUND AT THE STORE
PHONY PET TEETH!
HAR! HAR! HAR! HAR!
LET'S BITE HIM IN THE NECK
JIM DAVIS 12-31
© 1986 United Feature Syndicate, Inc.

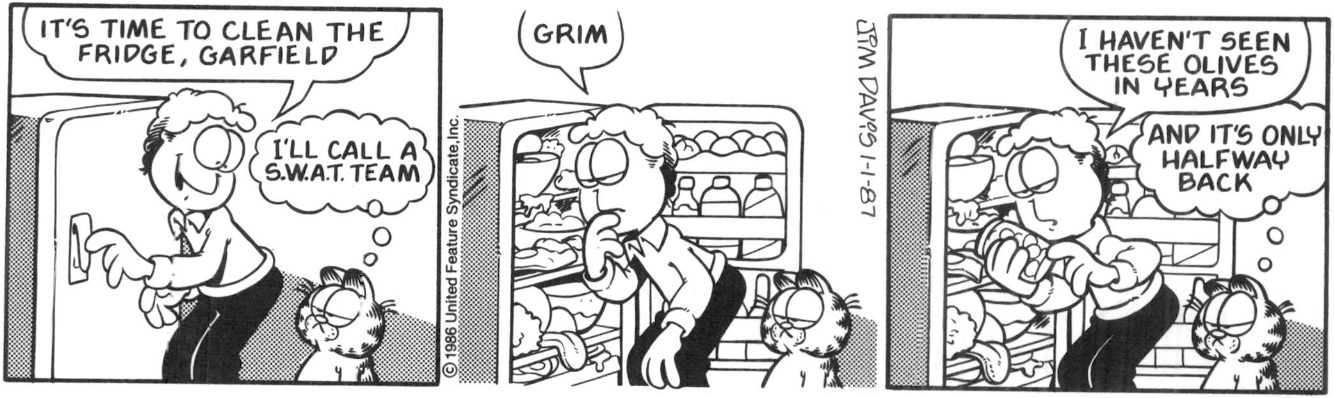
IT'S TIME TO CLEAN THE FRIDGE, GARFIELD
I'LL CALL A S.W.A.T. TEAM
GRIM
I HAVEN'T SEEN THESE OLIVES IN YEARS
AND IT'S ONLY HALFWAY BACK
JIM DAVIS 1-1-87
© 1986 United Feature Syndicate, Inc.

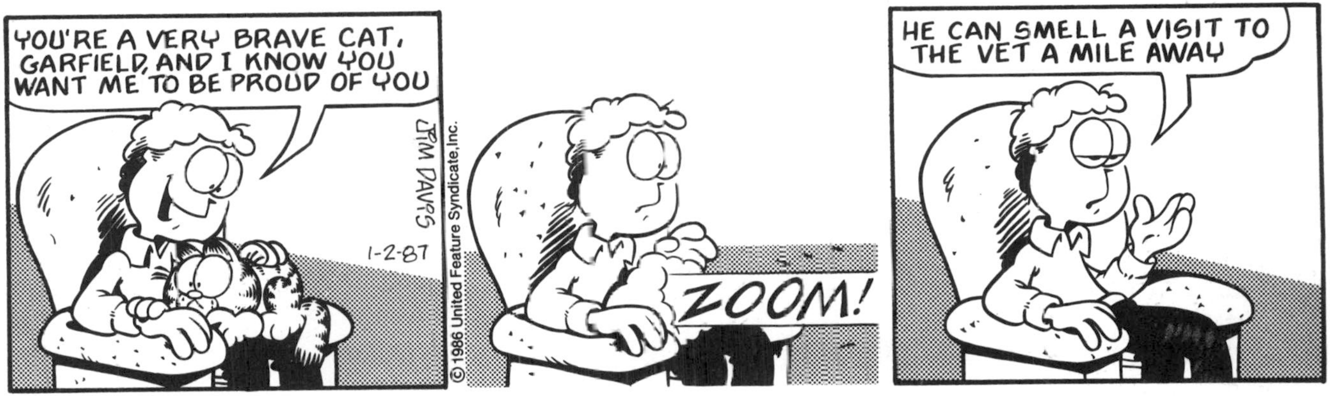
YOU'RE A VERY BRAVE CAT, GARFIELD, AND I KNOW YOU WANT ME TO BE PROUD OF YOU
ZOOM!
HE CAN SMELL A VISIT TO THE VET A MILE AWAY


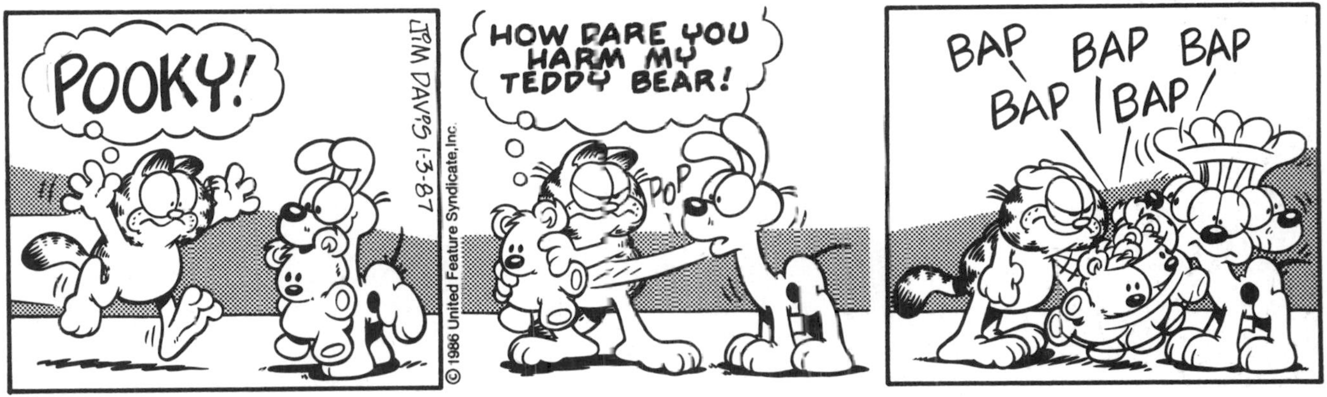
POOKY!
HOW DARE YOU HARM MY TEDDY BEAR!
POP
BAP BAP BAP BAP BAP BAP

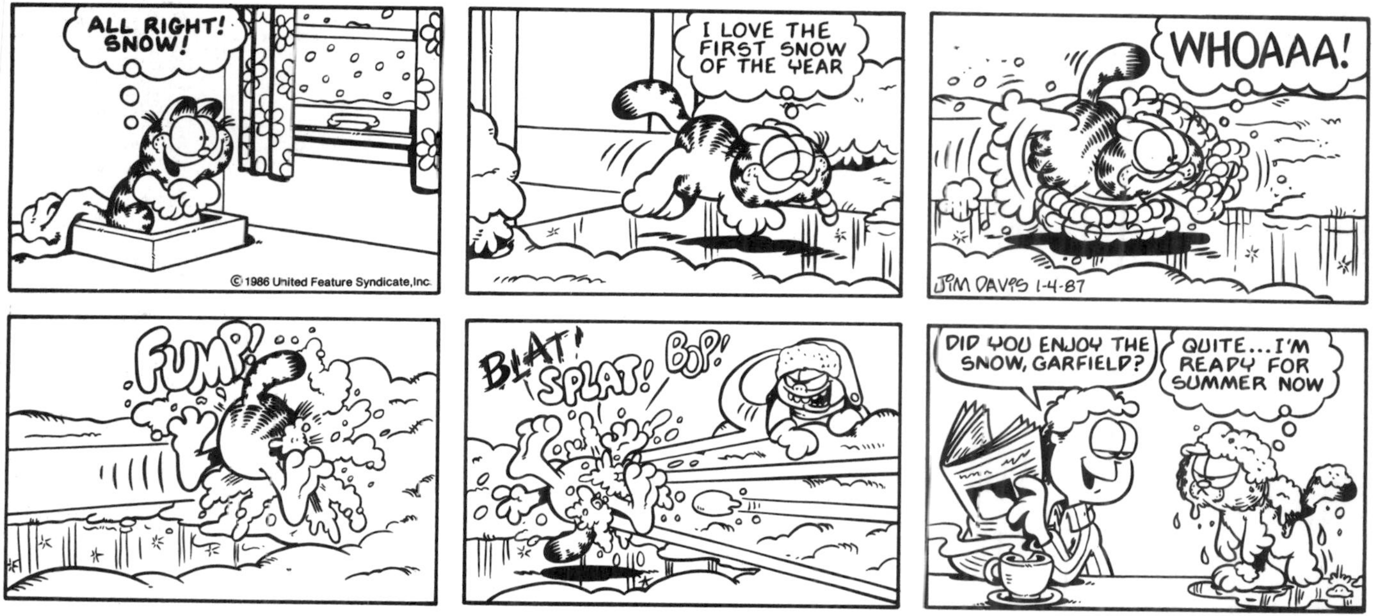
ALL RIGHT! SNOW!
© 1986 United Feature Syndicate, Inc.
I LOVE THE FIRST SNOW OF THE YEAR
WHOAAA!
JIM DAVIS 1-4-87
FUMP!
BLAT!
SPLAT!
BOP!
DID YOU ENJOY THE SNOW, GARFIELD?
QUITE... I'M READY FOR SUMMER NOW

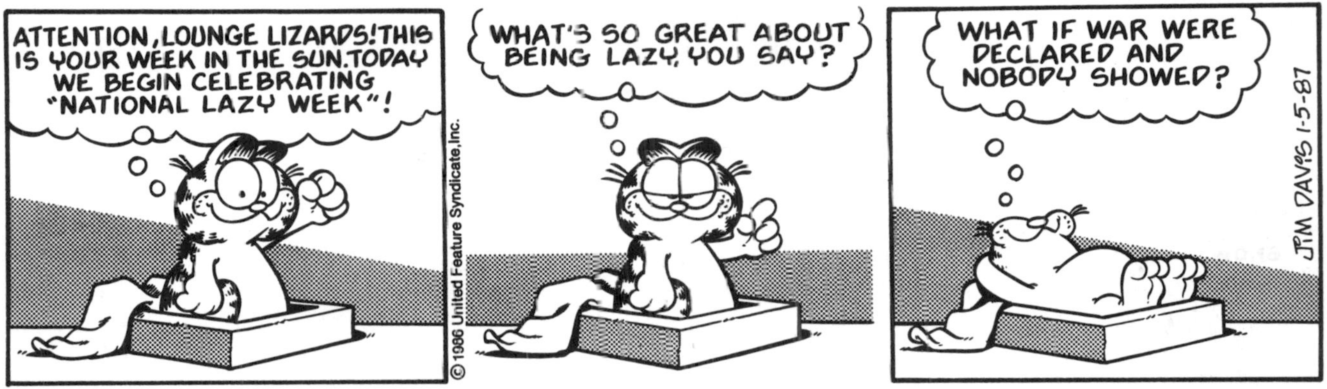
ATTENTION, LOUNGE LIZARDS! THIS IS YOUR WEEK IN THE SUN. TODAY WE BEGIN CELEBRATING "NATIONAL LAZY WEEK"!
© 1986 United Feature Syndicate, Inc.
WHAT'S SO GREAT ABOUT BEING LAZY, YOU SAY?
WHAT IF WAR WERE DECLARED AND NOBODY SHOWED?
JIM DAVIS 1-5-87

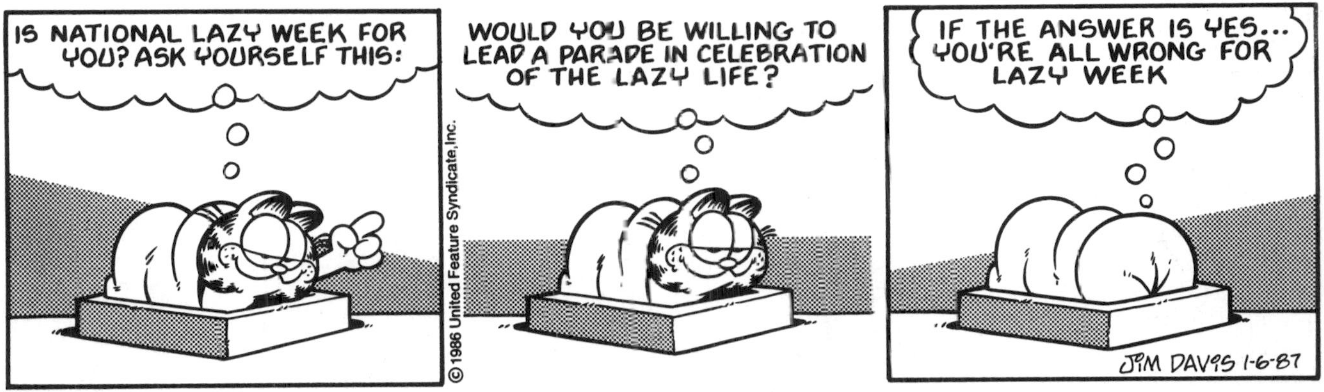
IS NATIONAL LAZY WEEK FOR YOU? ASK YOURSELF THIS:
© 1986 United Feature Syndicate, Inc.
WOULD YOU BE WILLING TO LEAD A PARADE IN CELEBRATION OF THE LAZY LIFE?
IF THE ANSWER IS YES... YOU'RE ALL WRONG FOR LAZY WEEK
JIM DAVIS 1-6-87

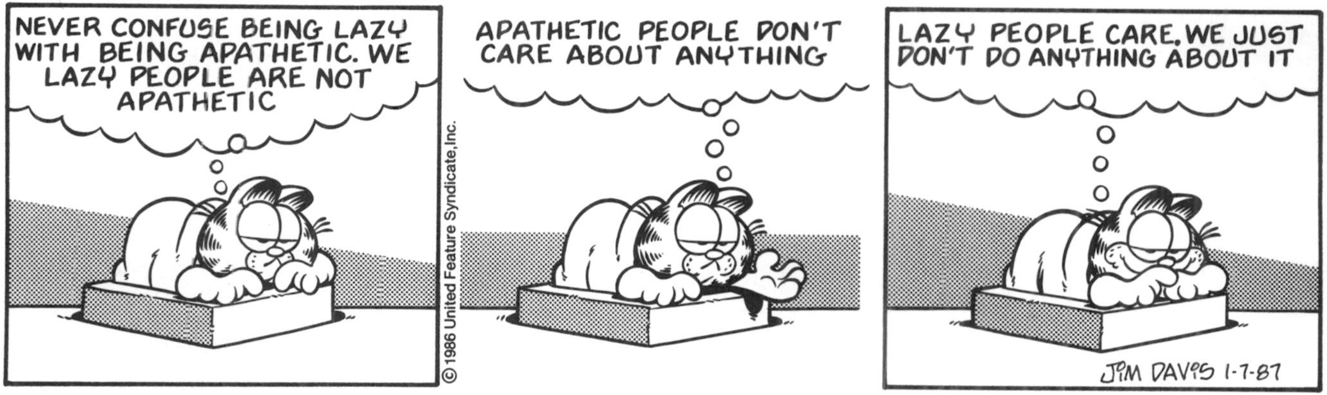
NEVER CONFUSE BEING LAZY WITH BEING APATHETIC. WE LAZY PEOPLE ARE NOT APATHETIC
APATHETIC PEOPLE DON'T CARE ABOUT ANYTHING
LAZY PEOPLE CARE. WE JUST DON'T DO ANYTHING ABOUT IT
© 1986 United Feature Syndicate, Inc.
JIM DAVIS 1-7-87

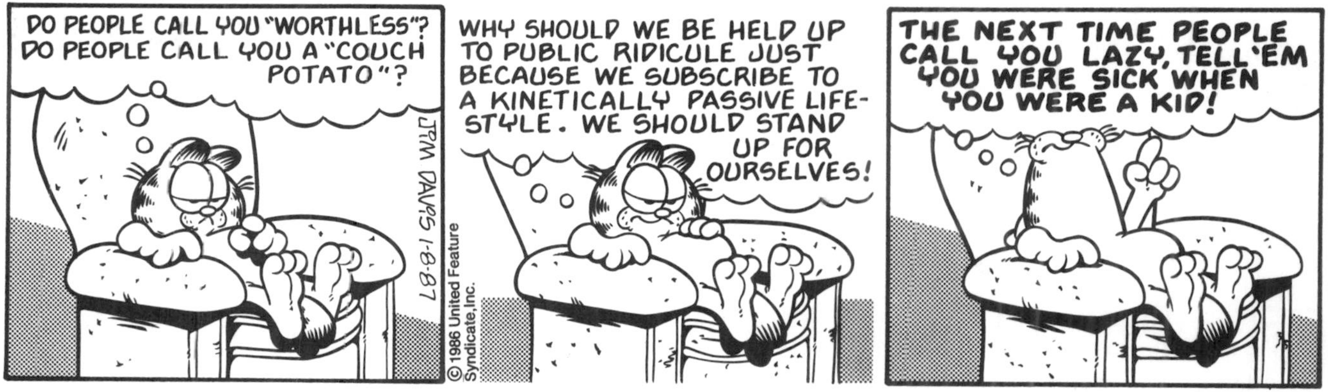
DO PEOPLE CALL YOU "WORTHLESS"? DO PEOPLE CALL YOU A "COUCH POTATO"?
JIM DAVIS 1-8-87
© 1986 United Feature Syndicate, Inc.
WHY SHOULD WE BE HELD UP TO PUBLIC RIDICULE JUST BECAUSE WE SUBSCRIBE TO A KINETICALLY PASSIVE LIFE-STYLE. WE SHOULD STAND UP FOR OURSELVES!
THE NEXT TIME PEOPLE CALL YOU LAZY, TELL 'EM YOU WERE SICK WHEN YOU WERE A KID!

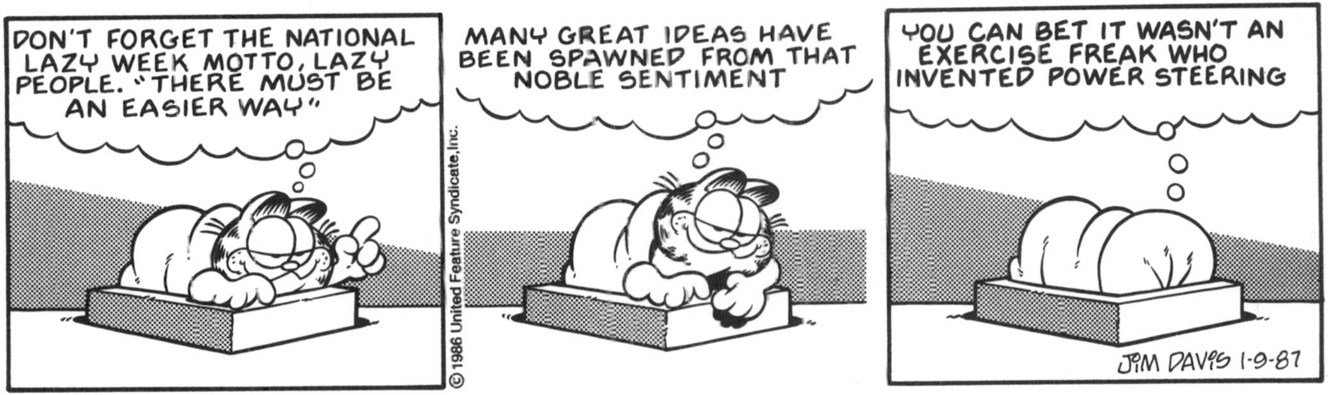
DON'T FORGET THE NATIONAL LAZY WEEK MOTTO, LAZY PEOPLE. "THERE MUST BE AN EASIER WAY"
MANY GREAT IDEAS HAVE BEEN SPAWNED FROM THAT NOBLE SENTIMENT
YOU CAN BET IT WASN'T AN EXERCISE FREAK WHO INVENTED POWER STEERING
© 1986 United Feature Syndicate, Inc.
JIM DAVIS 1-9-87

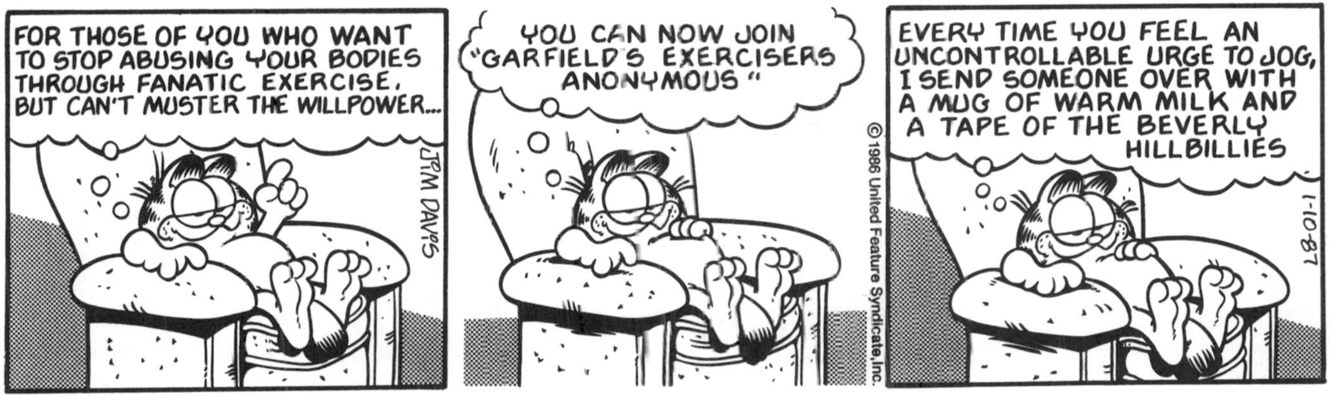
FOR THOSE OF YOU WHO WANT TO STOP ABUSING YOUR BODIES THROUGH FANATIC EXERCISE, BUT CAN'T MUSTER THE WILLPOWER...
JIM DAVIS
YOU CAN NOW JOIN "GARFIELD'S EXERCISERS ANONYMOUS"
© 1986 United Feature Syndicate, Inc.
EVERY TIME YOU FEEL AN UNCONTROLLABLE URGE TO JOG, I SEND SOMEONE OVER WITH A MUG OF WARM MILK AND A TAPE OF THE BEVERLY HILLBILLIES
1-10-87

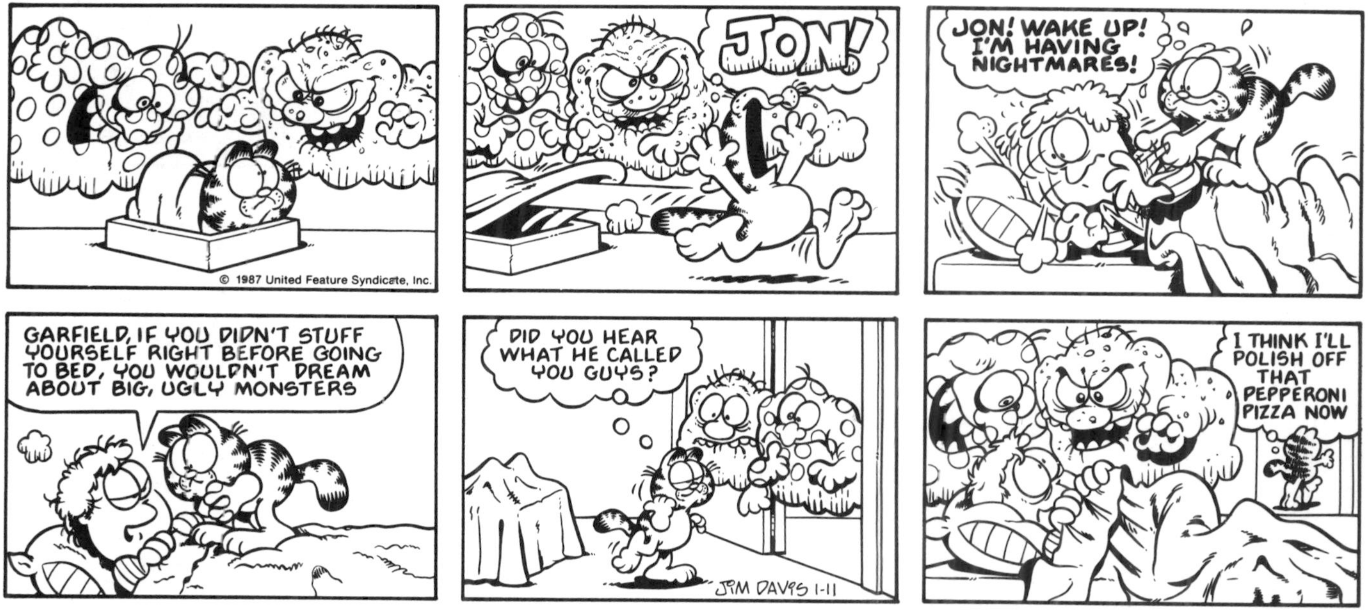
© 1987 United Feature Syndicate, Inc.
JON!
JON! WAKE UP! I'M HAVING NIGHTMARES!
GARFIELD, IF YOU DIDN'T STUFF YOURSELF RIGHT BEFORE GOING TO BED, YOU WOULDN'T DREAM ABOUT BIG, UGLY MONSTERS
DID YOU HEAR WHAT HE CALLED YOU GUYS?
JIM DAVIS 1-11
I THINK I'LL POLISH OFF THAT PEPPERONI PIZZA NOW

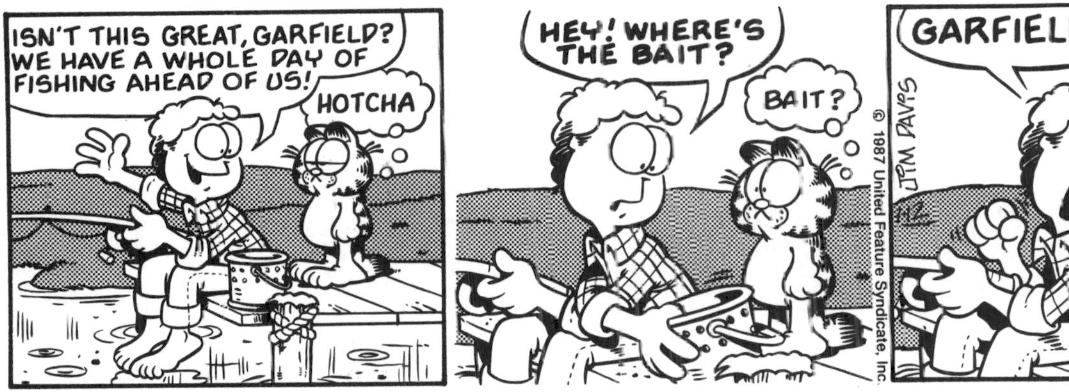
ISN'T THIS GREAT, GARFIELD? WE HAVE A WHOLE DAY OF FISHING AHEAD OF US!
HOTCHA
HEY! WHERE'S THE BAIT?
BAIT?
GARFIELD!
I THOUGHT IT WAS SUSHI
JIM DAVIS 1-12
© 1987 United Feature Syndicate, Inc.

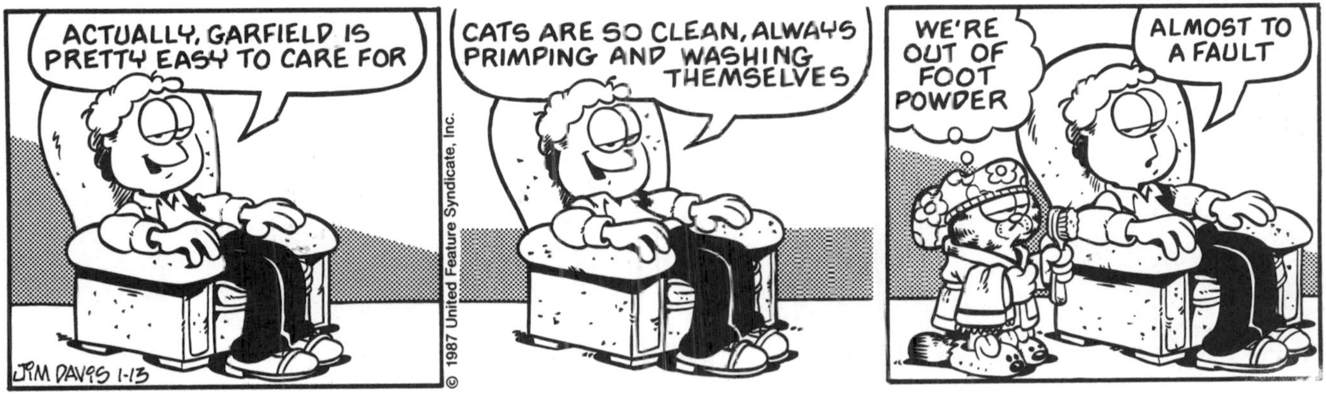
ACTUALLY, GARFIELD IS PRETTY EASY TO CARE FOR
CATS ARE SO CLEAN, ALWAYS PRIMPING AND WASHING THEMSELVES
WE'RE OUT OF FOOT POWDER
ALMOST TO A FAULT
JIM DAVIS 1-13
© 1987 United Feature Syndicate, Inc.

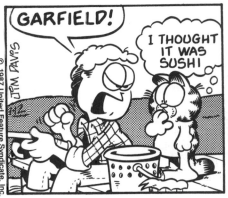

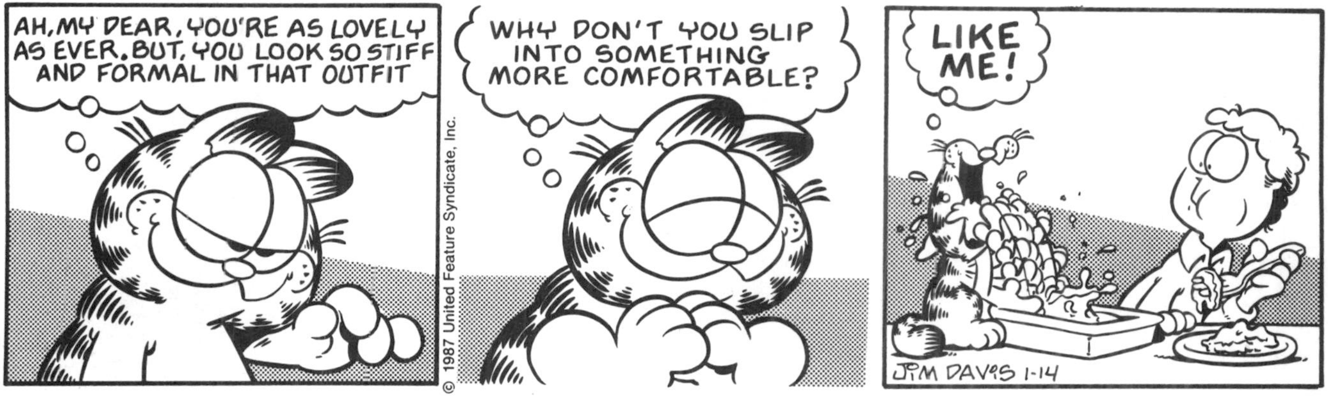
AH, MY DEAR, YOU'RE AS LOVELY AS EVER. BUT, YOU LOOK SO STIFF AND FORMAL IN THAT OUTFIT
© 1987 United Feature Syndicate, Inc.
WHY DON'T YOU SLIP INTO SOMETHING MORE COMFORTABLE?
LIKE ME!
JIM DAVIS 1-14

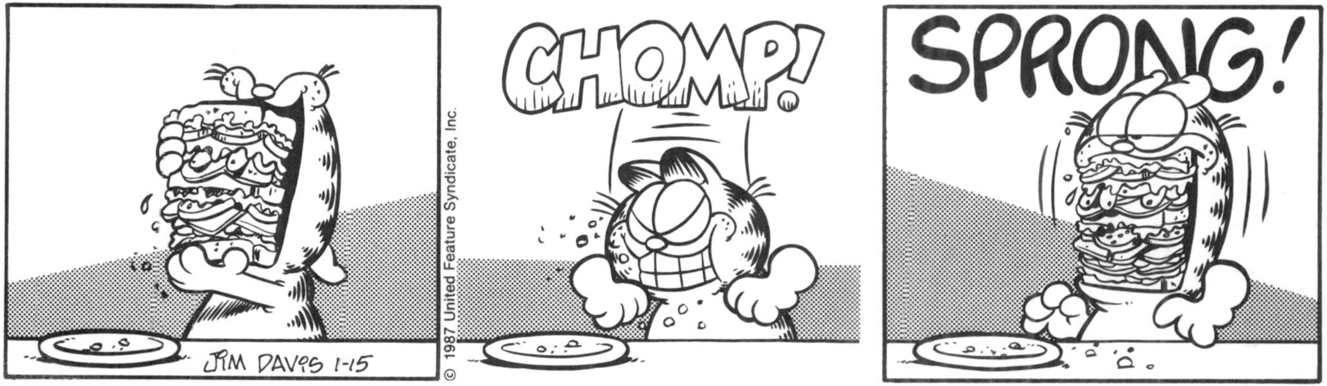
JIM DAVIS 1-15
© 1987 United Feature Syndicate, Inc.
CHOMP!
SPRONG!

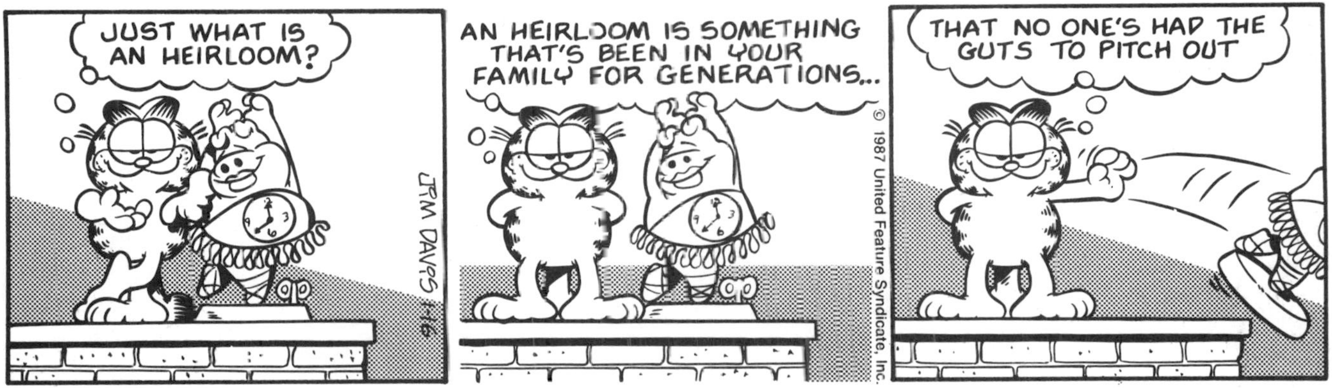
JUST WHAT IS AN HEIRLOOM?
JIM DAVIS 1-16
AN HEIRLOOM IS SOMETHING THAT'S BEEN IN YOUR FAMILY FOR GENERATIONS...
© 1987 United Feature Syndicate, Inc.
THAT NO ONE'S HAD THE GUTS TO PITCH OUT

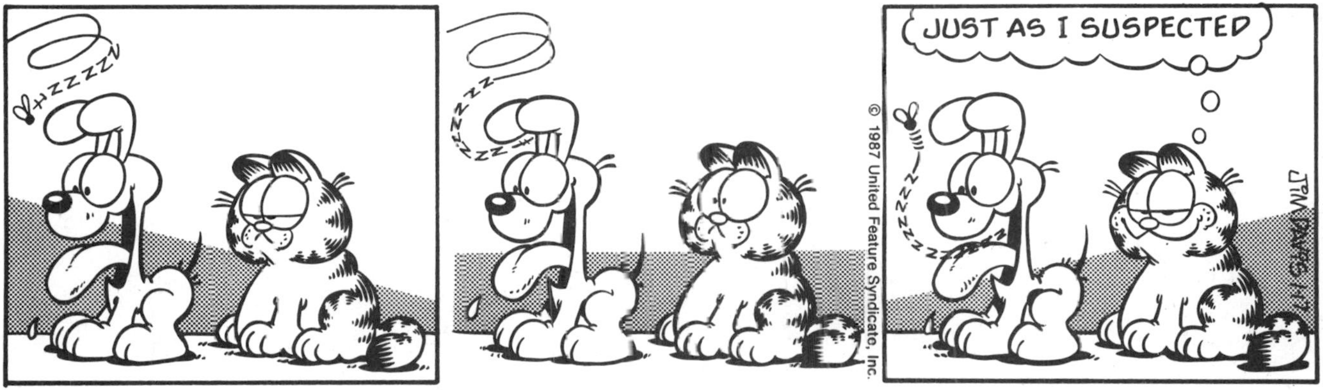
ZZZZZ
© 1987 United Feature Syndicate, Inc.
JUST AS I SUSPECTED
JIM DAVIS 1-17

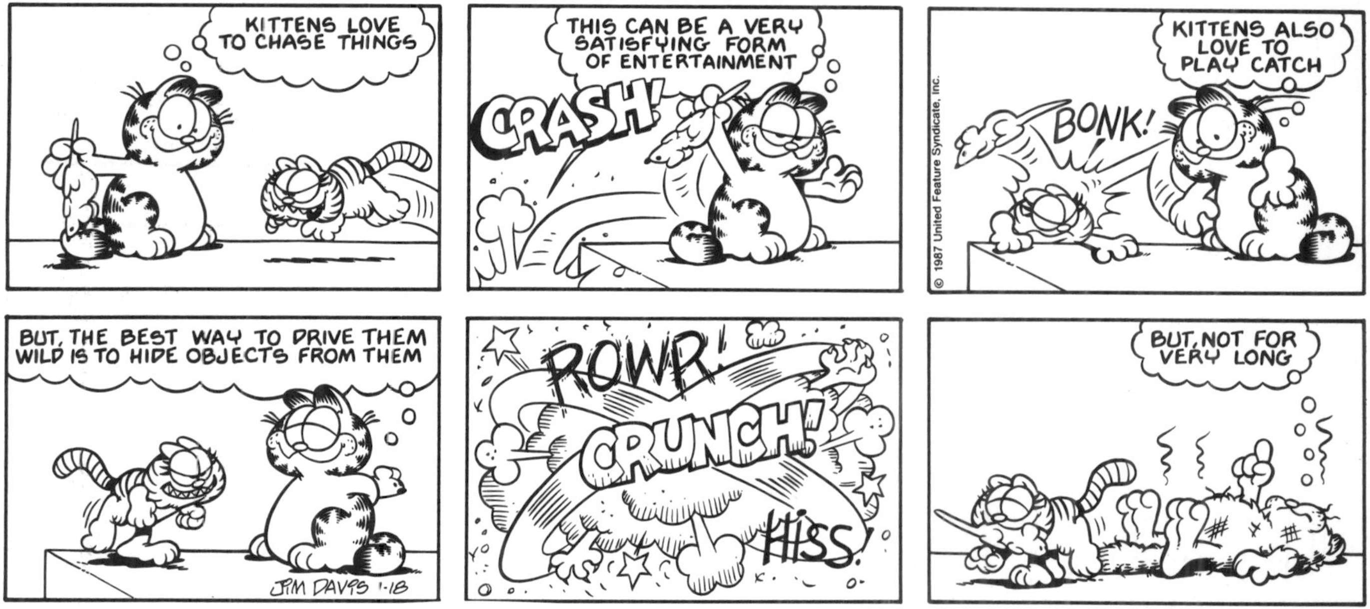
KITTENS LOVE TO CHASE THINGS
THIS CAN BE A VERY SATISFYING FORM OF ENTERTAINMENT
CRASH!
KITTENS ALSO LOVE TO PLAY CATCH
BONK!
© 1987 United Feature Syndicate, Inc.
BUT, THE BEST WAY TO DRIVE THEM WILD IS TO HIDE OBJECTS FROM THEM
JIM DAVIS 1-18
ROWR!
CRUNCH!
HISS!
BUT, NOT FOR VERY LONG

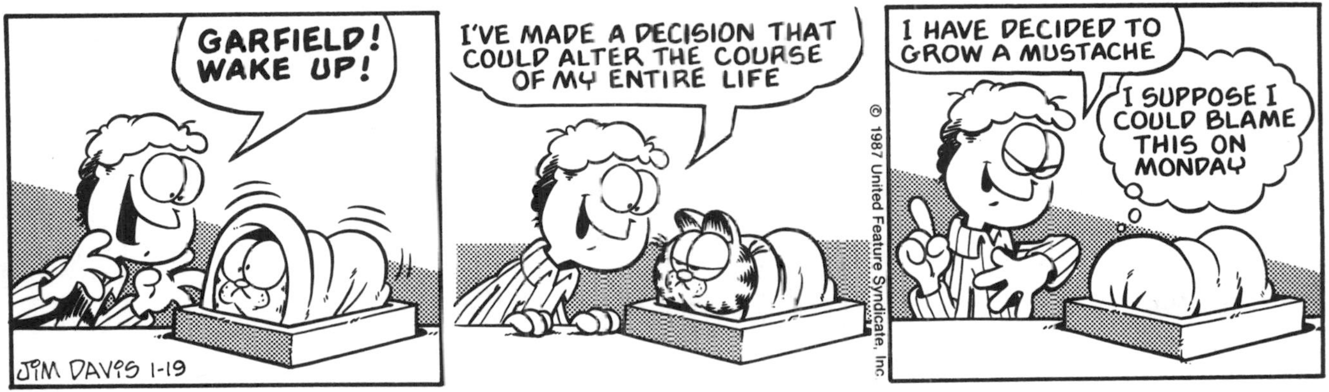
GARFIELD! WAKE UP!
JIM DAVIS 1-19
I'VE MADE A DECISION THAT COULD ALTER THE COURSE OF MY ENTIRE LIFE
© 1987 United Feature Syndicate, Inc.
I HAVE DECIDED TO GROW A MUSTACHE
I SUPPOSE I COULD BLAME THIS ON MONDAY

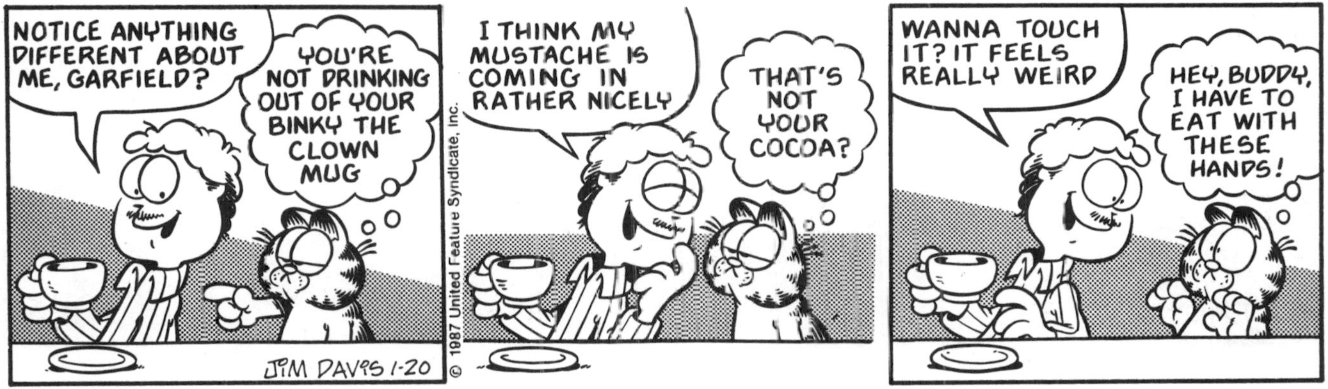
NOTICE ANYTHING DIFFERENT ABOUT ME, GARFIELD?
YOU'RE NOT DRINKING OUT OF YOUR BINKY THE CLOWN MUG
JIM DAVIS 1-20
© 1987 United Feature Syndicate, Inc.
I THINK MY MUSTACHE IS COMING IN RATHER NICELY
THAT'S NOT YOUR COCOA?
WANNA TOUCH IT? IT FEELS REALLY WEIRD
HEY, BUDDY, I HAVE TO EAT WITH THESE HANDS!

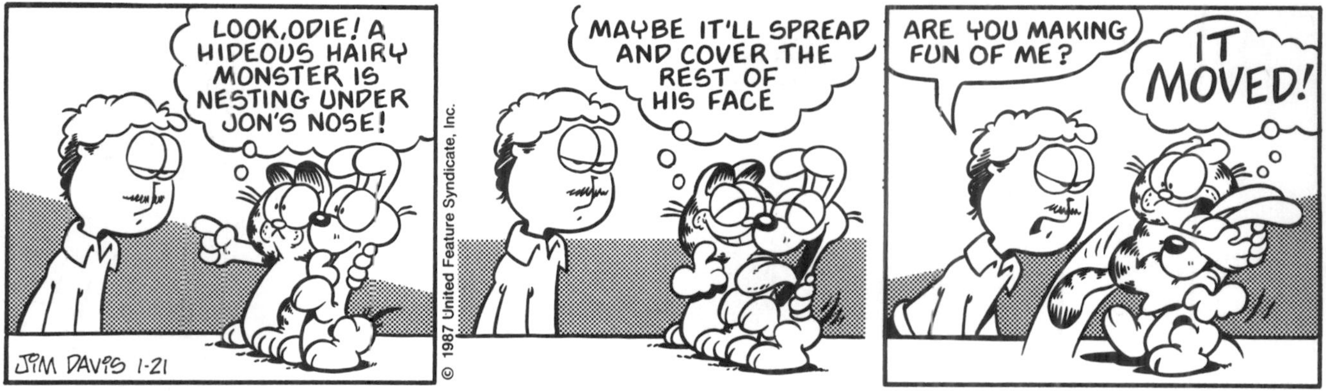
LOOK, ODIE! A HIDEOUS HAIRY MONSTER IS NESTING UNDER JON'S NOSE!
JIM DAVIS 1-21
© 1987 United Feature Syndicate, Inc.
MAYBE IT'LL SPREAD AND COVER THE REST OF HIS FACE
ARE YOU MAKING FUN OF ME?
IT MOVED!

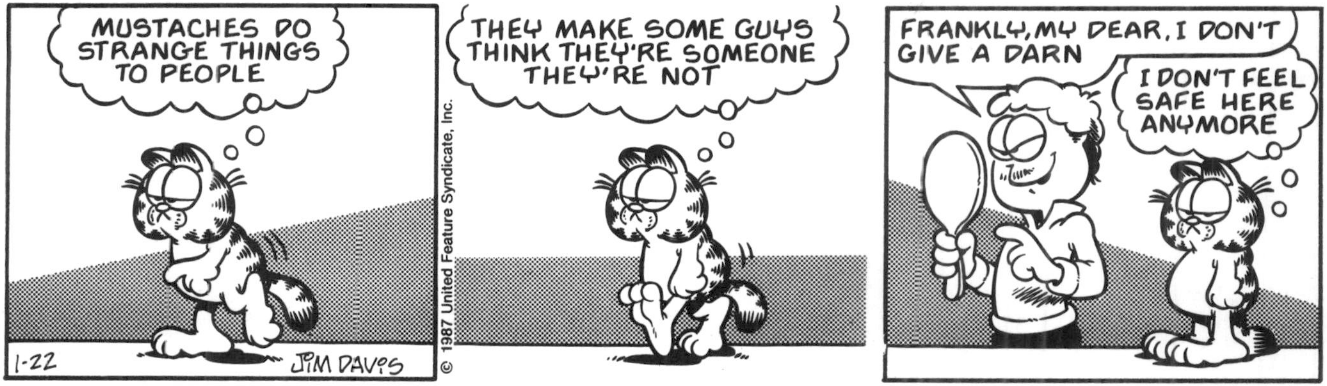
MUSTACHES DO STRANGE THINGS TO PEOPLE
1-22
JIM DAVIS
© 1987 United Feature Syndicate, Inc.
THEY MAKE SOME GUYS THINK THEY'RE SOMEONE THEY'RE NOT
FRANKLY, MY DEAR, I DON'T GIVE A DARN
I DON'T FEEL SAFE HERE ANYMORE

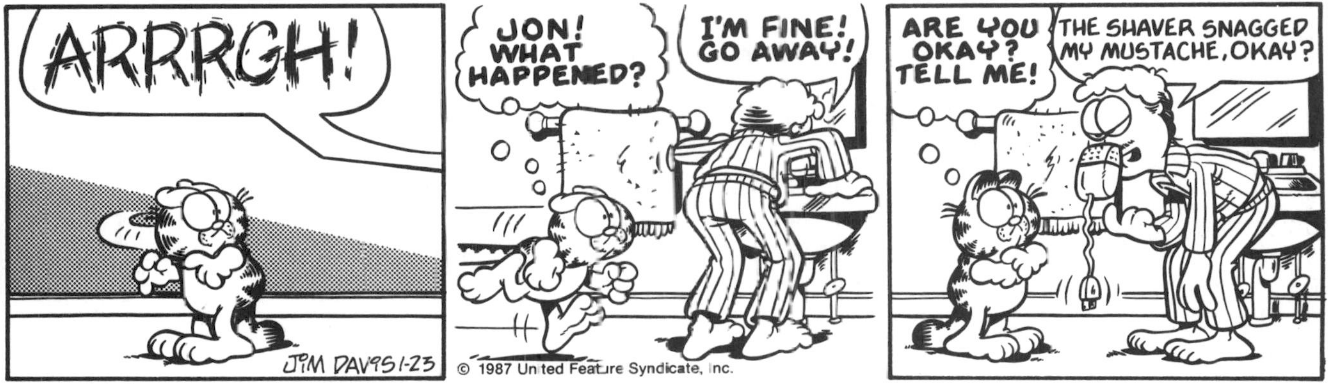
ARRRGH!
JIM DAVIS 1-23
JON! WHAT HAPPENED?
I'M FINE! GO AWAY!
© 1987 United Feature Syndicate, Inc.
ARE YOU OKAY? TELL ME!
THE SHAVER SNAGGED MY MUSTACHE, OKAY?

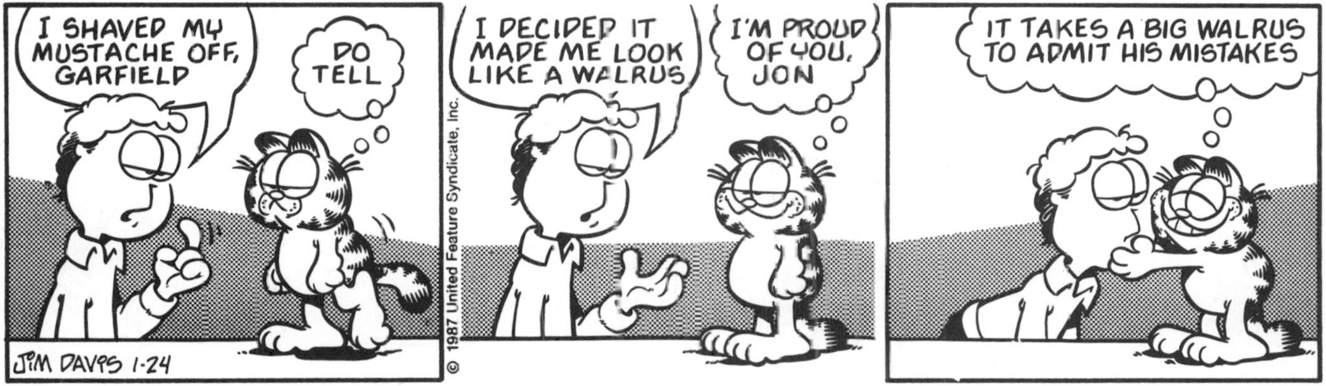
I SHAVED MY MUSTACHE OFF, GARFIELD
DO TELL
JIM DAVIS 1-24
© 1987 United Feature Syndicate, Inc.
I DECIDED IT MADE ME LOOK LIKE A WALRUS
I'M PROUD OF YOU, JON
IT TAKES A BIG WALRUS TO ADMIT HIS MISTAKES

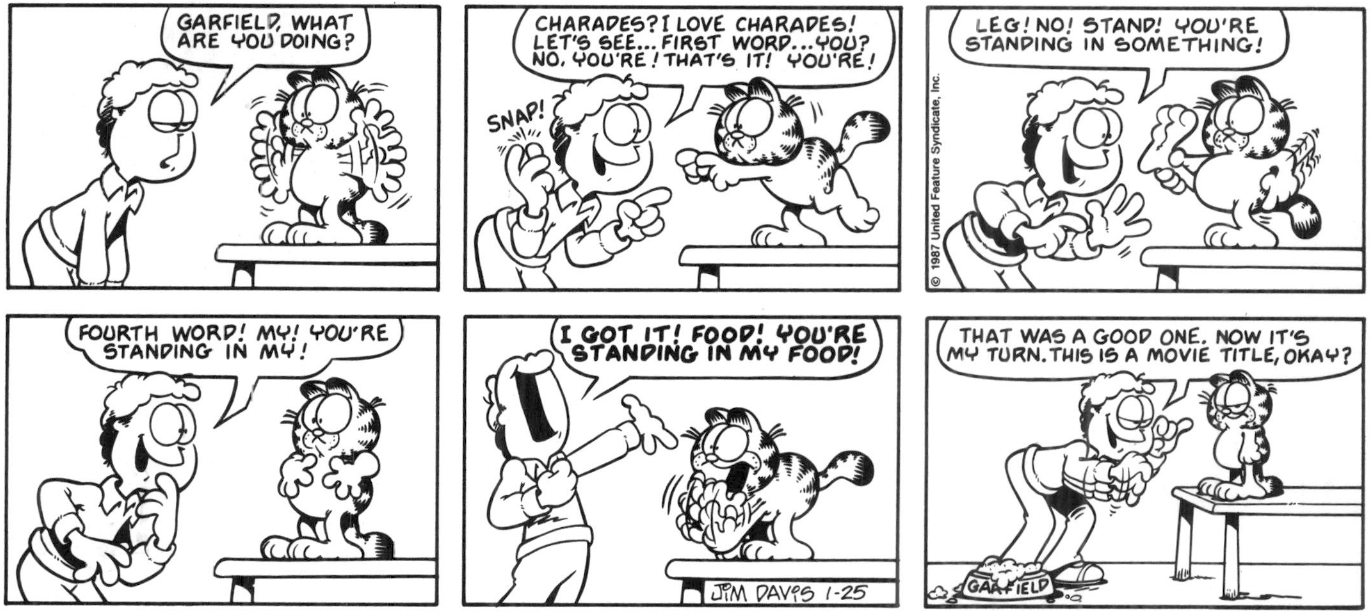
GARFIELD, WHAT ARE YOU DOING?
CHARADES? I LOVE CHARADES! LET'S SEE... FIRST WORD...YOU? NO, YOU'RE! THAT'S IT! YOU'RE!
SNAP!
LEG! NO! STAND! YOU'RE STANDING IN SOMETHING!
© 1987 United Feature Syndicate, Inc.
FOURTH WORD! MY! YOU'RE STANDING IN MY!
I GOT IT! FOOD! YOU'RE STANDING IN MY FOOD!
JIM DAVIS 1-25
THAT WAS A GOOD ONE. NOW IT'S MY TURN. THIS IS A MOVIE TITLE, OKAY?
GARFIELD

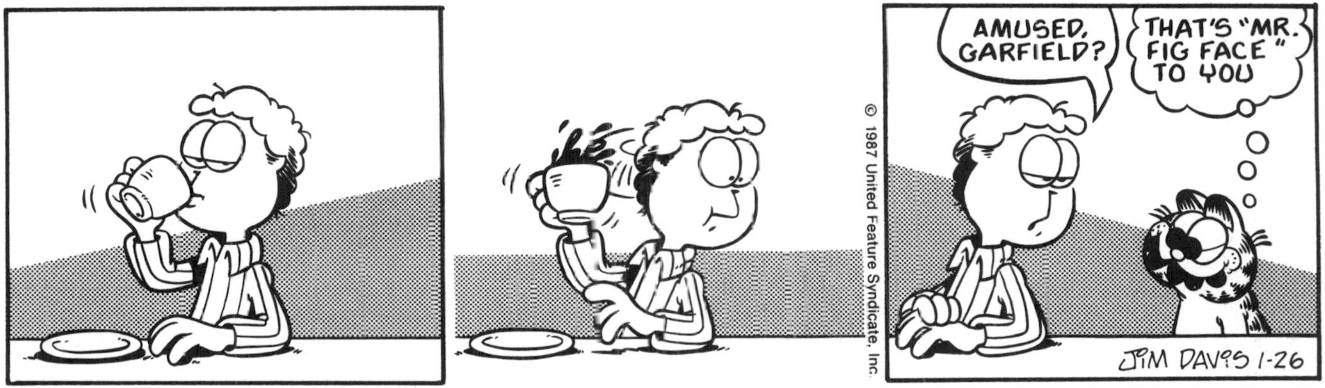
© 1987 United Feature Syndicate, Inc.
AMUSED, GARFIELD?
THAT'S "MR. FIG FACE" TO YOU
JIM DAVIS 1-26

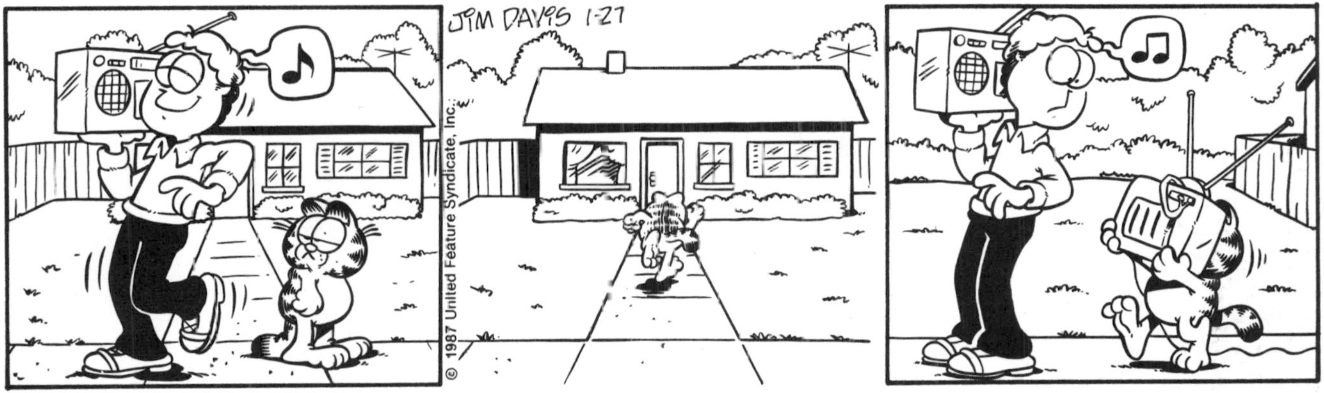
JIM DAVIS 1-27
© 1987 United Feature Syndicate, Inc.

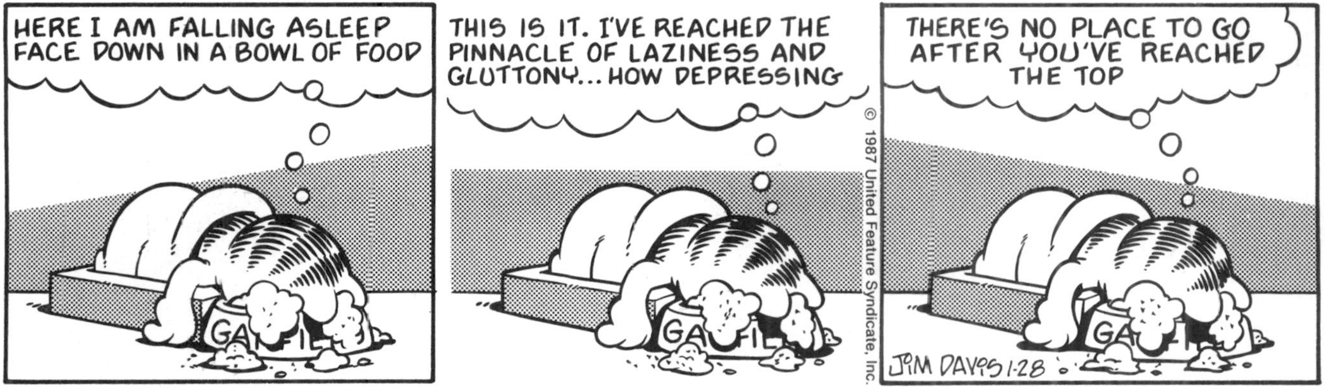
HERE I AM FALLING ASLEEP FACE DOWN IN A BOWL OF FOOD
THIS IS IT. I'VE REACHED THE PINNACLE OF LAZINESS AND GLUTTONY... HOW DEPRESSING
THERE'S NO PLACE TO GO AFTER YOU'VE REACHED THE TOP
© 1987 United Feature Syndicate, Inc.
JIM DAVIS 1·28

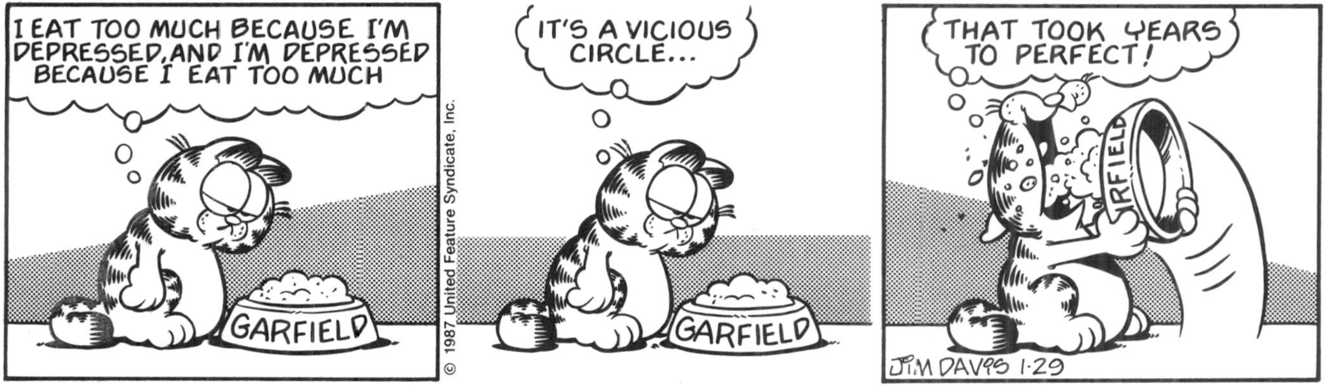
I EAT TOO MUCH BECAUSE I'M DEPRESSED, AND I'M DEPRESSED BECAUSE I EAT TOO MUCH
© 1987 United Feature Syndicate, Inc.
IT'S A VICIOUS CIRCLE...
THAT TOOK YEARS TO PERFECT!
JIM DAVIS 1·29

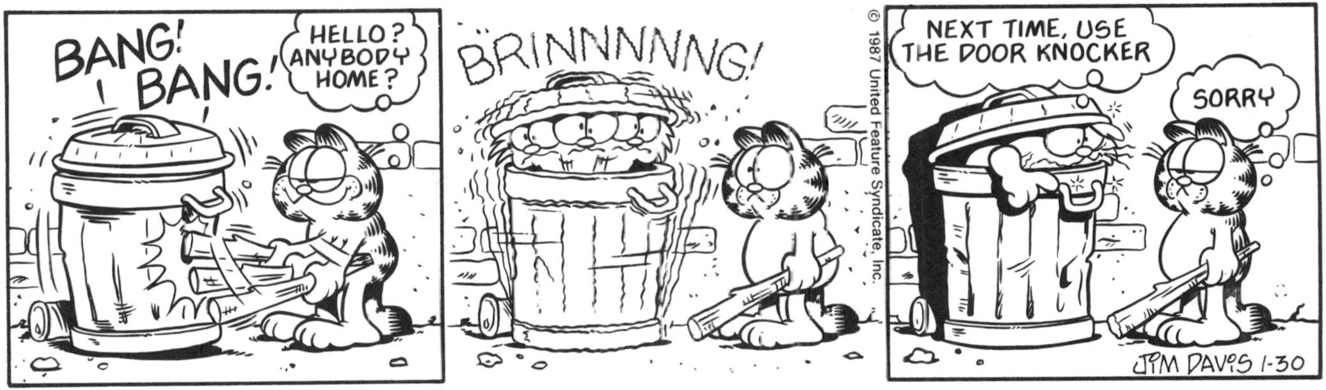
BANG! BANG!
HELLO? ANYBODY HOME?
BRINNNNNG!
NEXT TIME, USE THE DOOR KNOCKER
SORRY
© 1987 United Feature Syndicate, Inc.
JIM DAVIS 1-30

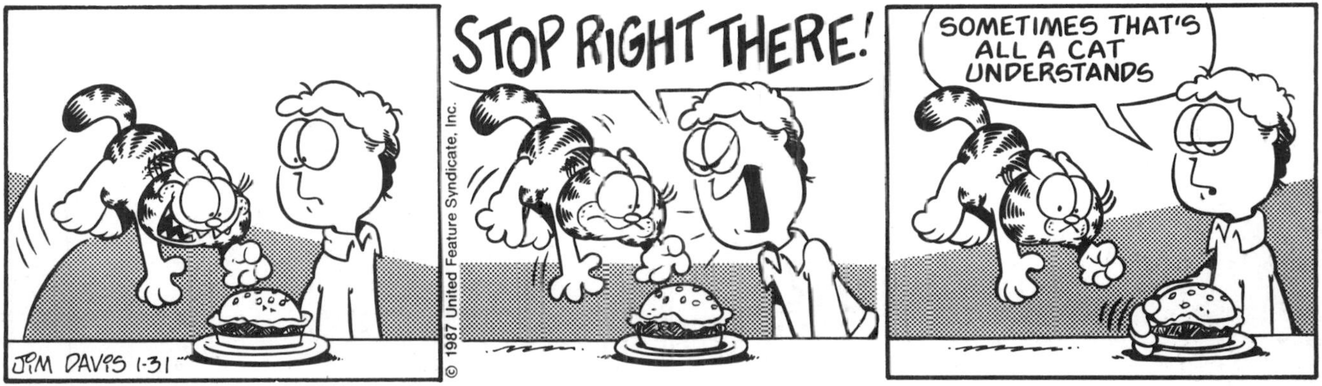
JIM DAVIS 1-31
© 1987 United Feature Syndicate, Inc.
STOP RIGHT THERE!
SOMETIMES THAT'S ALL A CAT UNDERSTANDS

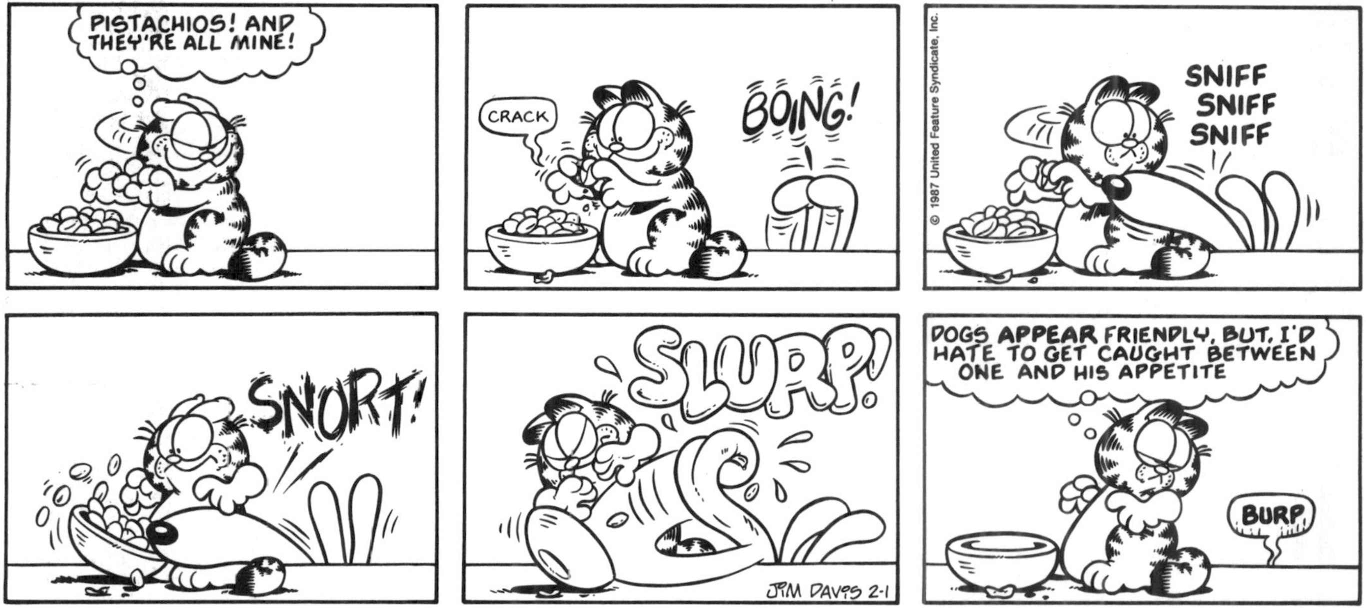
PISTACHIOS! AND THEY'RE ALL MINE!
CRACK
BOING!
© 1987 United Feature Syndicate, Inc.
SNIFF SNIFF SNIFF
SNORT!
SLURP!
JIM DAVIS 2-1
DOGS APPEAR FRIENDLY, BUT, I'D HATE TO GET CAUGHT BETWEEN ONE AND HIS APPETITE
BURP

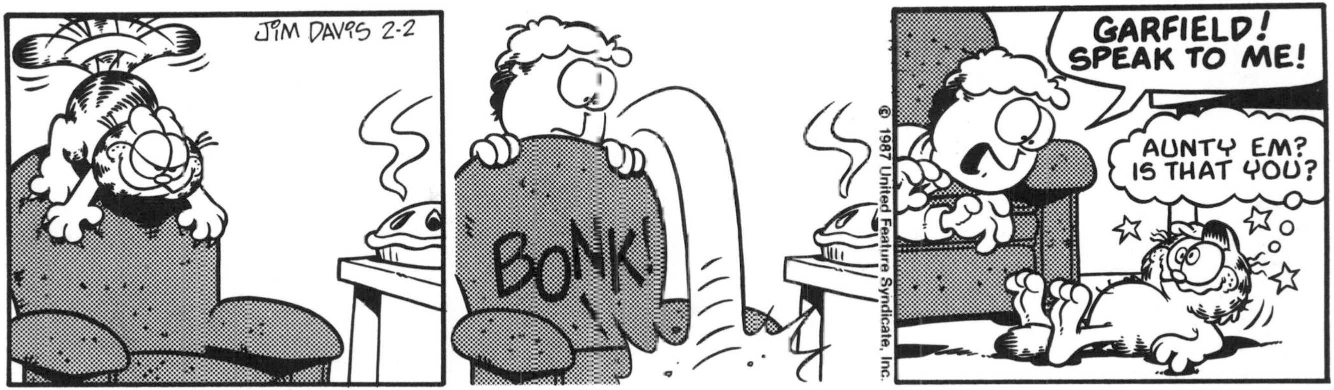
JIM DAVIS 2-2
BONK!
© 1987 United Feature Syndicate, Inc.
GARFIELD! SPEAK TO ME!
AUNTY EM? IS THAT YOU?

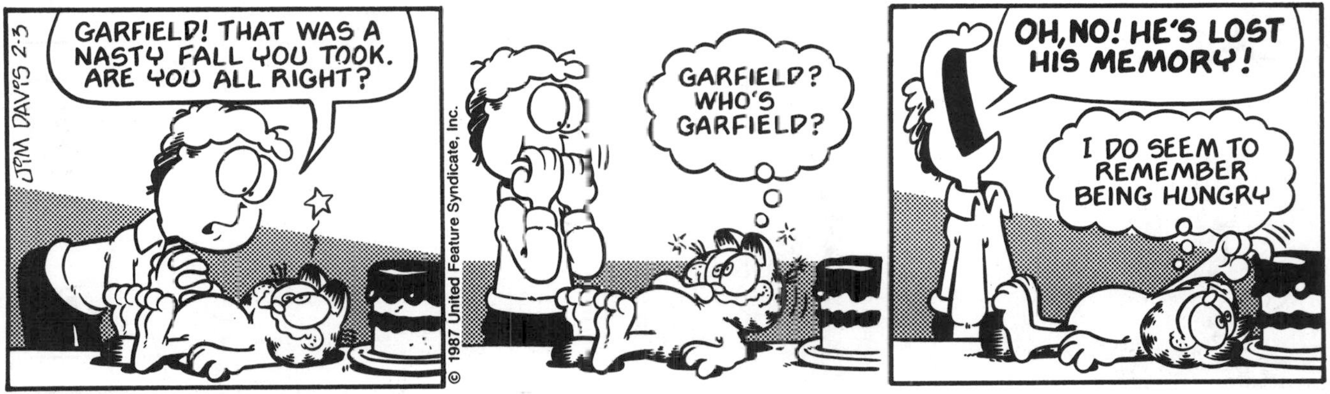
JIM DAVIS 2-3
GARFIELD! THAT WAS A NASTY FALL YOU TOOK. ARE YOU ALL RIGHT?
© 1987 United Feature Syndicate, Inc.
GARFIELD? WHO'S GARFIELD?
OH, NO! HE'S LOST HIS MEMORY!
I DO SEEM TO REMEMBER BEING HUNGRY

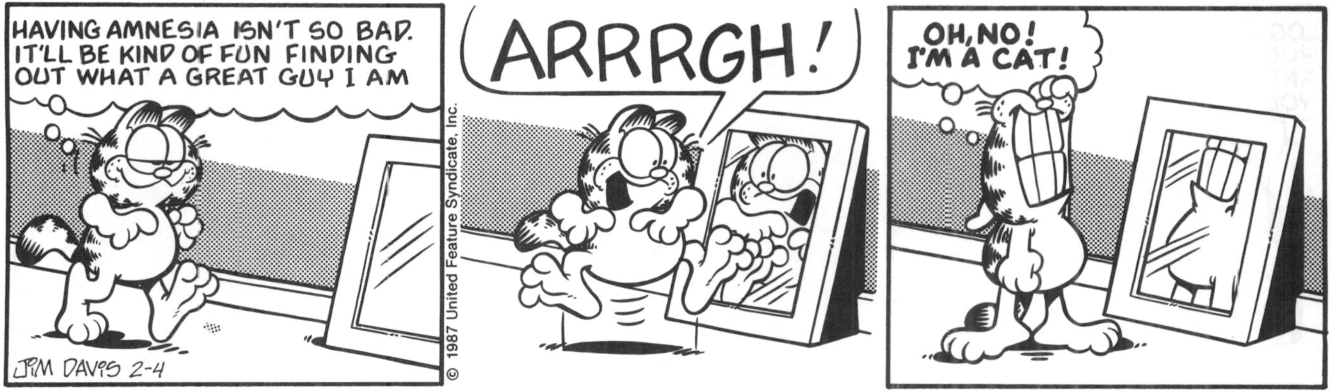
HAVING AMNESIA ISN'T SO BAD. IT'LL BE KIND OF FUN FINDING OUT WHAT A GREAT GUY I AM
JIM DAVIS 2-4
© 1987 United Feature Syndicate, Inc.
ARRRGH!
OH, NO! I'M A CAT!

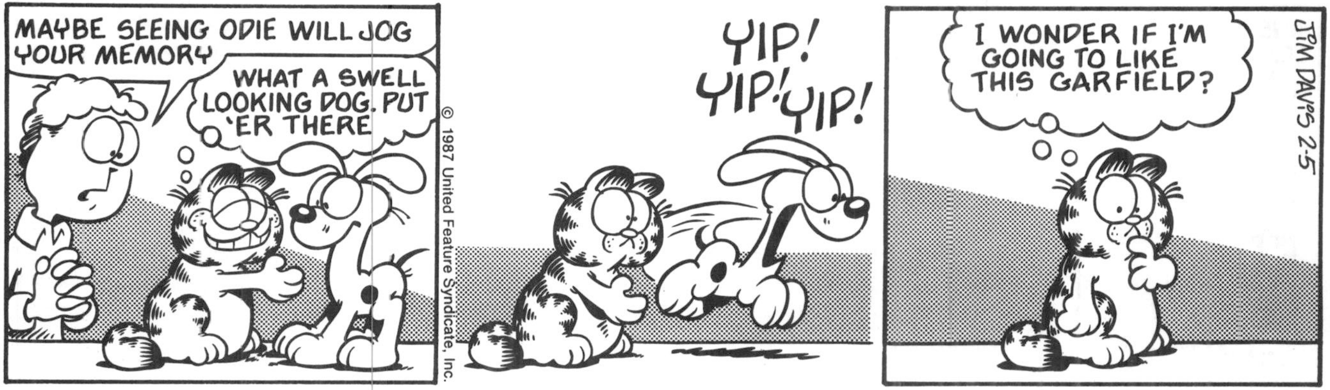
MAYBE SEEING ODIE WILL JOG YOUR MEMORY
WHAT A SWELL LOOKING DOG. PUT 'ER THERE
© 1987 United Feature Syndicate, Inc.
YIP! YIP! YIP!
I WONDER IF I'M GOING TO LIKE THIS GARFIELD?
JIM DAVIS 2-5

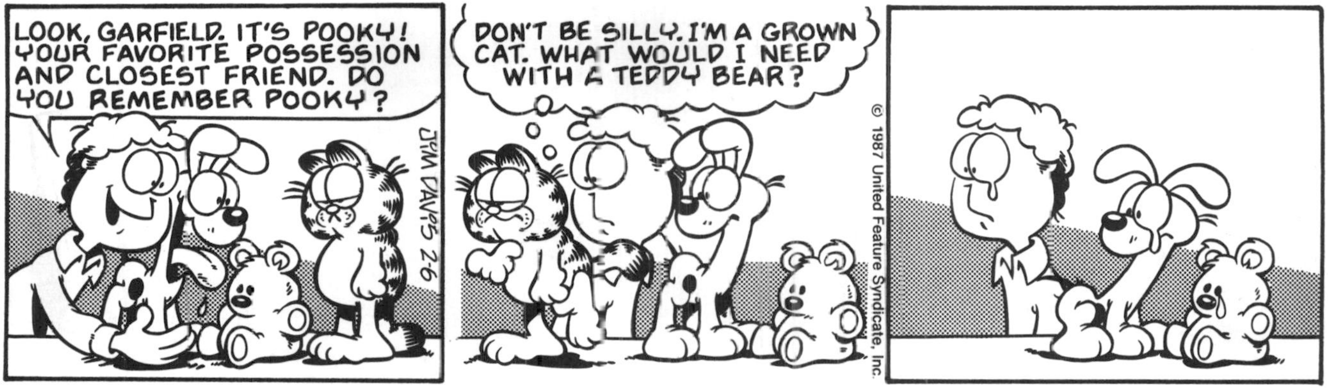
LOOK, GARFIELD. IT'S POOKY! YOUR FAVORITE POSSESSION AND CLOSEST FRIEND. DO YOU REMEMBER POOKY?
JIM DAVIS 2-6
DON'T BE SILLY. I'M A GROWN CAT. WHAT WOULD I NEED WITH A TEDDY BEAR?
© 1987 United Feature Syndicate, Inc.

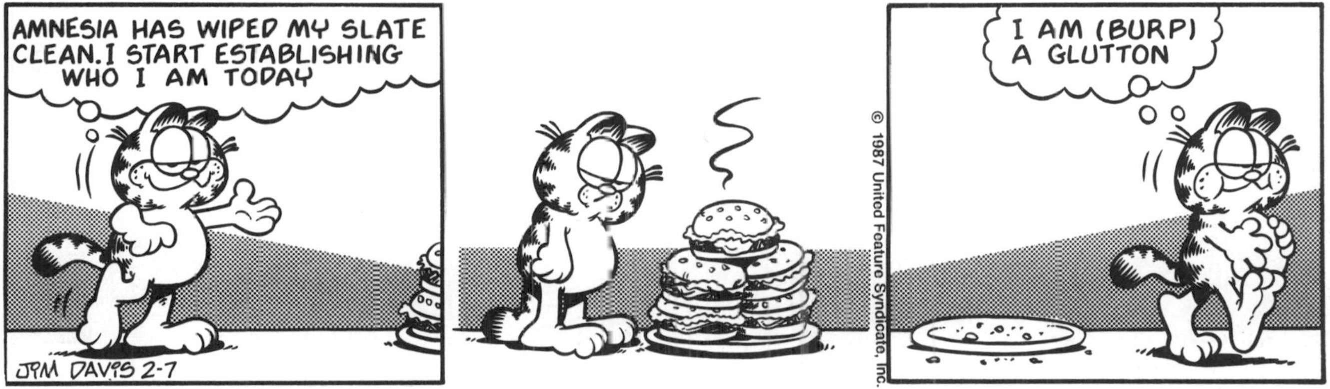
AMNESIA HAS WIPED MY SLATE CLEAN. I START ESTABLISHING WHO I AM TODAY
JIM DAVIS 2-7
© 1987 United Feature Syndicate, Inc.
I AM (BURP) A GLUTTON

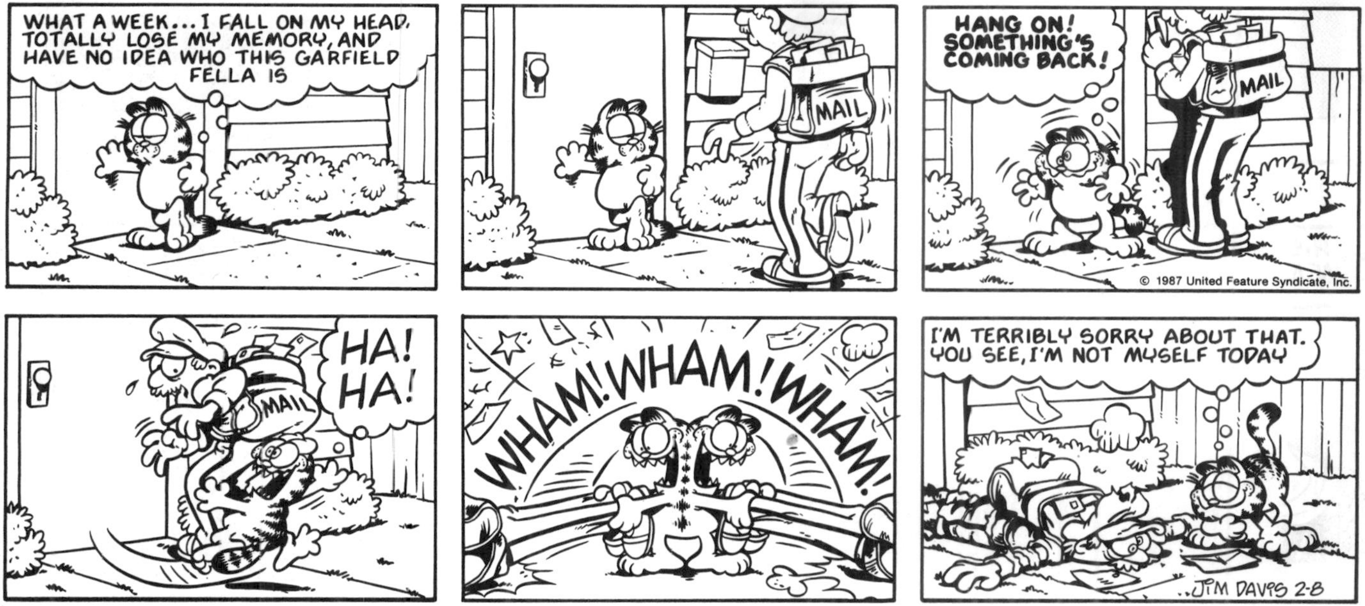
WHAT A WEEK... I FALL ON MY HEAD, TOTALLY LOSE MY MEMORY, AND HAVE NO IDEA WHO THIS GARFIELD FELLA IS
MAIL
HANG ON! SOMETHING'S COMING BACK!
MAIL
© 1987 United Feature Syndicate, Inc.
MAIL
HA! HA!
WHAM! WHAM! WHAM!
I'M TERRIBLY SORRY ABOUT THAT. YOU SEE, I'M NOT MYSELF TODAY
JIM DAVIS 2-8

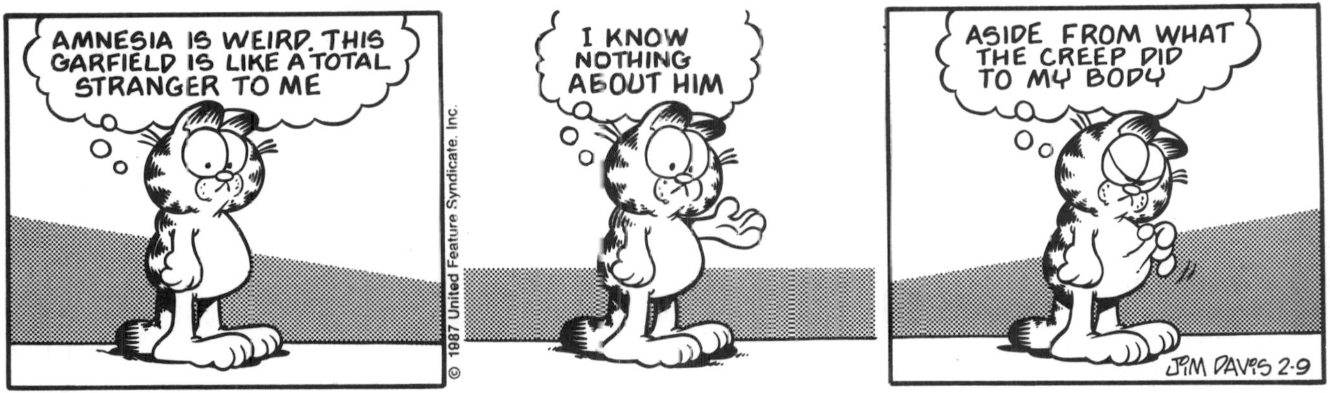
AMNESIA IS WEIRD. THIS GARFIELD IS LIKE A TOTAL STRANGER TO ME
I KNOW NOTHING ABOUT HIM
ASIDE FROM WHAT THE CREEP DID TO MY BODY
JIM DAVIS 2-9
© 1987 United Feature Syndicate, Inc.

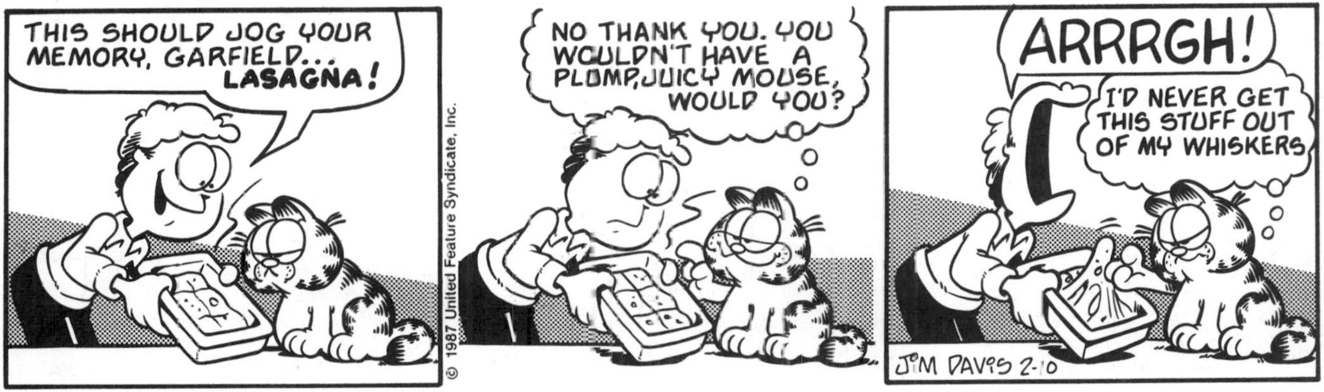
THIS SHOULD JOG YOUR MEMORY, GARFIELD... LASAGNA!
NO THANK YOU. YOU WOULDN'T HAVE A PLUMP, JUICY MOUSE, WOULD YOU?
ARRRGH!
I'D NEVER GET THIS STUFF OUT OF MY WHISKERS
JIM DAVIS 2-10
© 1987 United Feature Syndicate, Inc.

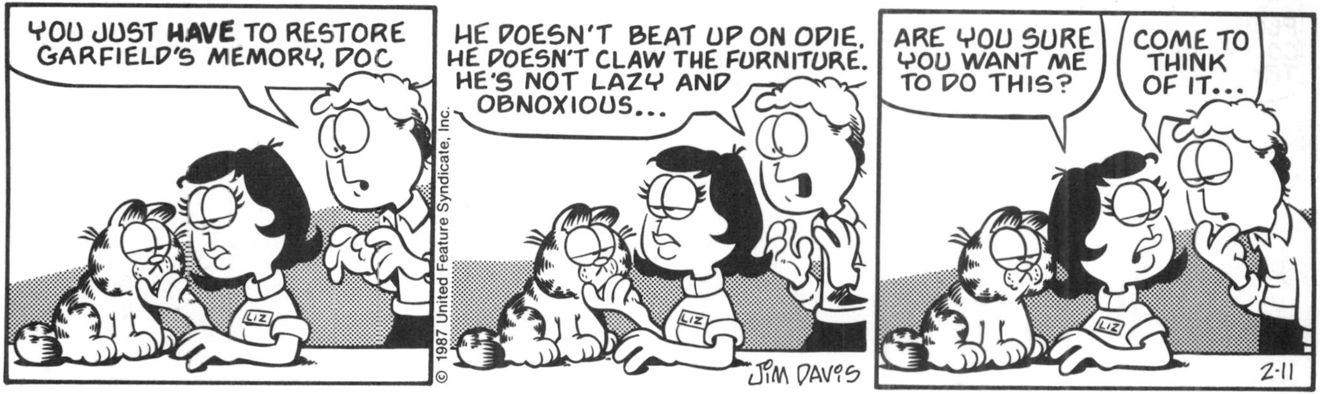
YOU JUST HAVE TO RESTORE GARFIELD'S MEMORY, DOC
© 1987 United Feature Syndicate, Inc.
HE DOESN'T BEAT UP ON ODIE. HE DOESN'T CLAW THE FURNITURE. HE'S NOT LAZY AND OBNOXIOUS...
JIM DAVIS
ARE YOU SURE YOU WANT ME TO DO THIS?
COME TO THINK OF IT...
2-11

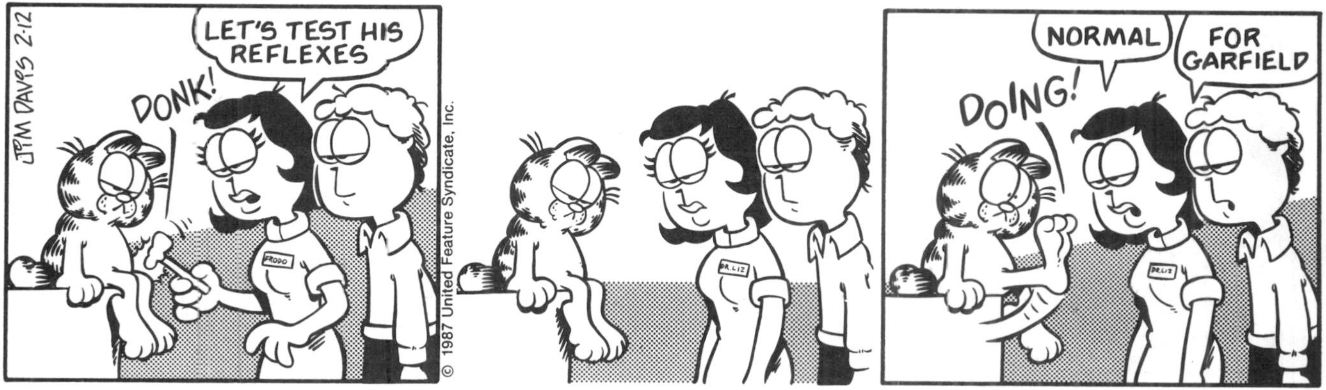
JIM DAVIS 2-12
LET'S TEST HIS REFLEXES
DONK!
© 1987 United Feature Syndicate, Inc.
DOING!
NORMAL
FOR GARFIELD

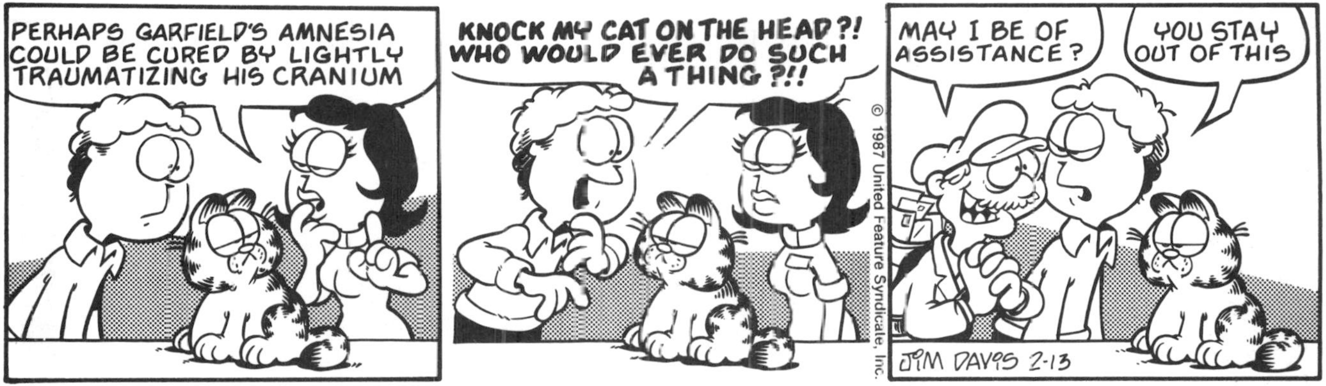
PERHAPS GARFIELD'S AMNESIA COULD BE CURED BY LIGHTLY TRAUMATIZING HIS CRANIUM
KNOCK MY CAT ON THE HEAD?! WHO WOULD EVER DO SUCH A THING?!!
MAY I BE OF ASSISTANCE?
YOU STAY OUT OF THIS
© 1987 United Feature Syndicate, Inc.
JIM DAVIS 2-13

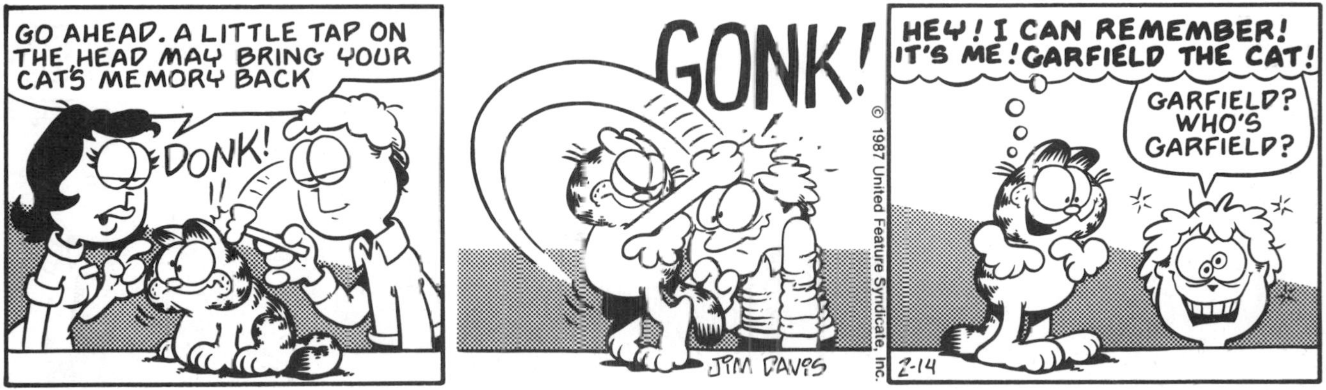
GO AHEAD. A LITTLE TAP ON THE HEAD MAY BRING YOUR CAT'S MEMORY BACK
DONK!
GONK!
JIM DAVIS
© 1987 United Feature Syndicate, Inc.
HEY! I CAN REMEMBER! IT'S ME! GARFIELD THE CAT!
GARFIELD? WHO'S GARFIELD?
2-14

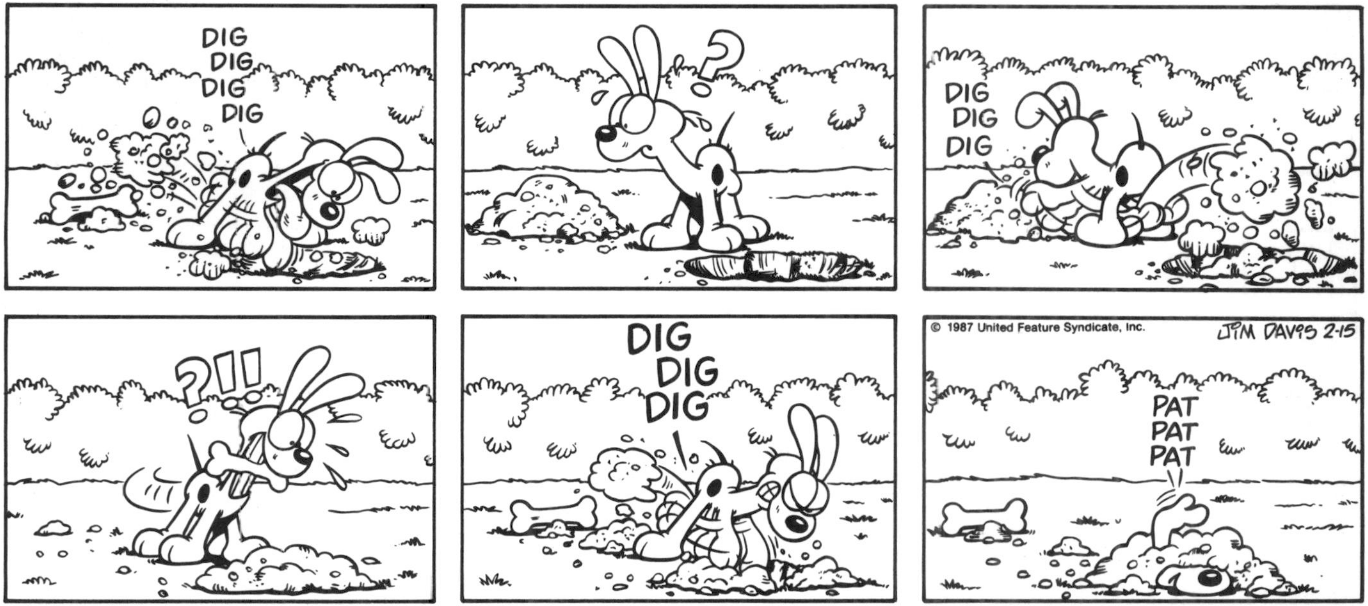
DIG
DIG
DIG
DIG
?
DIG
DIG
DIG
?!!
DIG
DIG
DIG
© 1987 United Feature Syndicate, Inc.
JIM DAVIS 2-15
PAT
PAT
PAT

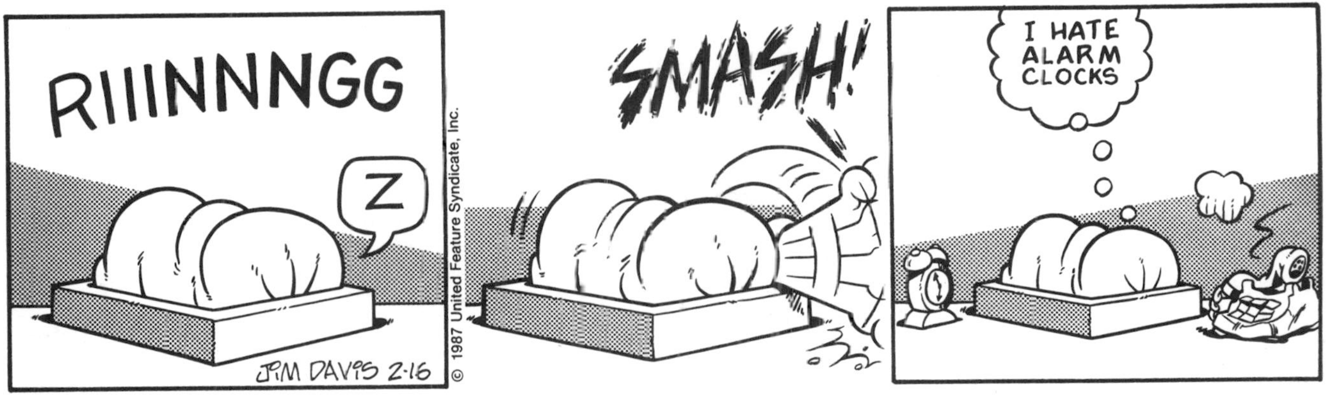
RIIINNNGG
Z
JIM DAVIS 2·16
© 1987 United Feature Syndicate, Inc.
SMASH!
I HATE ALARM CLOCKS

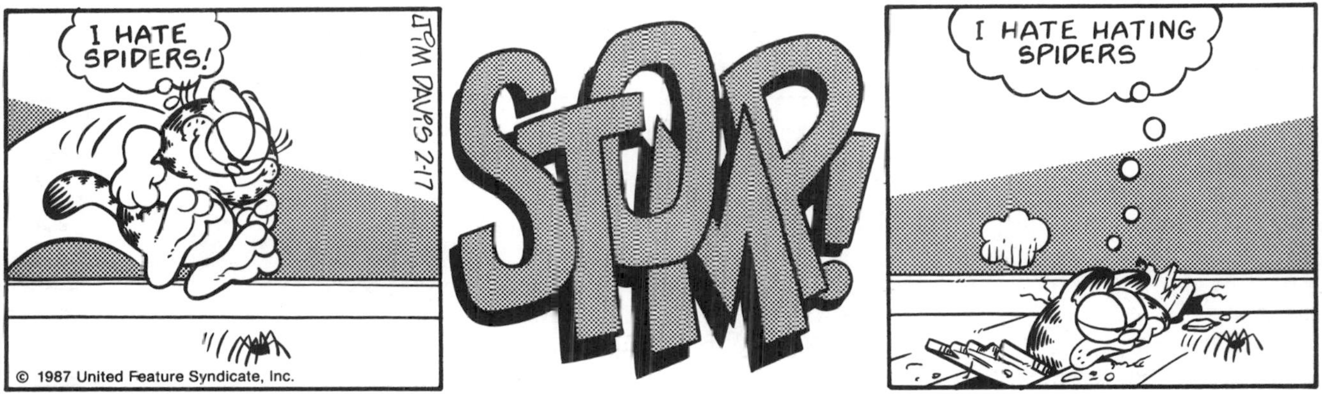
I HATE SPIDERS!
JIM DAVIS 2·17
© 1987 United Feature Syndicate, Inc.
STOMP!
I HATE HATING SPIDERS

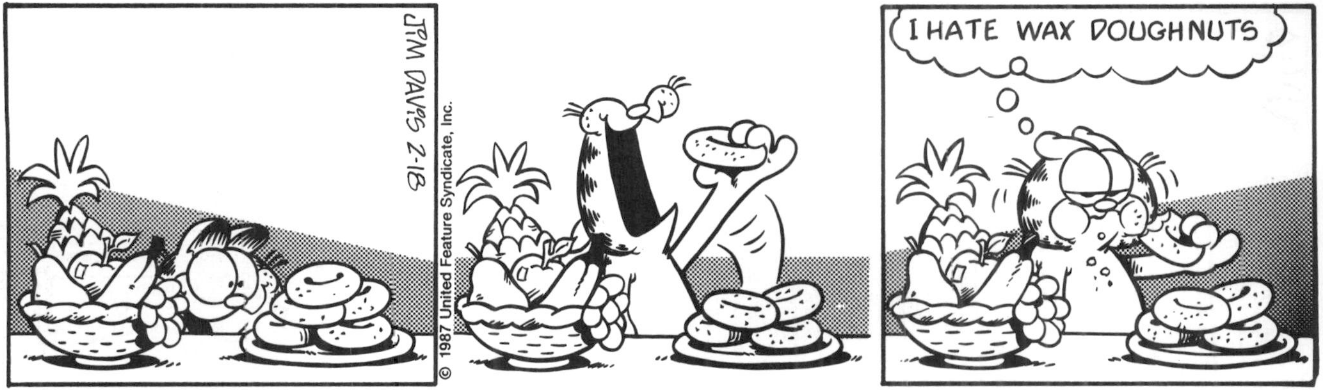
JIM DAVIS 2-18
© 1987 United Feature Syndicate, Inc.
I HATE WAX DOUGHNUTS

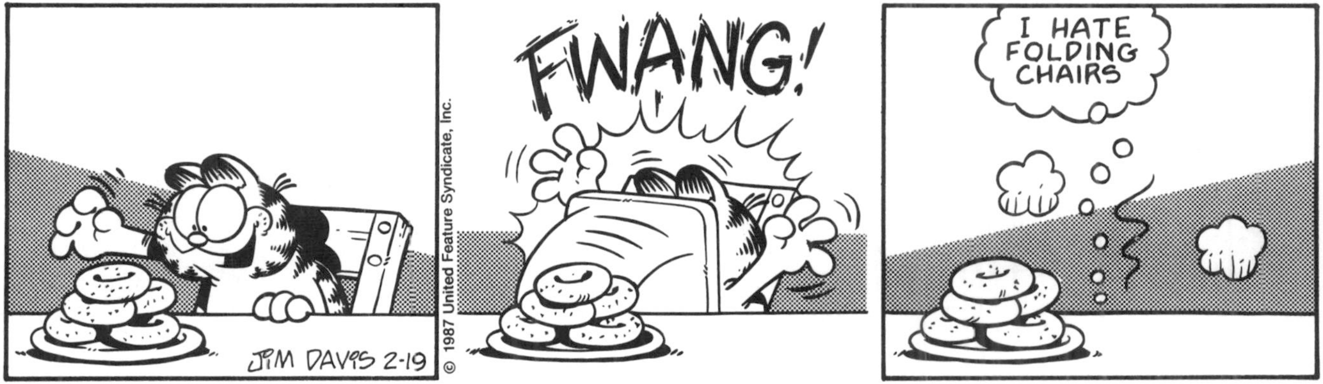
© 1987 United Feature Syndicate, Inc.
JIM DAVIS 2-19
FWANG!
I HATE FOLDING CHAIRS

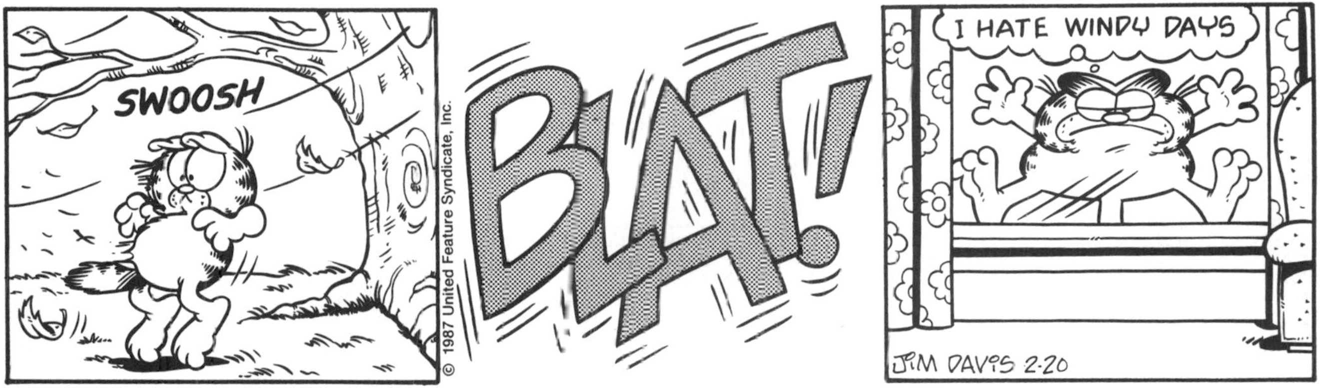
SWOOSH
© 1987 United Feature Syndicate, Inc.
BLAT!
I HATE WINDY DAYS
JIM DAVIS 2-20

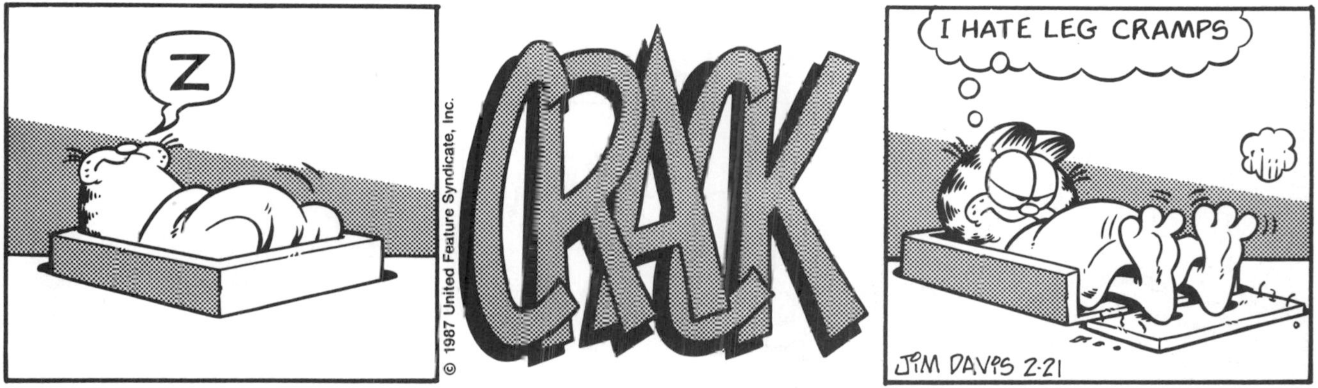
Z
© 1987 United Feature Syndicate, Inc.
CRACK
I HATE LEG CRAMPS
JIM DAVIS 2-21

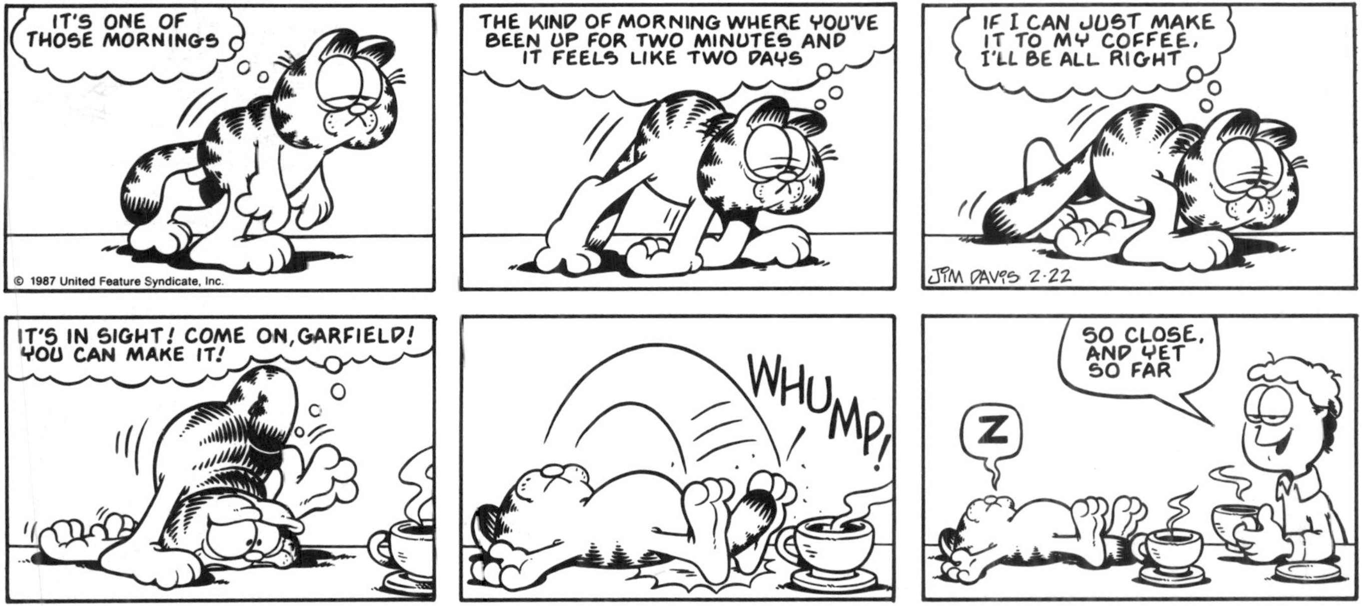
IT'S ONE OF THOSE MORNINGS
© 1987 United Feature Syndicate, Inc.
THE KIND OF MORNING WHERE YOU'VE BEEN UP FOR TWO MINUTES AND IT FEELS LIKE TWO DAYS
IF I CAN JUST MAKE IT TO MY COFFEE, I'LL BE ALL RIGHT
JIM DAVIS 2-22
IT'S IN SIGHT! COME ON, GARFIELD! YOU CAN MAKE IT!
WHUMP!
Z
SO CLOSE, AND YET SO FAR

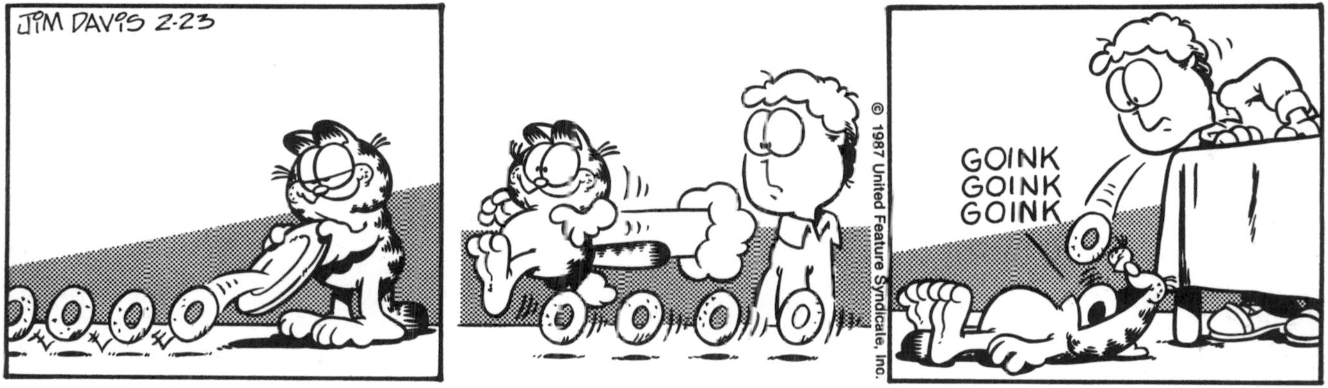
JIM DAVIS 2-23
GOINK
GOINK
GOINK
© 1987 United Feature Syndicate, Inc.

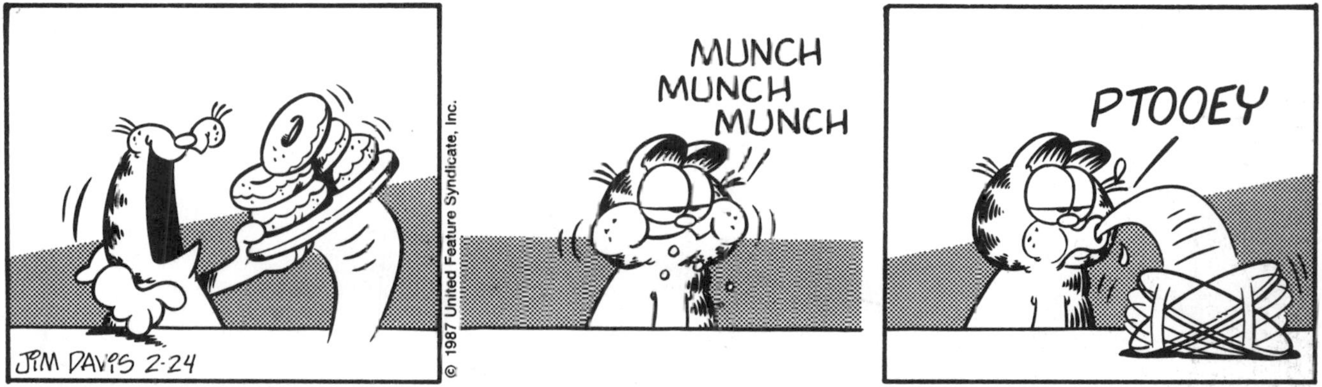
JIM DAVIS 2-24
© 1987 United Feature Syndicate, Inc.
MUNCH
MUNCH
MUNCH
PTOOEY

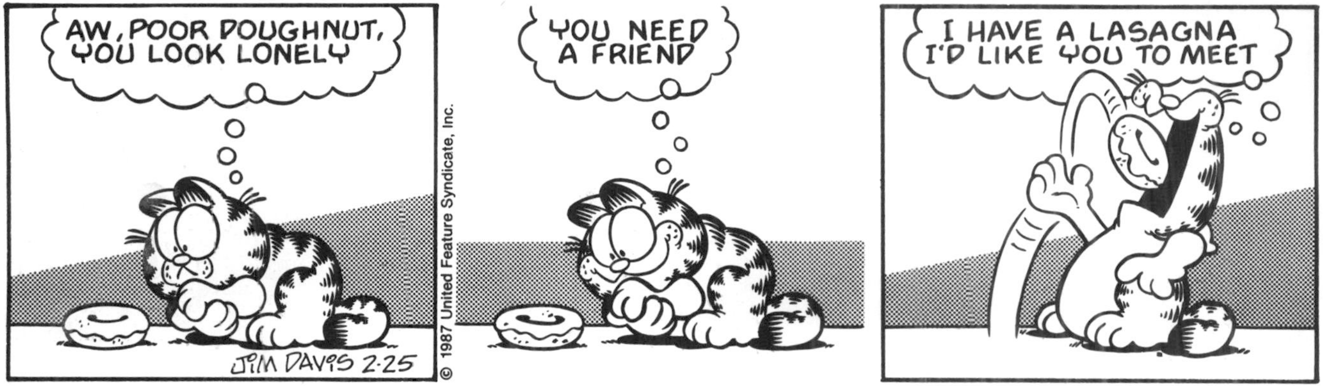
AW, POOR DOUGHNUT, YOU LOOK LONELY
JIM DAVIS 2-25
© 1987 United Feature Syndicate, Inc.
YOU NEED A FRIEND
I HAVE A LASAGNA I'D LIKE YOU TO MEET

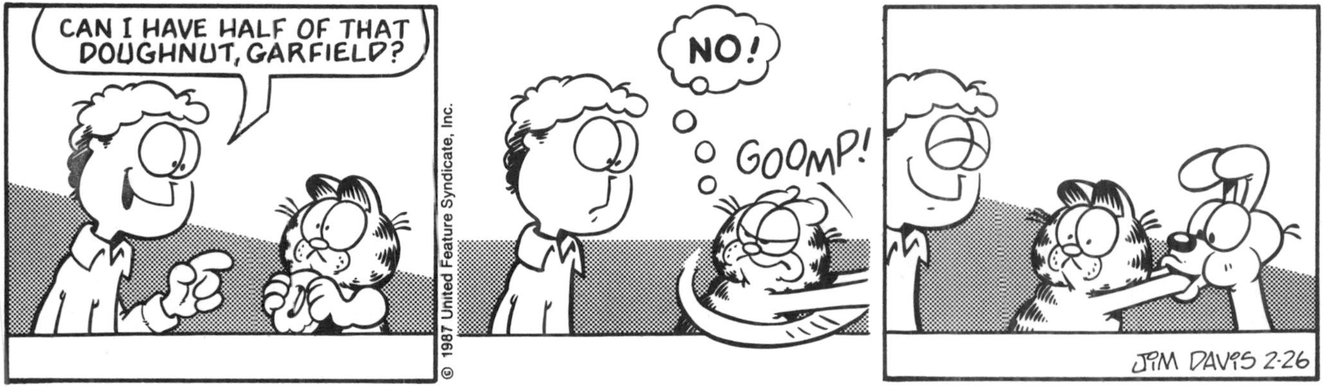
CAN I HAVE HALF OF THAT DOUGHNUT, GARFIELD?
© 1987 United Feature Syndicate, Inc.
NO!
GOOMP!
JIM DAVIS 2-26

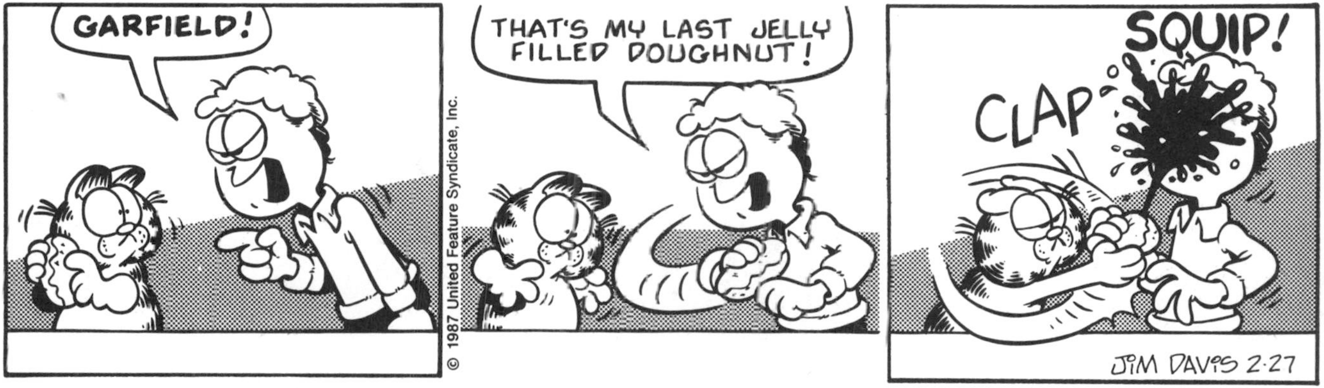
GARFIELD!
THAT'S MY LAST JELLY FILLED DOUGHNUT!
CLAP
SQUIP!
© 1987 United Feature Syndicate, Inc.
JIM DAVIS 2-27

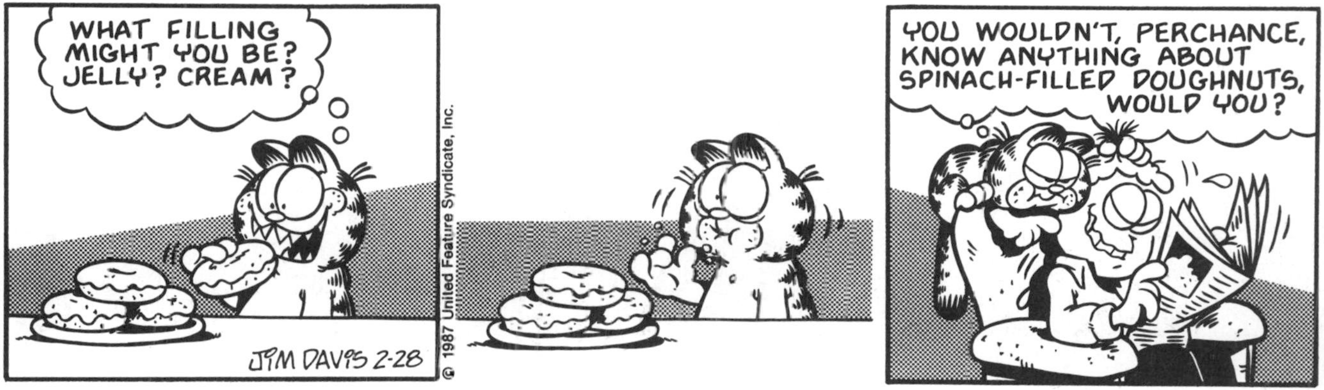
WHAT FILLING MIGHT YOU BE? JELLY? CREAM?
YOU WOULDN'T, PERCHANCE, KNOW ANYTHING ABOUT SPINACH-FILLED DOUGHNUTS, WOULD YOU?
© 1987 United Feature Syndicate, Inc.
JIM DAVIS 2-28

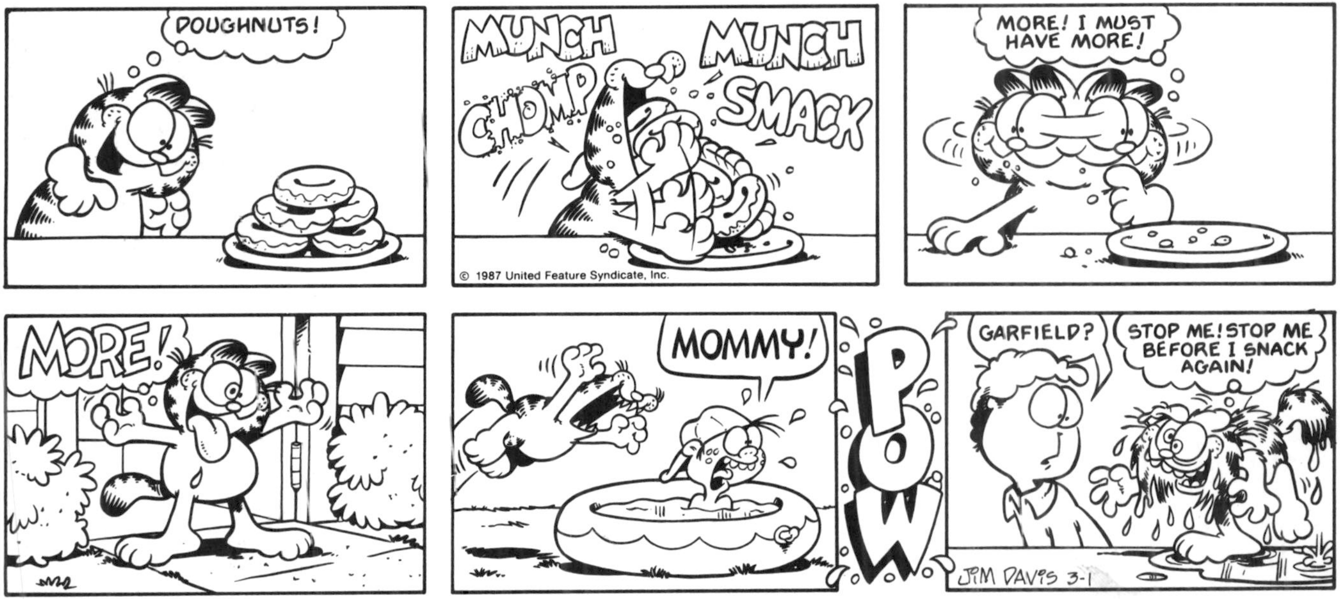
DOUGHNUTS!
MUNCH
MUNCH
CHOMP
SMACK
© 1987 United Feature Syndicate, Inc.
MORE! I MUST HAVE MORE!
MORE!
MOMMY!
POW
GARFIELD?
STOP ME! STOP ME BEFORE I SNACK AGAIN!
JIM DAVIS 3-1

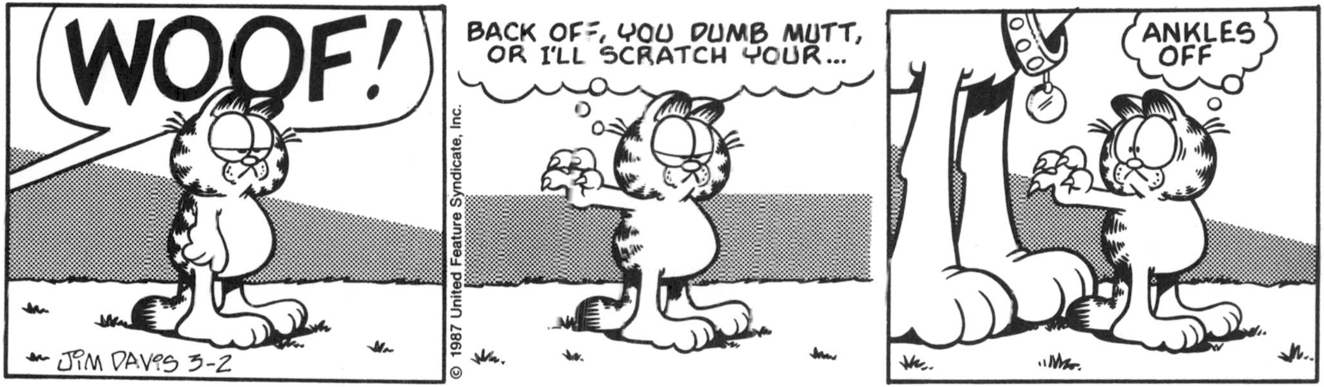
WOOF!
JIM DAVIS 3-2
© 1987 United Feature Syndicate, Inc.
BACK OFF, YOU DUMB MUTT, OR I'LL SCRATCH YOUR...
ANKLES OFF

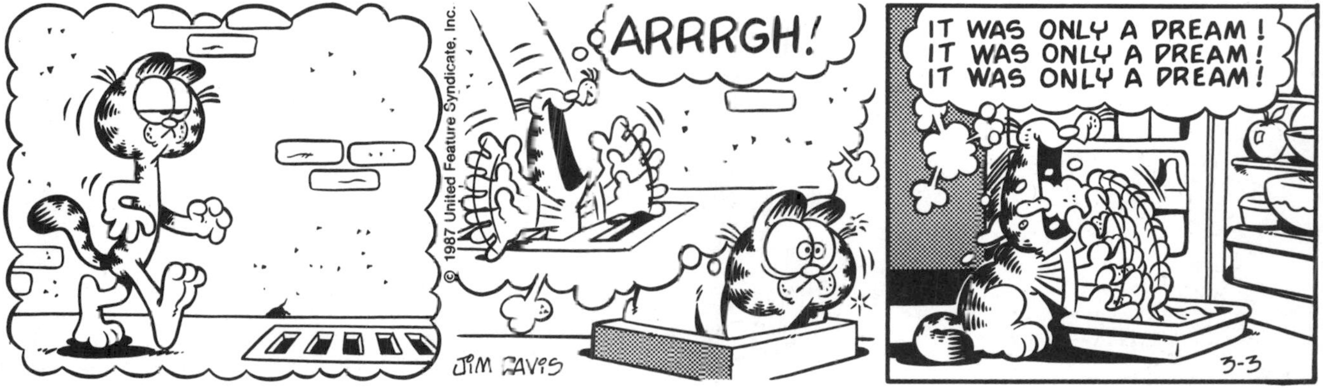
© 1987 United Feature Syndicate, Inc.
ARRRGH!
JIM DAVIS
IT WAS ONLY A DREAM! IT WAS ONLY A DREAM! IT WAS ONLY A DREAM!
3-3

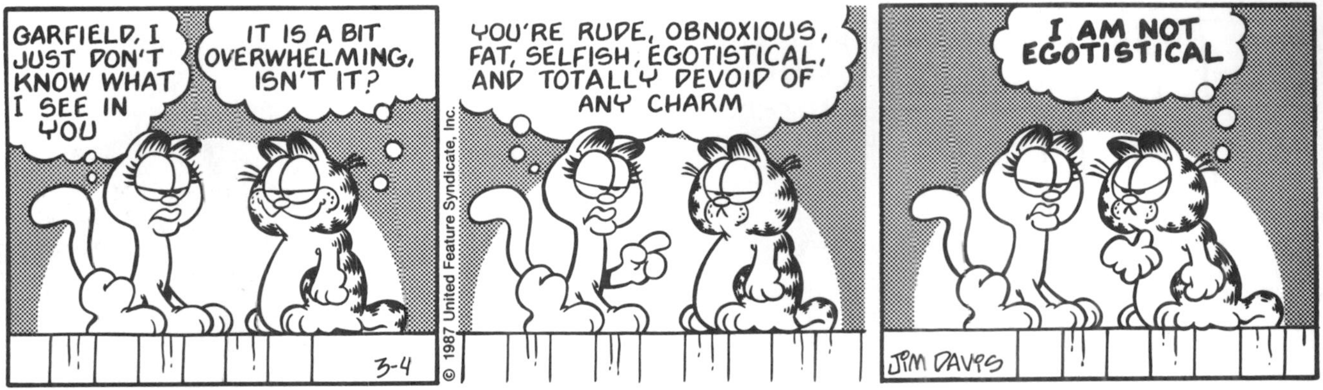

GARFIELD, I JUST DON'T KNOW WHAT I SEE IN YOU
IT IS A BIT OVERWHELMING, ISN'T IT?
3-4
© 1987 United Feature Syndicate, Inc.
YOU'RE RUDE, OBNOXIOUS, FAT, SELFISH, EGOTISTICAL, AND TOTALLY DEVOID OF ANY CHARM
I AM NOT EGOTISTICAL
JIM DAVIS


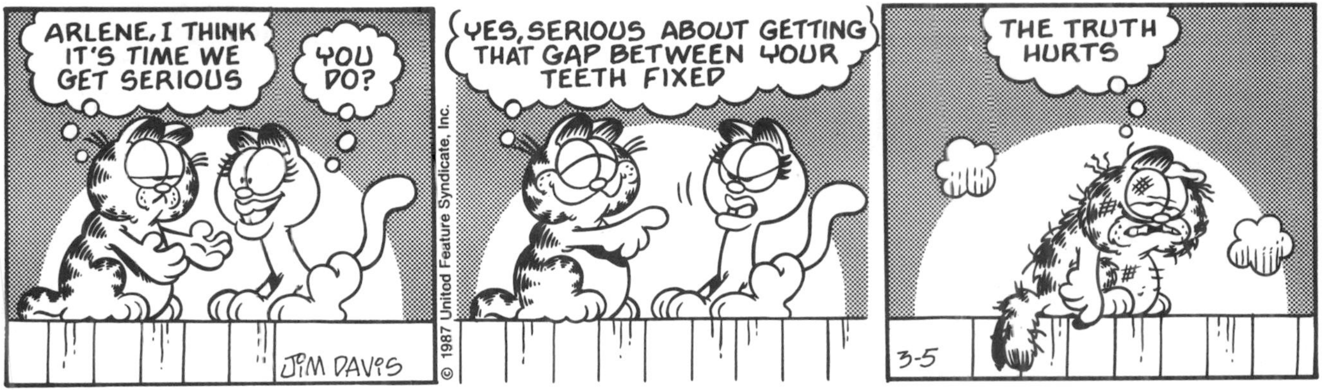

ARLENE, I THINK IT'S TIME WE GET SERIOUS
YOU DO?
JIM DAVIS
© 1987 United Feature Syndicate, Inc.
YES, SERIOUS ABOUT GETTING THAT GAP BETWEEN YOUR TEETH FIXED
THE TRUTH HURTS
3-5

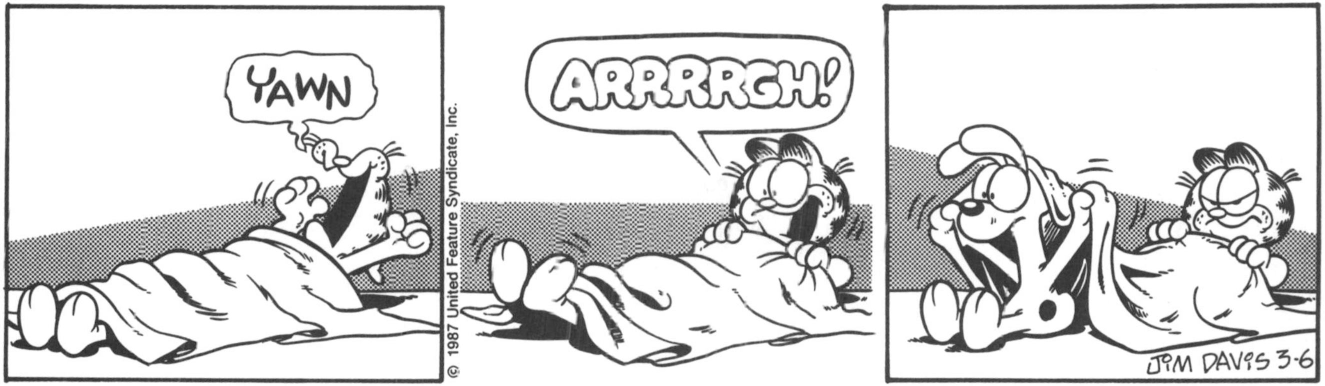
YAWN
ARRRRGH!
© 1987 United Feature Syndicate, Inc.
JIM DAVIS 3-6

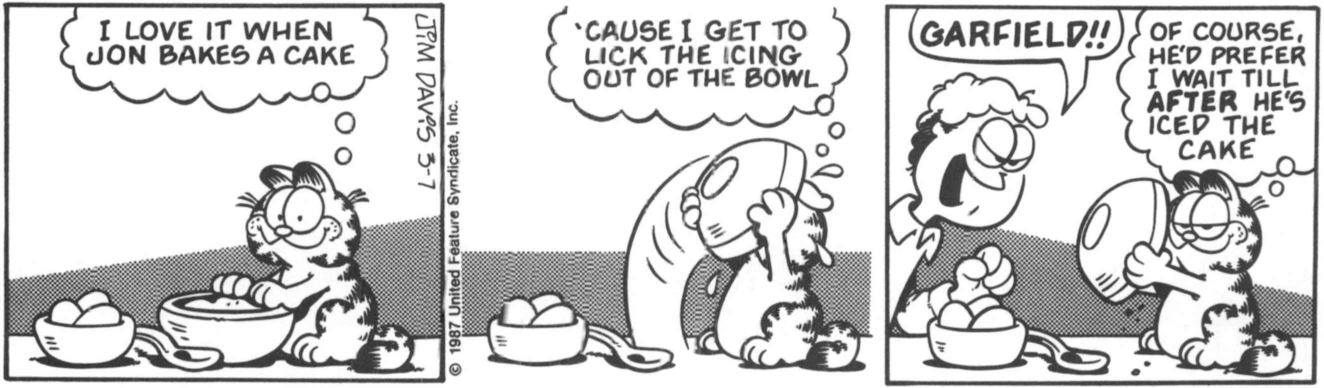
I LOVE IT WHEN JON BAKES A CAKE
JIM DAVIS 3-7
© 1987 United Feature Syndicate, Inc.
'CAUSE I GET TO LICK THE ICING OUT OF THE BOWL
GARFIELD!!
OF COURSE, HE'D PREFER I WAIT TILL **AFTER** HE'S ICED THE CAKE

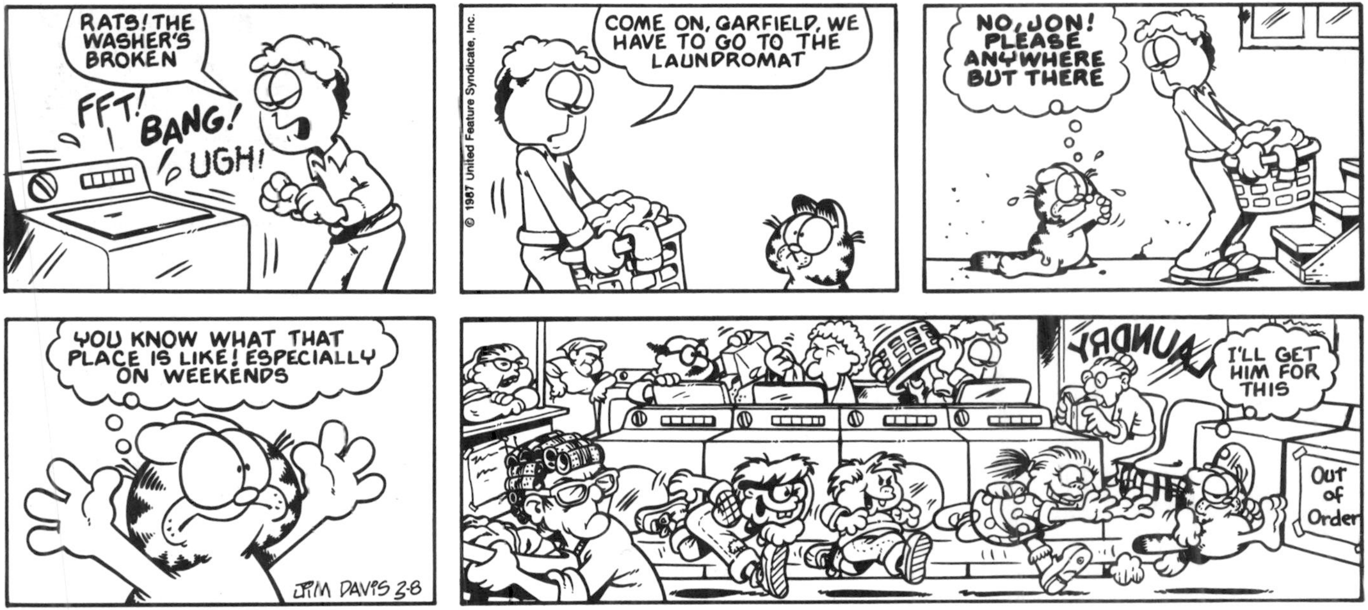
RATS! THE WASHER'S BROKEN
FFT!
BANG!
UGH!
© 1987 United Feature Syndicate, Inc.
COME ON, GARFIELD, WE HAVE TO GO TO THE LAUNDROMAT
NO, JON! PLEASE ANYWHERE BUT THERE
YOU KNOW WHAT THAT PLACE IS LIKE! ESPECIALLY ON WEEKENDS
JIM DAVIS 3-8
LAUNDRY
I'LL GET HIM FOR THIS
Out of Order

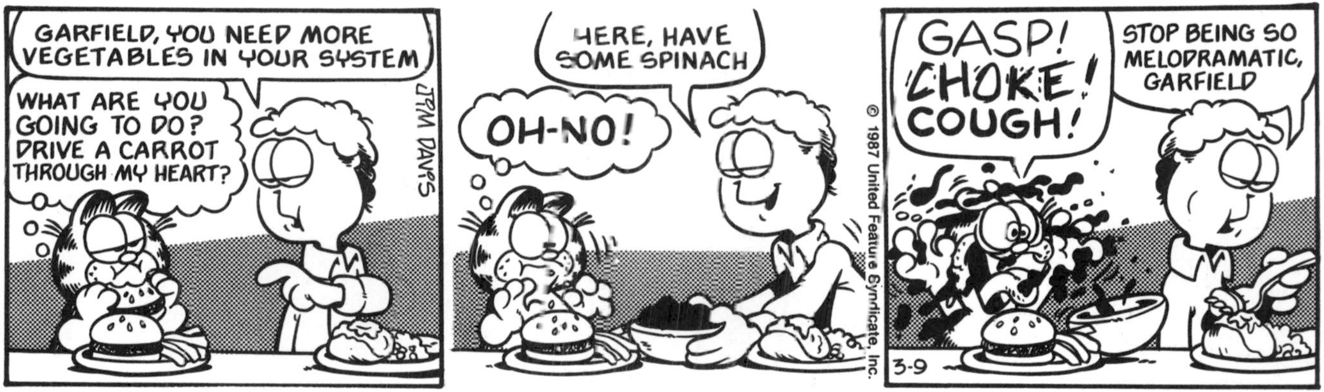
GARFIELD, YOU NEED MORE VEGETABLES IN YOUR SYSTEM
WHAT ARE YOU GOING TO DO? DRIVE A CARROT THROUGH MY HEART?
JIM DAVIS
OH-NO!
HERE, HAVE SOME SPINACH
© 1987 United Feature Syndicate, Inc.
GASP! CHOKE! COUGH!
STOP BEING SO MELODRAMATIC, GARFIELD
3-9

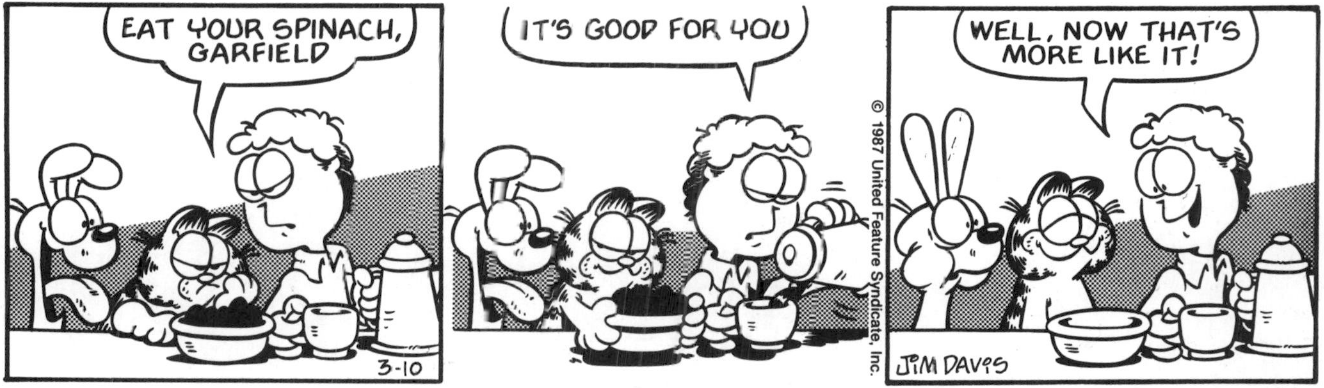
EAT YOUR SPINACH, GARFIELD
3-10
IT'S GOOD FOR YOU
© 1987 United Feature Syndicate, Inc.
WELL, NOW THAT'S MORE LIKE IT!
JIM DAVIS

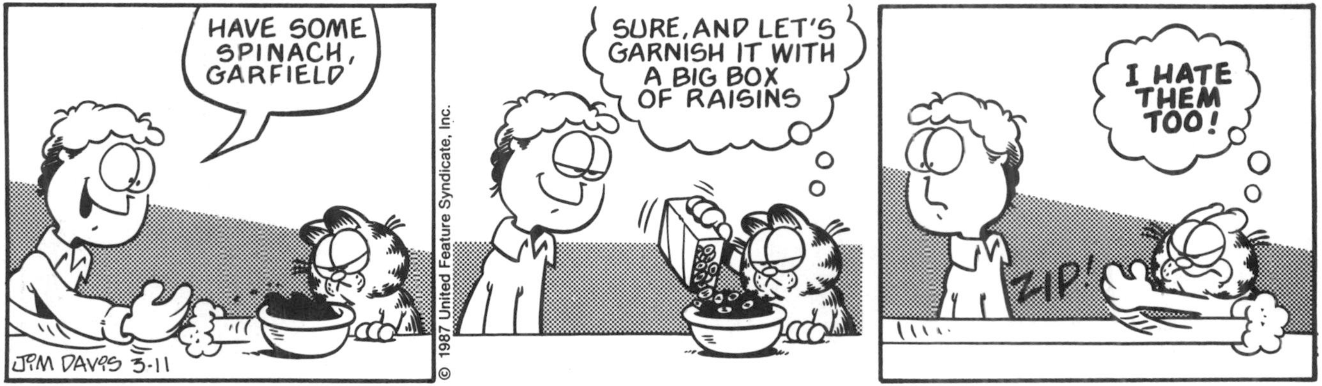
HAVE SOME SPINACH, GARFIELD
JIM DAVIS 3-11
© 1987 United Feature Syndicate, Inc.
SURE, AND LET'S GARNISH IT WITH A BIG BOX OF RAISINS
I HATE THEM TOO!
ZIP!

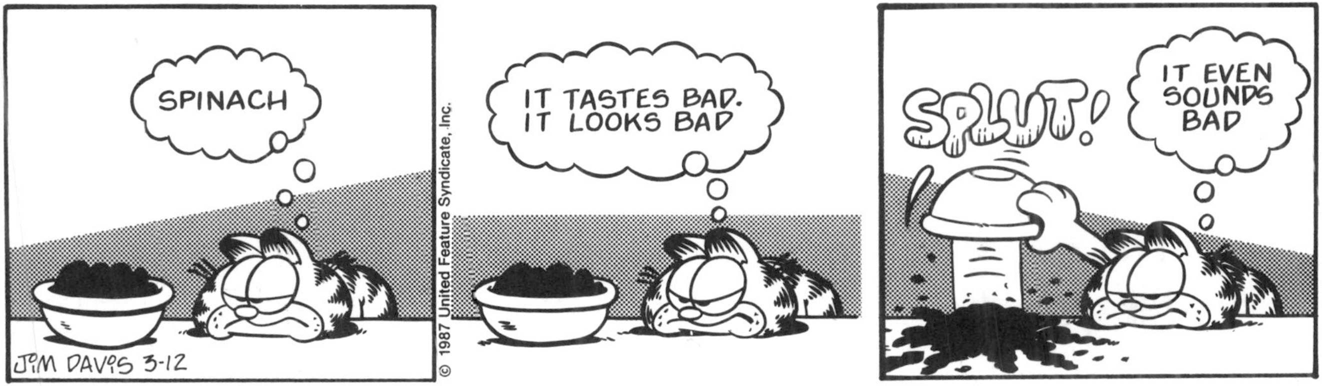
SPINACH
JIM DAVIS 3-12
© 1987 United Feature Syndicate, Inc.
IT TASTES BAD. IT LOOKS BAD
SPLUT!
IT EVEN SOUNDS BAD

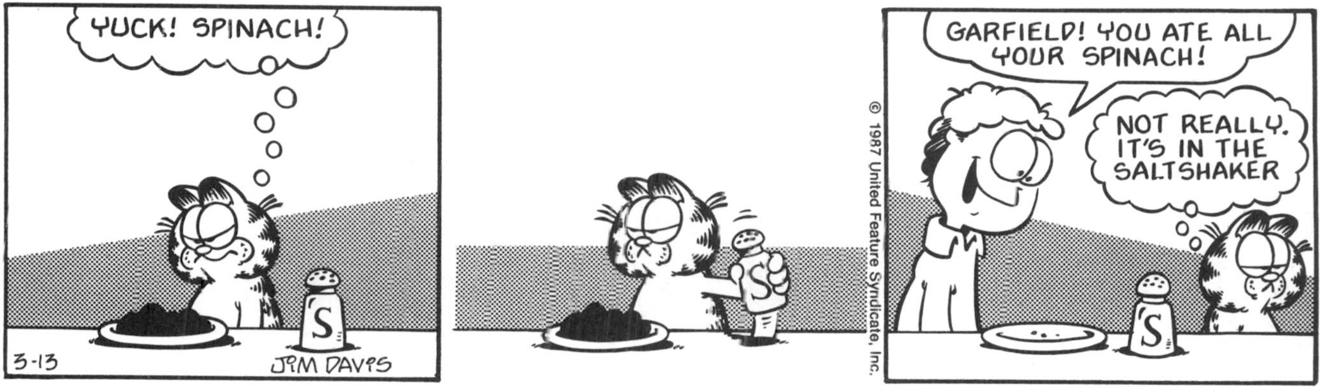
YUCK! SPINACH!
3-13
JIM DAVIS
© 1987 United Feature Syndicate, Inc.
GARFIELD! YOU ATE ALL YOUR SPINACH!
NOT REALLY. IT'S IN THE SALTSHAKER

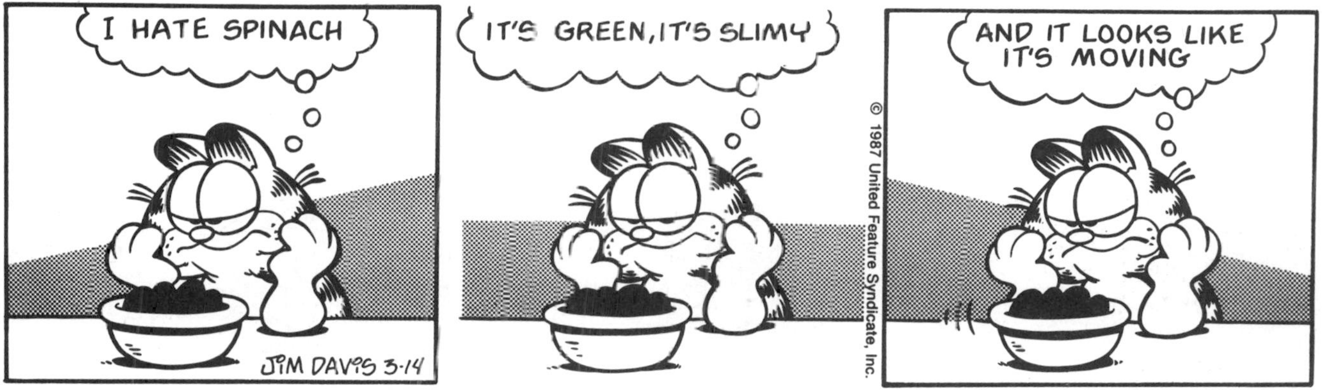
I HATE SPINACH
JIM DAVIS 3-14
IT'S GREEN, IT'S SLIMY
© 1987 United Feature Syndicate, Inc.
AND IT LOOKS LIKE IT'S MOVING

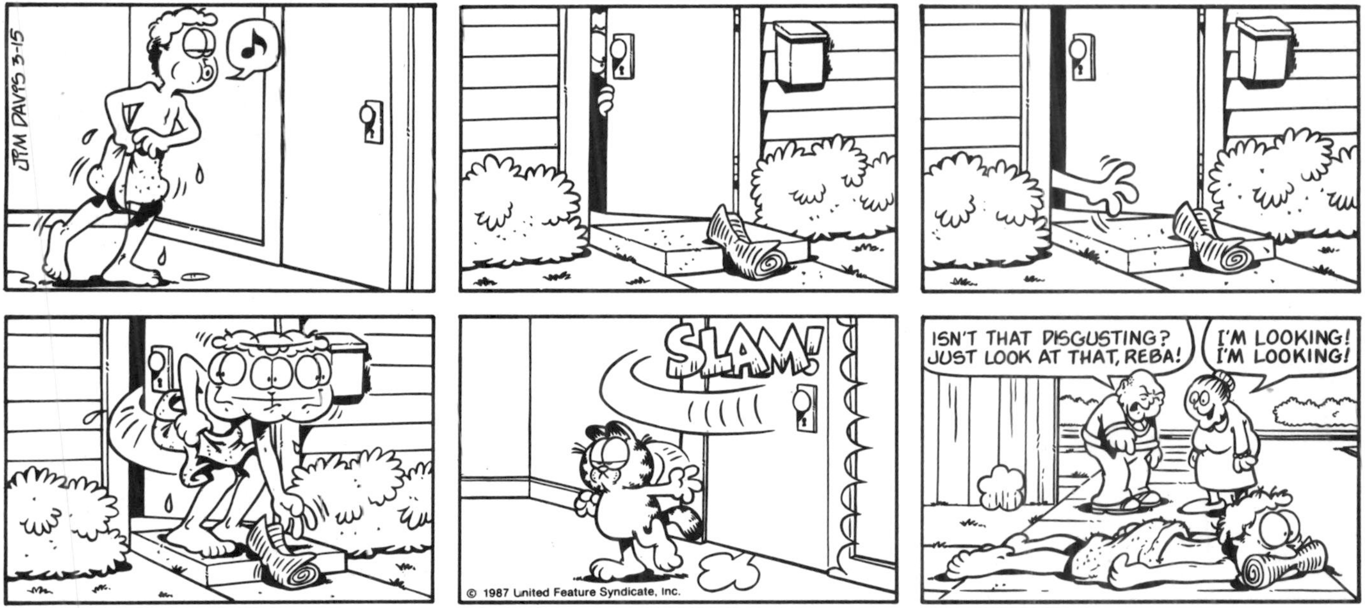
JIM DAVIS 3-15
SLAM!
© 1987 United Feature Syndicate, Inc.
ISN'T THAT DISGUSTING? JUST LOOK AT THAT, REBA!
I'M LOOKING! I'M LOOKING!

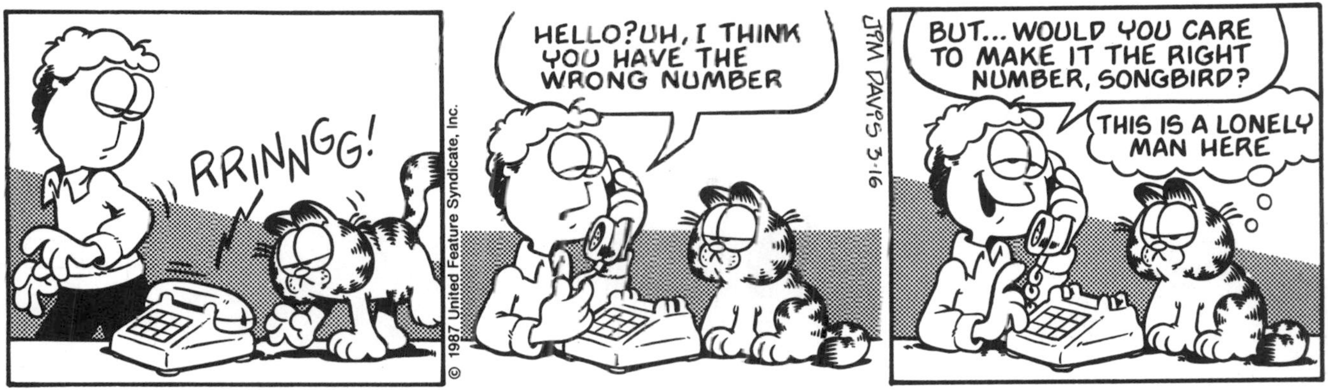
RRINNGG!
HELLO? UH, I THINK YOU HAVE THE WRONG NUMBER
BUT... WOULD YOU CARE TO MAKE IT THE RIGHT NUMBER, SONGBIRD?
THIS IS A LONELY MAN HERE
JIM DAVIS 3-16
© 1987 United Feature Syndicate, Inc.

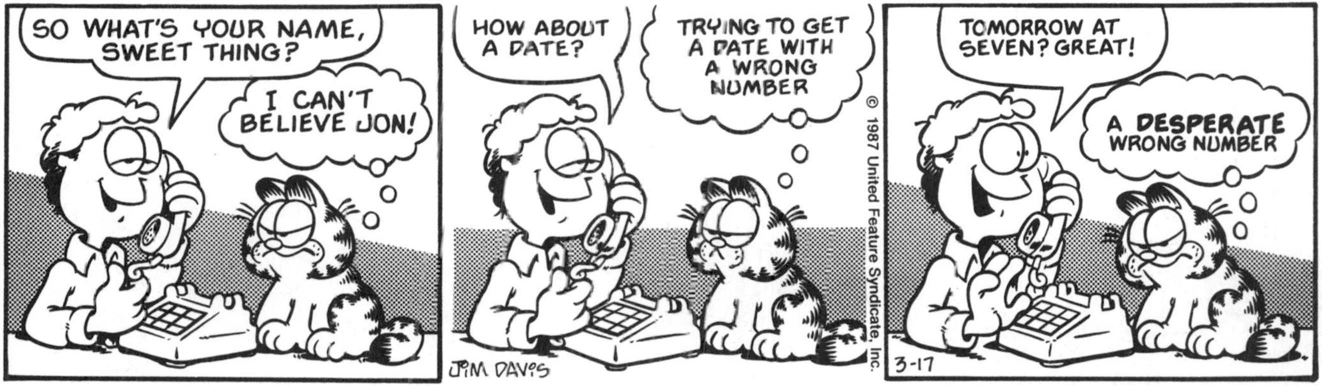
SO WHAT'S YOUR NAME, SWEET THING?
I CAN'T BELIEVE JON!
HOW ABOUT A DATE?
TRYING TO GET A DATE WITH A WRONG NUMBER
TOMORROW AT SEVEN? GREAT!
A DESPERATE WRONG NUMBER
JIM DAVIS
3-17
© 1987 United Feature Syndicate, Inc.

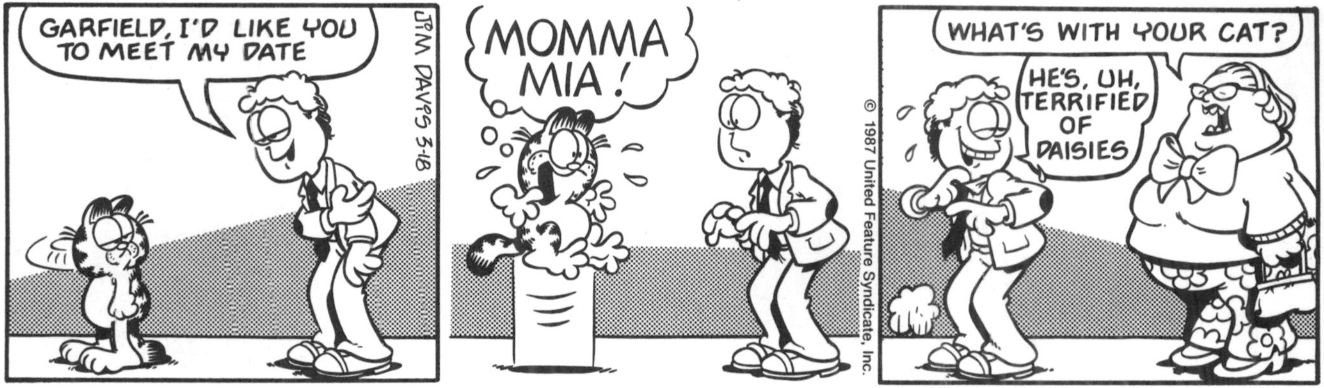
GARFIELD, I'D LIKE YOU TO MEET MY DATE
JIM DAVIS 3-18
MOMMA MIA!
WHAT'S WITH YOUR CAT?
HE'S, UH, TERRIFIED OF DAISIES
© 1987 United Feature Syndicate, Inc.

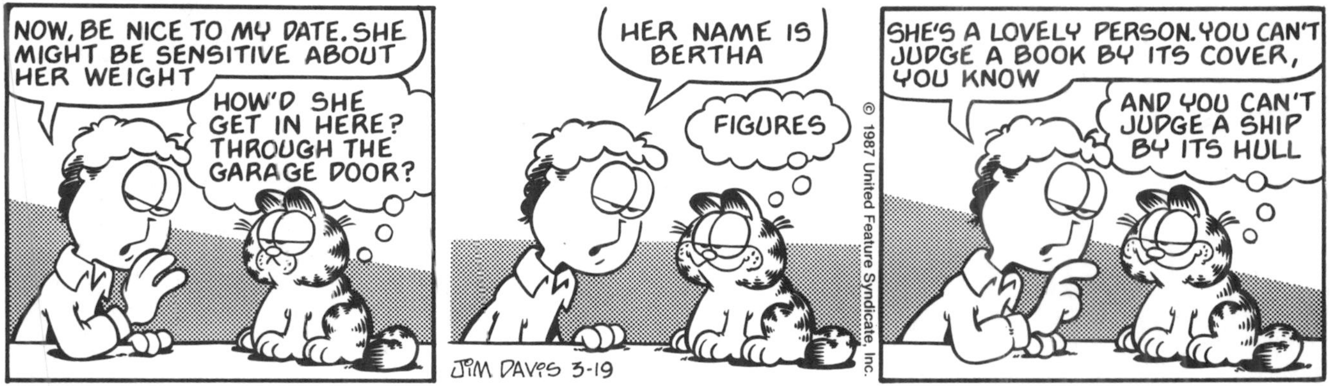
NOW, BE NICE TO MY DATE. SHE MIGHT BE SENSITIVE ABOUT HER WEIGHT
HOW'D SHE GET IN HERE? THROUGH THE GARAGE DOOR?
HER NAME IS BERTHA
FIGURES
JIM DAVIS 3-19
SHE'S A LOVELY PERSON. YOU CAN'T JUDGE A BOOK BY ITS COVER, YOU KNOW
AND YOU CAN'T JUDGE A SHIP BY ITS HULL
© 1987 United Feature Syndicate, Inc.

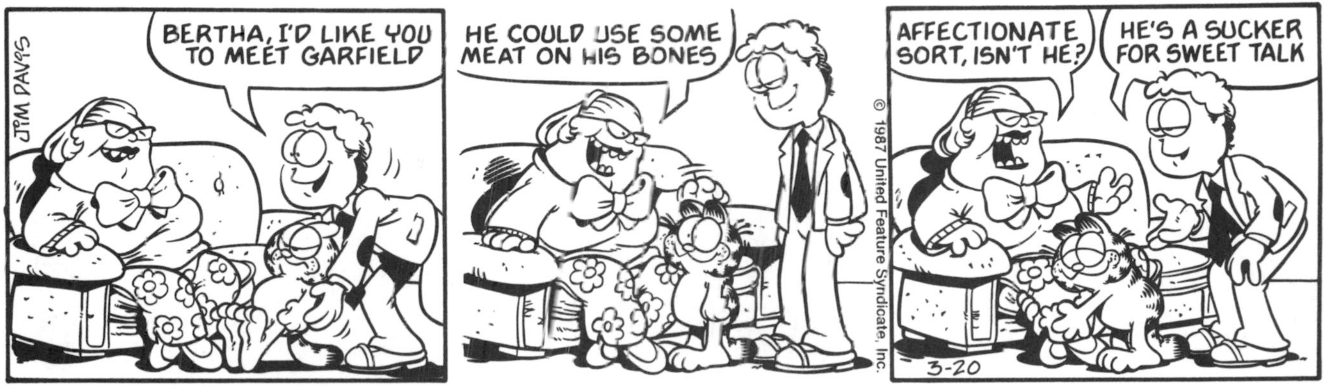
JIM DAVIS
BERTHA, I'D LIKE YOU TO MEET GARFIELD
HE COULD USE SOME MEAT ON HIS BONES
© 1987 United Feature Syndicate, Inc.
AFFECTIONATE SORT, ISN'T HE?
HE'S A SUCKER FOR SWEET TALK
3-20

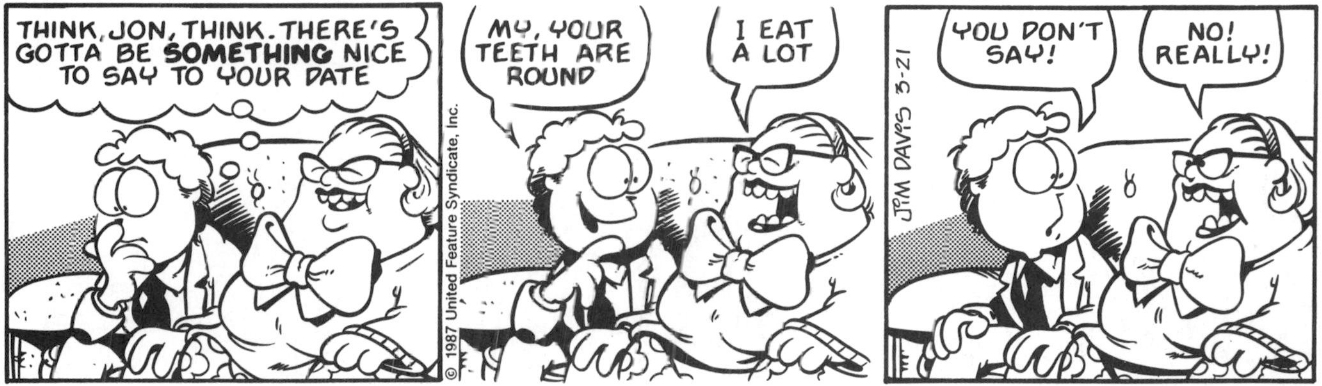
THINK, JON, THINK. THERE'S GOTTA BE **SOMETHING** NICE TO SAY TO YOUR DATE
© 1987 United Feature Syndicate, Inc.
MY, YOUR TEETH ARE ROUND
I EAT A LOT
JIM DAVIS 3-21
YOU DON'T SAY!
NO! REALLY!

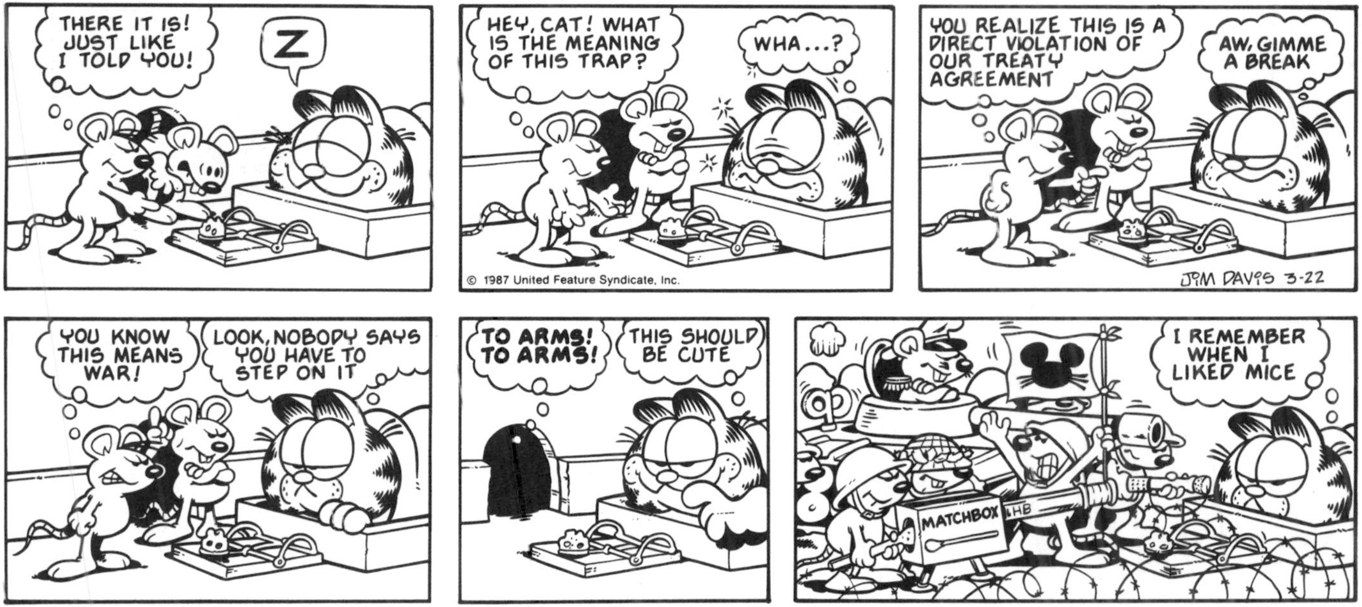

THERE IT IS! JUST LIKE I TOLD YOU!
Z
HEY, CAT! WHAT IS THE MEANING OF THIS TRAP?
WHA...?
© 1987 United Feature Syndicate, Inc.
YOU REALIZE THIS IS A DIRECT VIOLATION OF OUR TREATY AGREEMENT
AW, GIMME A BREAK
JIM DAVIS 3-22
YOU KNOW THIS MEANS WAR!
LOOK, NOBODY SAYS YOU HAVE TO STEP ON IT
TO ARMS! TO ARMS!
THIS SHOULD BE CUTE
MATCHBOX
HB
I REMEMBER WHEN I LIKED MICE

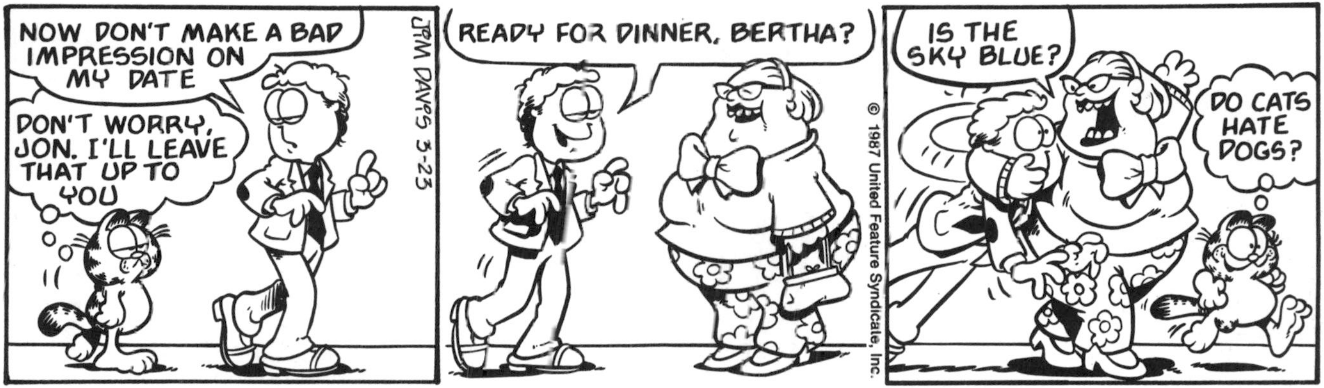
NOW DON'T MAKE A BAD IMPRESSION ON MY DATE
DON'T WORRY, JON. I'LL LEAVE THAT UP TO YOU
JIM DAVIS 3-23
READY FOR DINNER, BERTHA?
© 1987 United Feature Syndicate, Inc.
IS THE SKY BLUE?
DO CATS HATE DOGS?

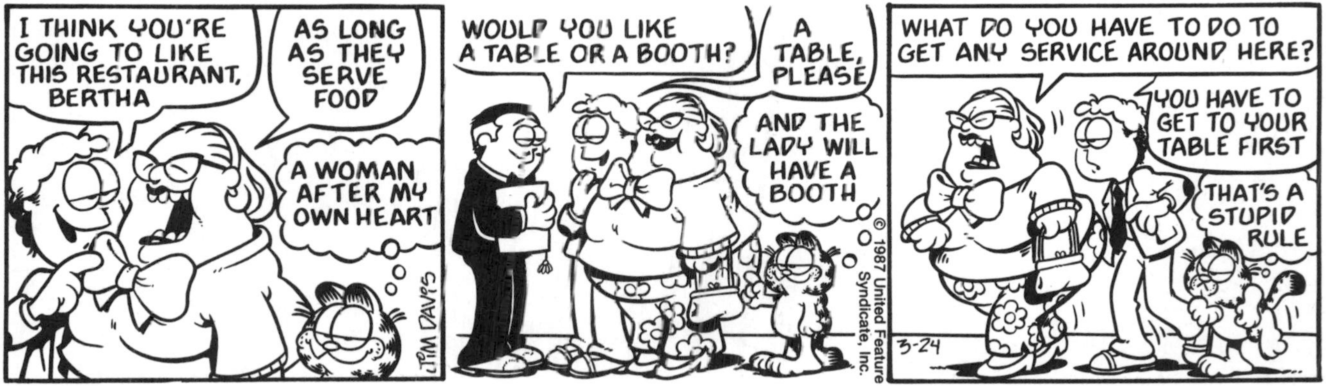
I THINK YOU'RE GOING TO LIKE THIS RESTAURANT, BERTHA
AS LONG AS THEY SERVE FOOD
A WOMAN AFTER MY OWN HEART
JIM DAVIS
WOULD YOU LIKE A TABLE OR A BOOTH?
A TABLE, PLEASE
AND THE LADY WILL HAVE A BOOTH
© 1987 United Feature Syndicate, Inc.
3-24
WHAT DO YOU HAVE TO DO TO GET ANY SERVICE AROUND HERE?
YOU HAVE TO GET TO YOUR TABLE FIRST
THAT'S A STUPID RULE

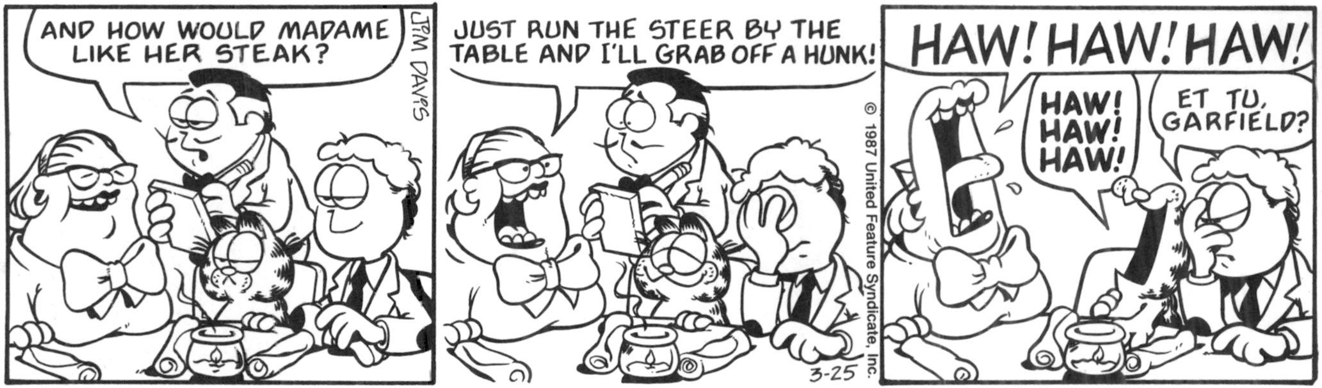
AND HOW WOULD MADAME LIKE HER STEAK?
JIM DAVIS
JUST RUN THE STEER BY THE TABLE AND I'LL GRAB OFF A HUNK!
© 1987 United Feature Syndicate, Inc.
3-25
HAW! HAW! HAW!
HAW! HAW! HAW!
ET TU, GARFIELD?

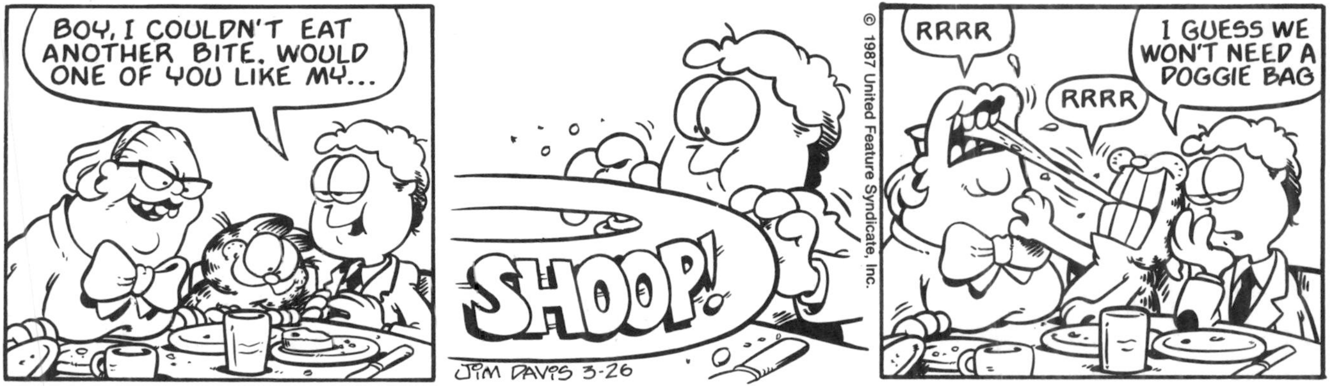
BOY, I COULDN'T EAT ANOTHER BITE. WOULD ONE OF YOU LIKE MY...
SHOOP!
JIM DAVIS 3-26
© 1987 United Feature Syndicate, Inc.
RRRR
RRRR
I GUESS WE WON'T NEED A DOGGIE BAG

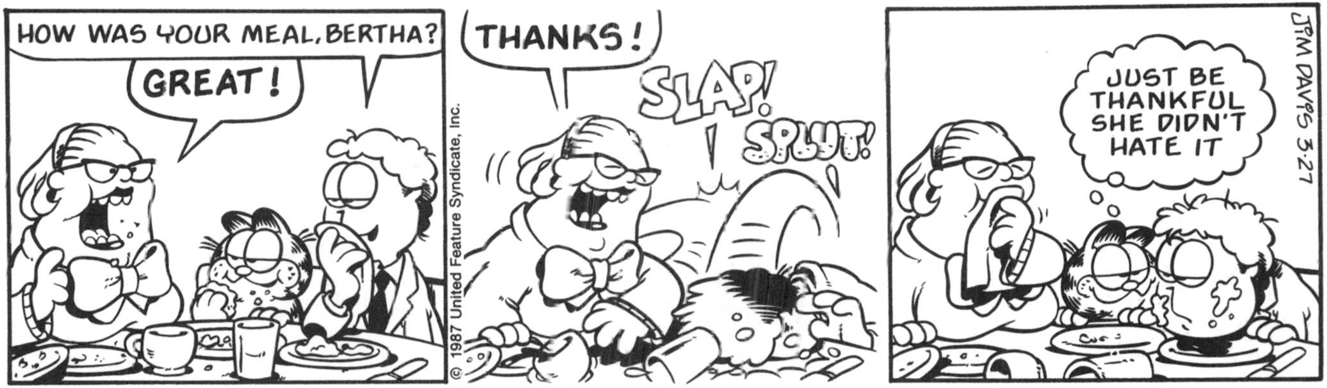
HOW WAS YOUR MEAL, BERTHA?
GREAT!
© 1987 United Feature Syndicate, Inc.
THANKS!
SLAP!
SPLUT!
JUST BE THANKFUL SHE DIDN'T HATE IT
JIM DAVIS 3-27

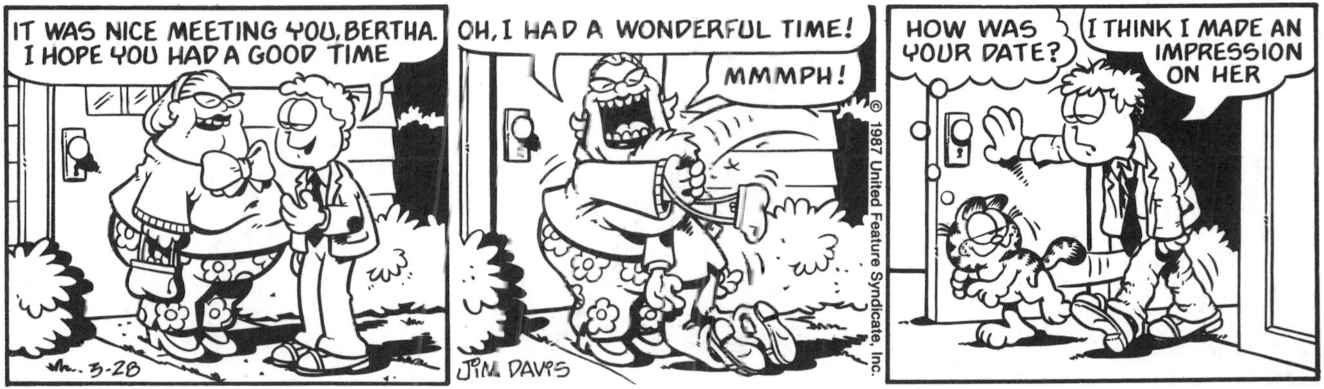
IT WAS NICE MEETING YOU, BERTHA. I HOPE YOU HAD A GOOD TIME
3-28
OH, I HAD A WONDERFUL TIME!
MMMPH!
JIM DAVIS
© 1987 United Feature Syndicate, Inc.
HOW WAS YOUR DATE?
I THINK I MADE AN IMPRESSION ON HER

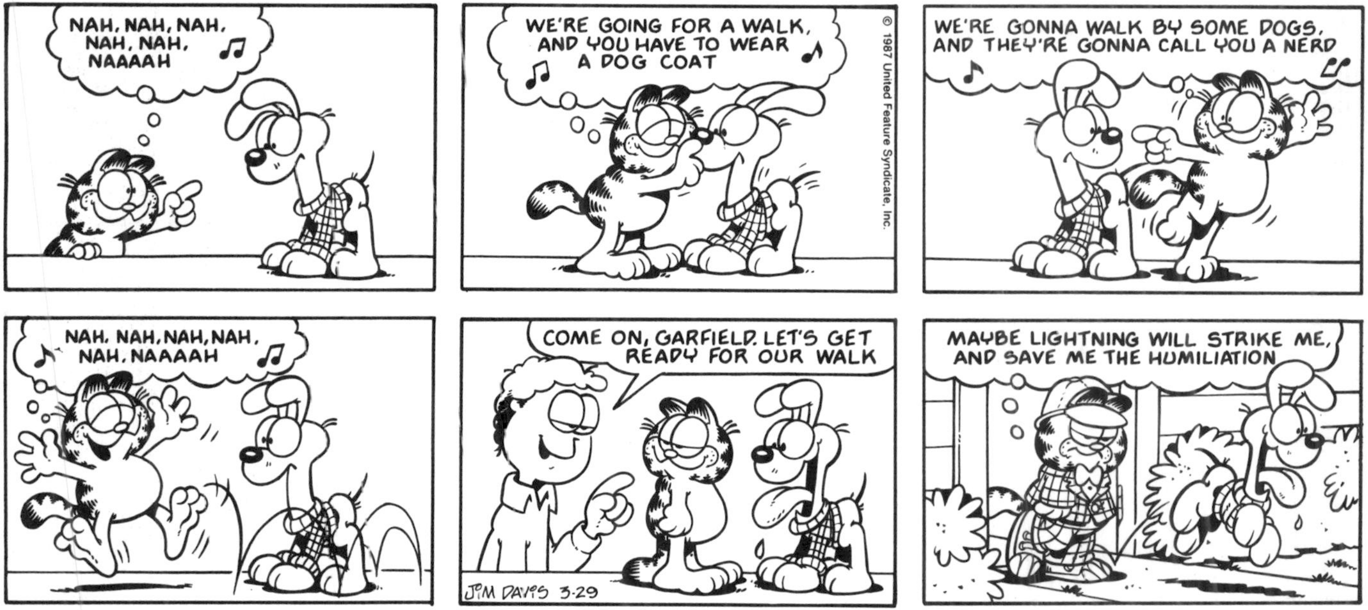
NAH, NAH, NAH, NAH, NAH, NAAAAH
WE'RE GOING FOR A WALK, AND YOU HAVE TO WEAR A DOG COAT
© 1987 United Feature Syndicate, Inc.
WE'RE GONNA WALK BY SOME DOGS, AND THEY'RE GONNA CALL YOU A NERD
NAH, NAH, NAH, NAH, NAH, NAAAAH
COME ON, GARFIELD. LET'S GET READY FOR OUR WALK
JIM DAVIS 3-29
MAYBE LIGHTNING WILL STRIKE ME, AND SAVE ME THE HUMILIATION

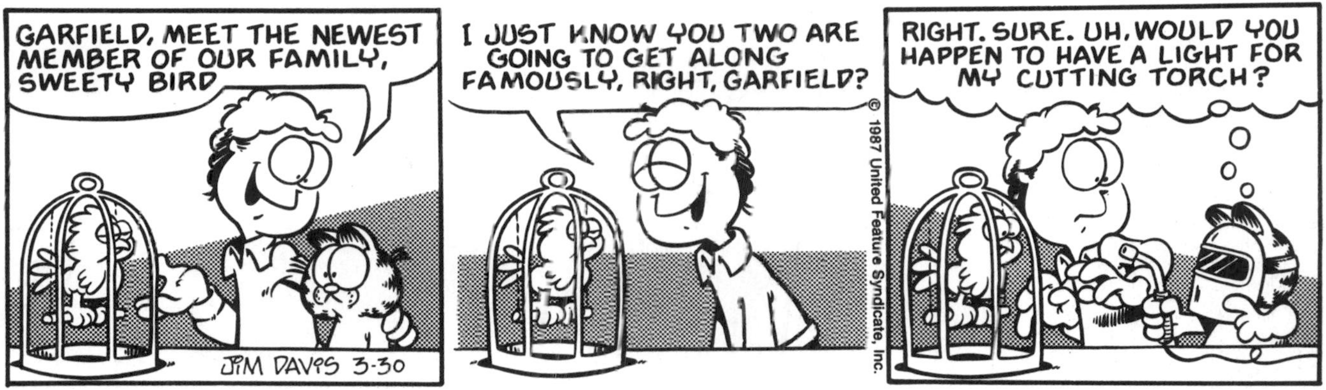
GARFIELD, MEET THE NEWEST MEMBER OF OUR FAMILY, SWEETY BIRD
JIM DAVIS 3-30
I JUST KNOW YOU TWO ARE GOING TO GET ALONG FAMOUSLY, RIGHT, GARFIELD?
© 1987 United Feature Syndicate, Inc.
RIGHT. SURE. UH, WOULD YOU HAPPEN TO HAVE A LIGHT FOR MY CUTTING TORCH?

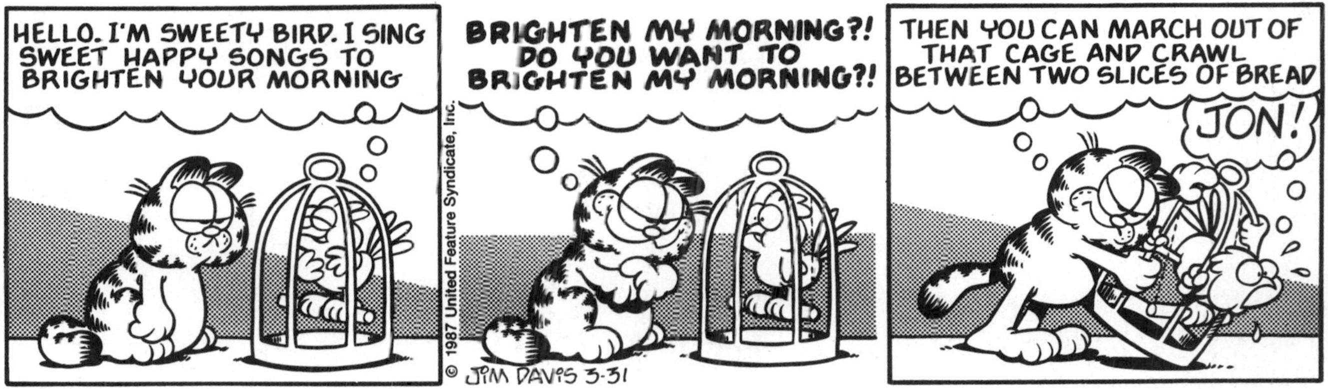
HELLO. I'M SWEETY BIRD. I SING SWEET HAPPY SONGS TO BRIGHTEN YOUR MORNING
© 1987 United Feature Syndicate, Inc.
BRIGHTEN MY MORNING?! DO YOU WANT TO BRIGHTEN MY MORNING?!
JIM DAVIS 3-31
THEN YOU CAN MARCH OUT OF THAT CAGE AND CRAWL BETWEEN TWO SLICES OF BREAD
JON!

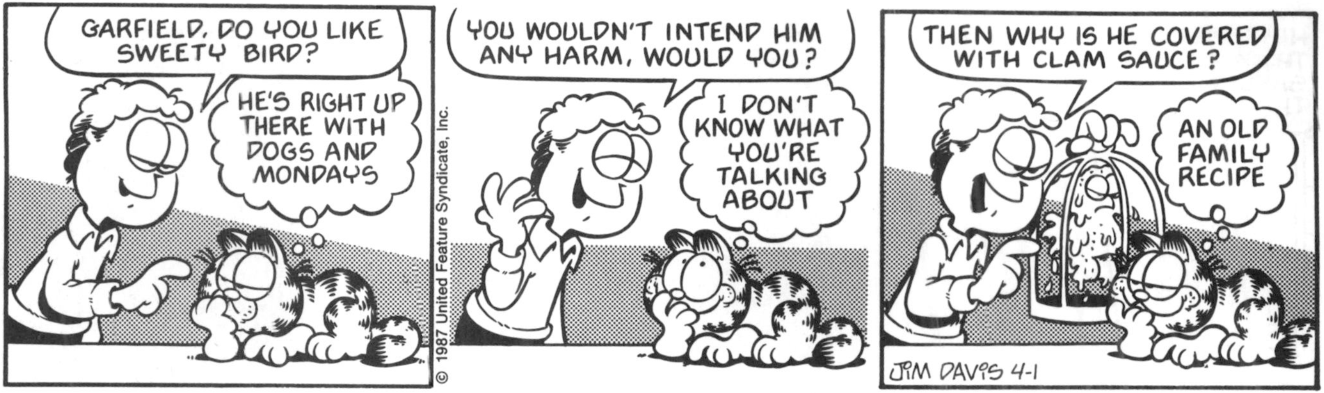
GARFIELD, DO YOU LIKE SWEETY BIRD?
HE'S RIGHT UP THERE WITH DOGS AND MONDAYS
YOU WOULDN'T INTEND HIM ANY HARM, WOULD YOU?
I DON'T KNOW WHAT YOU'RE TALKING ABOUT
THEN WHY IS HE COVERED WITH CLAM SAUCE?
AN OLD FAMILY RECIPE
© 1987 United Feature Syndicate, Inc.
JIM DAVIS 4-1

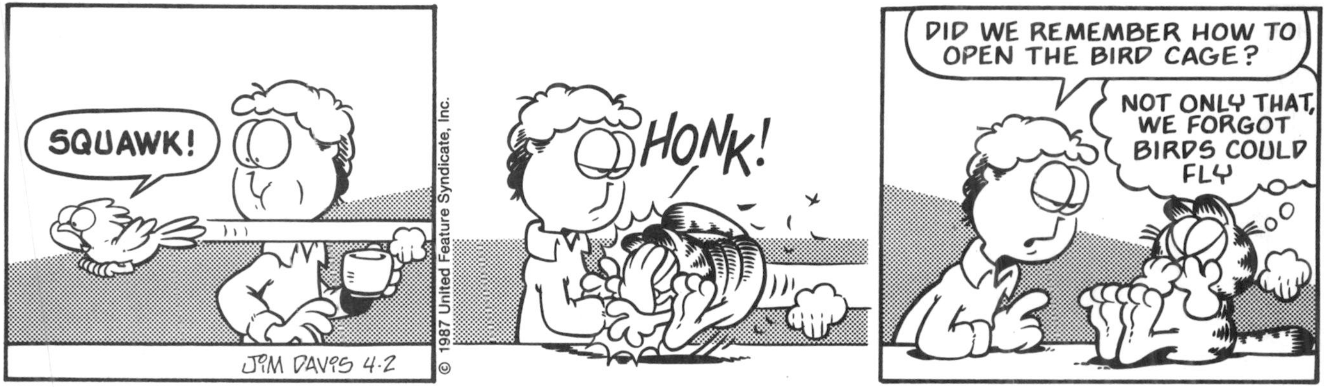
SQUAWK!
HONK!
DID WE REMEMBER HOW TO OPEN THE BIRD CAGE?
NOT ONLY THAT, WE FORGOT BIRDS COULD FLY
© 1987 United Feature Syndicate, Inc.
JIM DAVIS 4-2

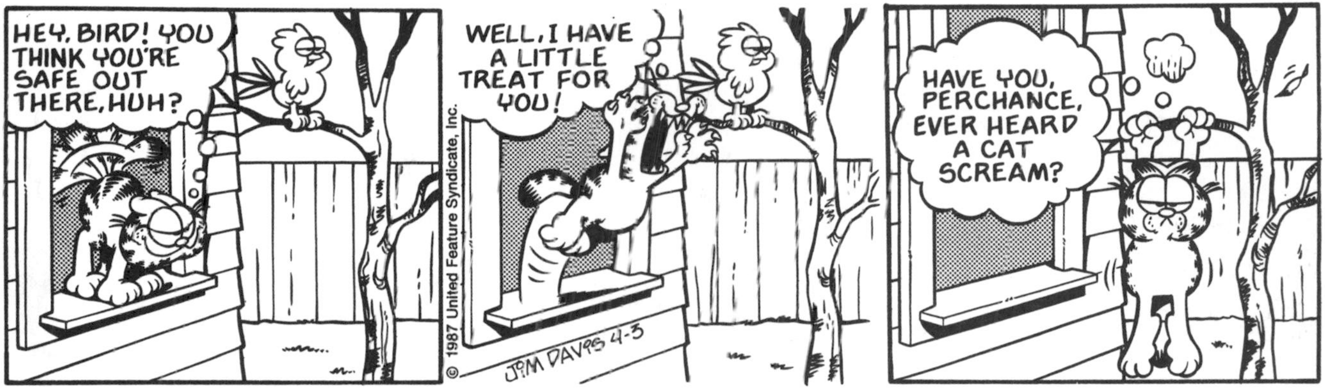
HEY, BIRD! YOU THINK YOU'RE SAFE OUT THERE, HUH?
WELL, I HAVE A LITTLE TREAT FOR YOU!
© 1987 United Feature Syndicate, Inc.
JIM DAVIS 4-3
HAVE YOU, PERCHANCE, EVER HEARD A CAT SCREAM?

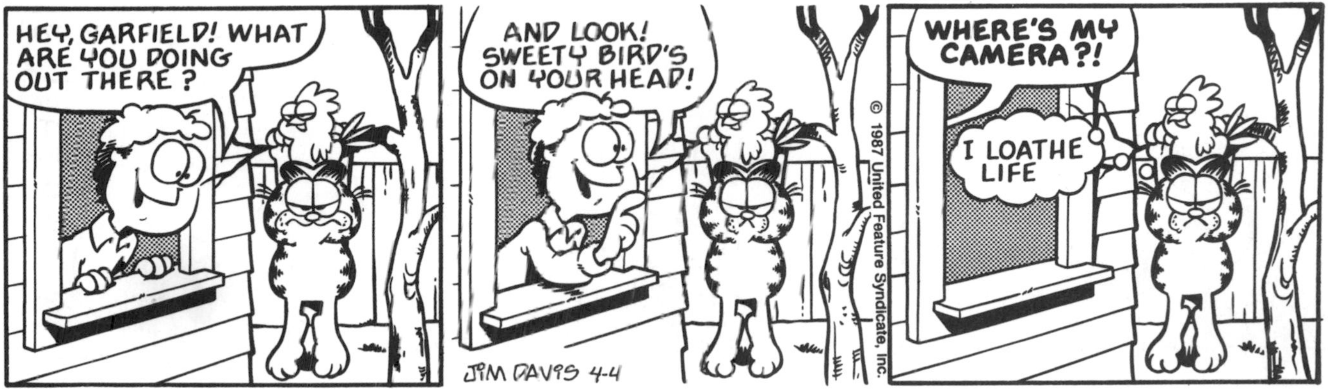
HEY, GARFIELD! WHAT ARE YOU DOING OUT THERE?
AND LOOK! SWEETY BIRD'S ON YOUR HEAD!
JIM DAVIS 4-4
© 1987 United Feature Syndicate, Inc.
WHERE'S MY CAMERA?!
I LOATHE LIFE

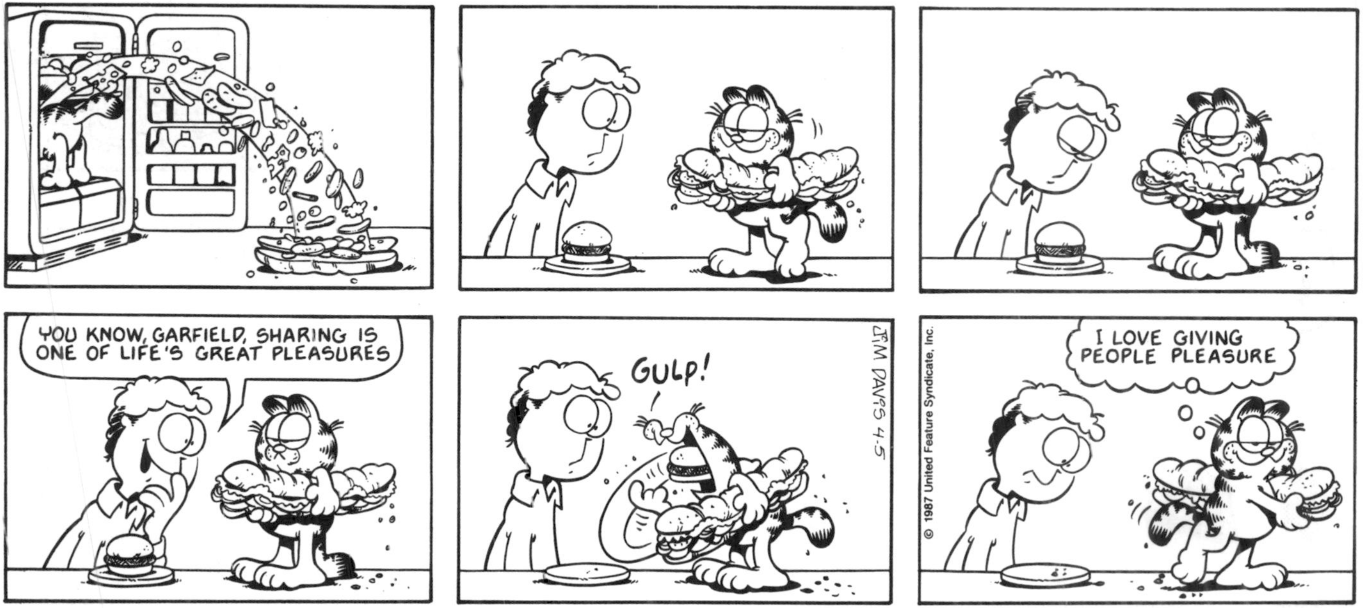
YOU KNOW, GARFIELD, SHARING IS ONE OF LIFE'S GREAT PLEASURES
GULP!
JIM DAVIS 4-5
© 1987 United Feature Syndicate, Inc.
I LOVE GIVING PEOPLE PLEASURE

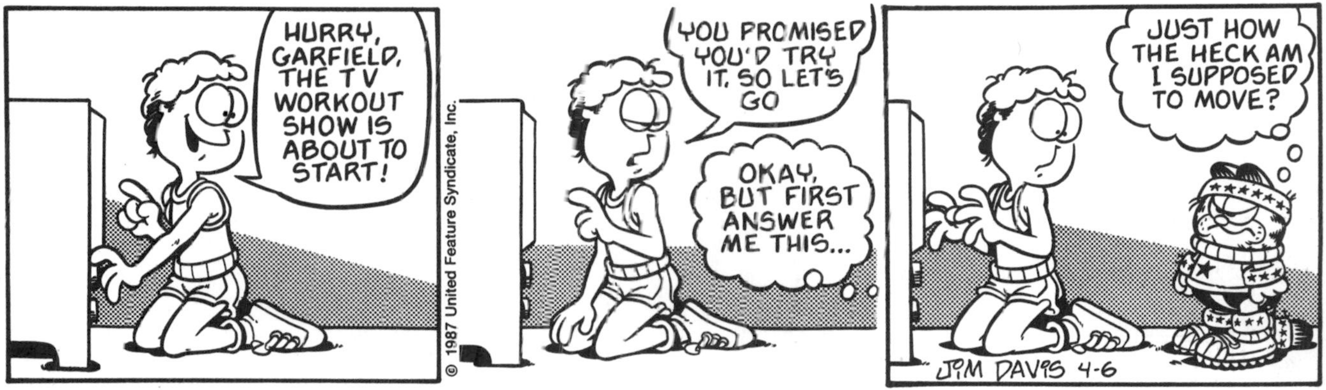
HURRY, GARFIELD, THE T V WORKOUT SHOW IS ABOUT TO START!
© 1987 United Feature Syndicate, Inc.
YOU PROMISED YOU'D TRY IT. SO LET'S GO
OKAY, BUT FIRST ANSWER ME THIS...
JUST HOW THE HECK AM I SUPPOSED TO MOVE?
JIM DAVIS 4-6

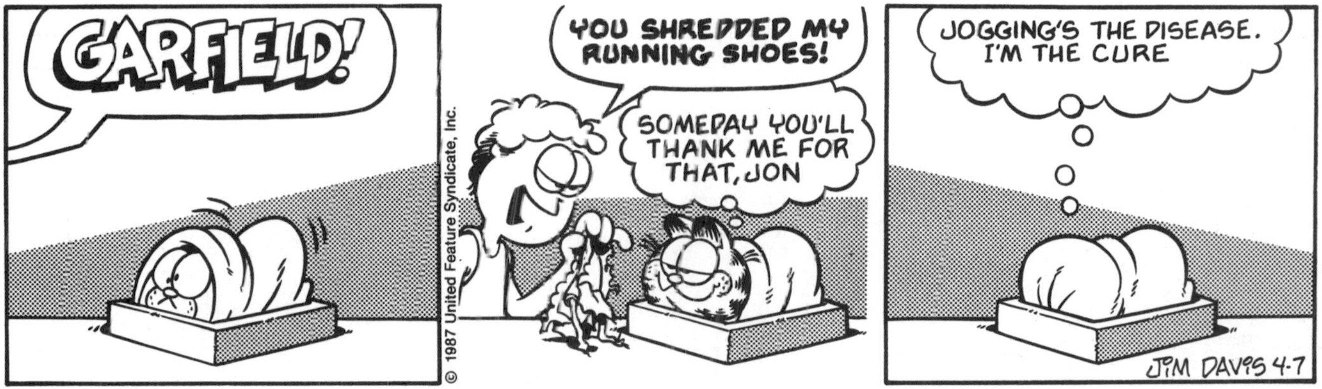
GARFIELD!
© 1987 United Feature Syndicate, Inc.
YOU SHREDDED MY RUNNING SHOES!
SOMEDAY YOU'LL THANK ME FOR THAT, JON
JOGGING'S THE DISEASE. I'M THE CURE
JIM DAVIS 4-7

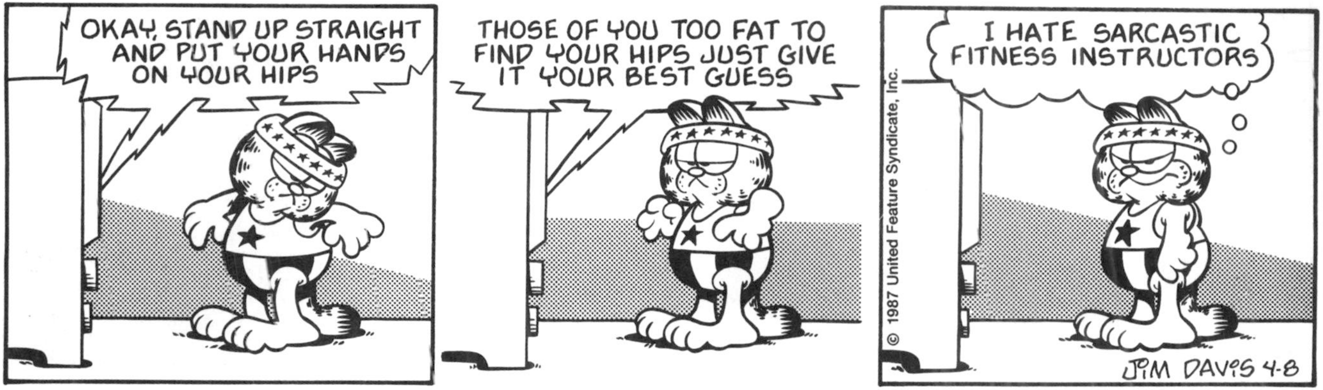
OKAY, STAND UP STRAIGHT AND PUT YOUR HANDS ON YOUR HIPS
THOSE OF YOU TOO FAT TO FIND YOUR HIPS JUST GIVE IT YOUR BEST GUESS
I HATE SARCASTIC FITNESS INSTRUCTORS
© 1987 United Feature Syndicate, Inc.
JIM DAVIS 4-8

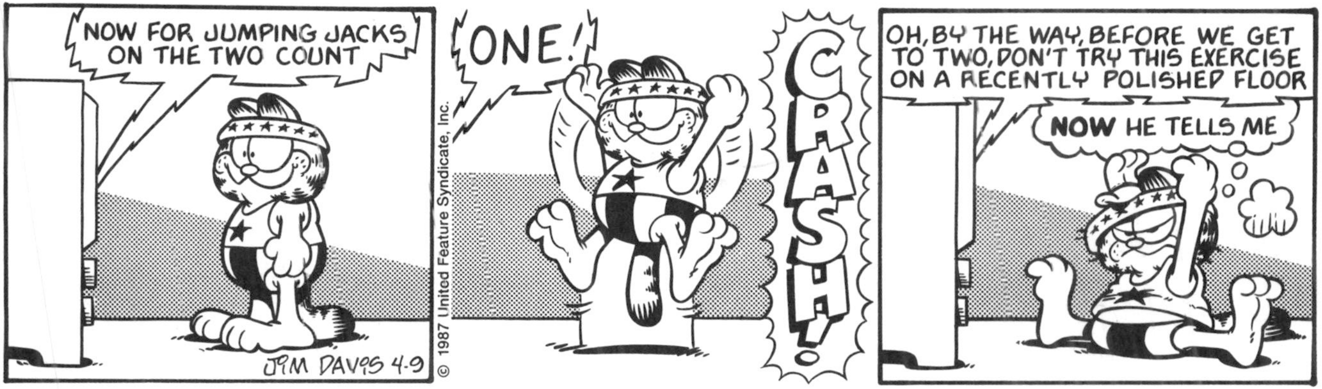
NOW FOR JUMPING JACKS ON THE TWO COUNT
JIM DAVIS 4-9
© 1987 United Feature Syndicate, Inc.
ONE!
CRASH!
OH, BY THE WAY, BEFORE WE GET TO TWO, DON'T TRY THIS EXERCISE ON A RECENTLY POLISHED FLOOR
NOW HE TELLS ME

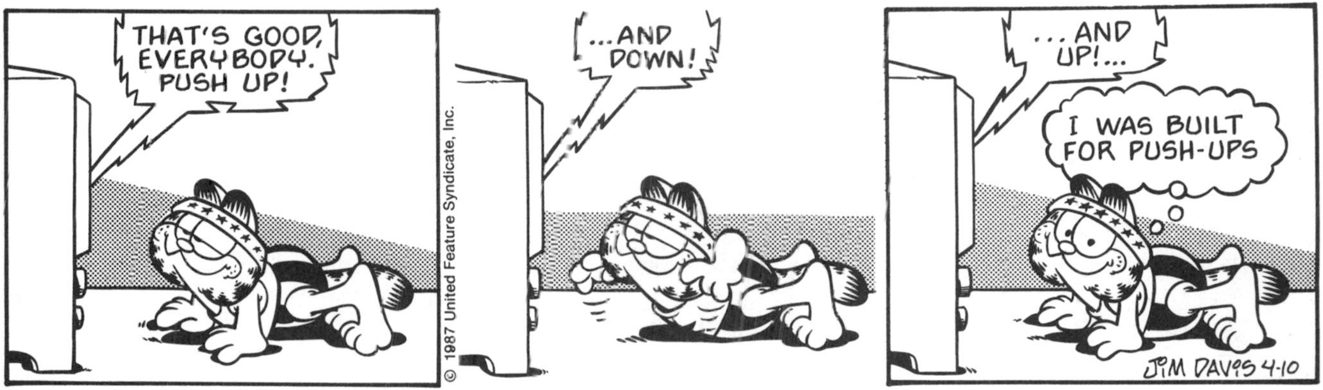
THAT'S GOOD, EVERYBODY. PUSH UP!
© 1987 United Feature Syndicate, Inc.
...AND DOWN!
...AND UP!...
I WAS BUILT FOR PUSH-UPS
JIM DAVIS 4-10

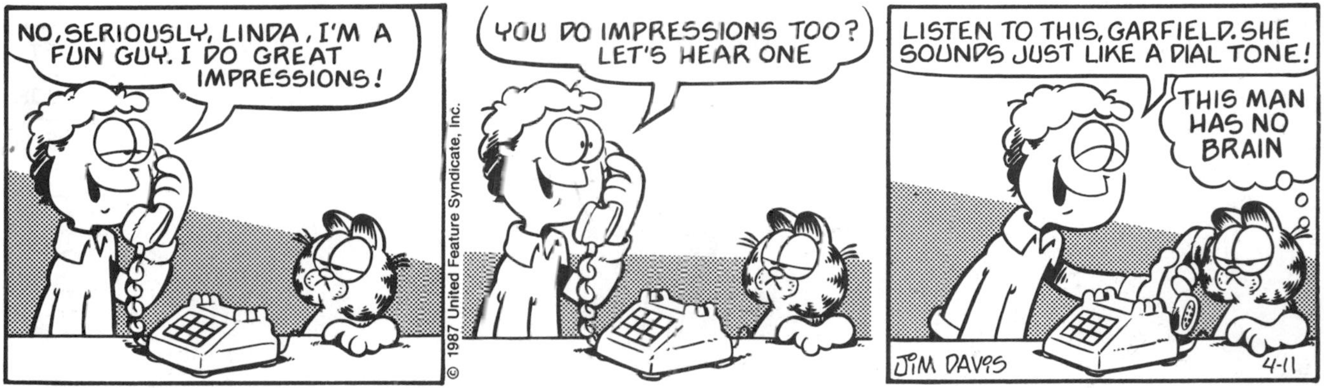
NO, SERIOUSLY, LINDA, I'M A FUN GUY. I DO GREAT IMPRESSIONS!
© 1987 United Feature Syndicate, Inc.
YOU DO IMPRESSIONS TOO? LET'S HEAR ONE
LISTEN TO THIS, GARFIELD. SHE SOUNDS JUST LIKE A DIAL TONE!
THIS MAN HAS NO BRAIN
JIM DAVIS
4-11

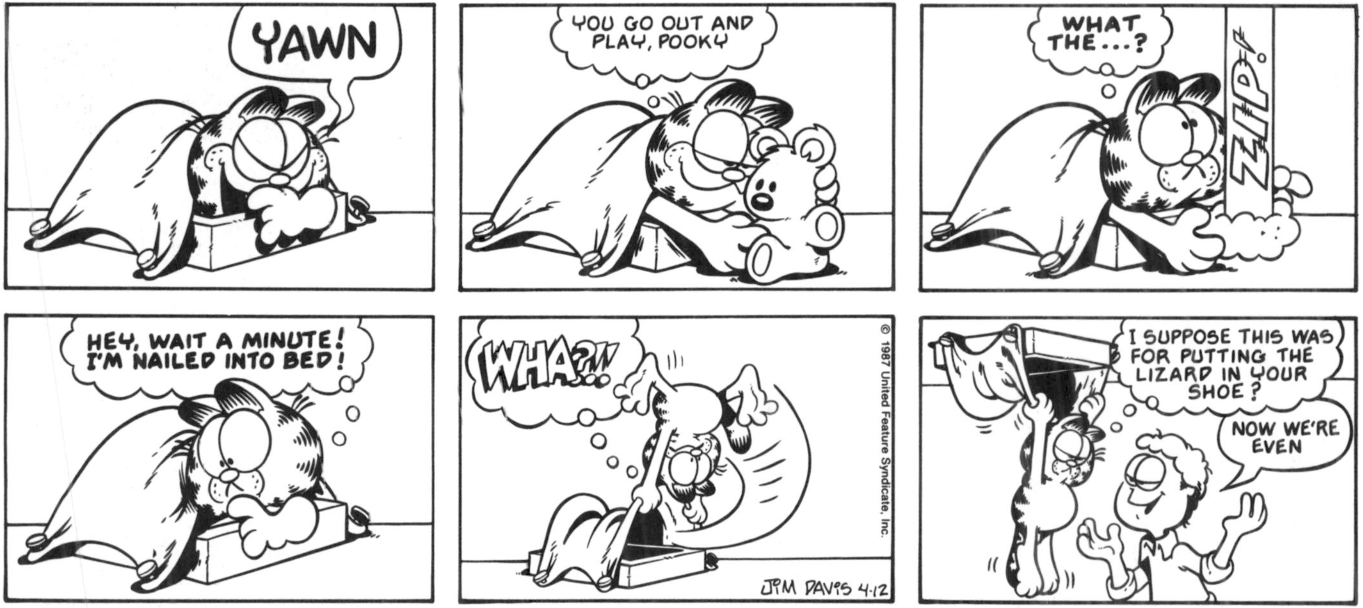
YAWN
YOU GO OUT AND PLAY, POOKY
WHAT THE...?
ZIP!
HEY, WAIT A MINUTE! I'M NAILED INTO BED!
WHA?!!
© 1987 United Feature Syndicate, Inc.
JIM DAVIS 4-12
I SUPPOSE THIS WAS FOR PUTTING THE LIZARD IN YOUR SHOE?
NOW WE'RE EVEN

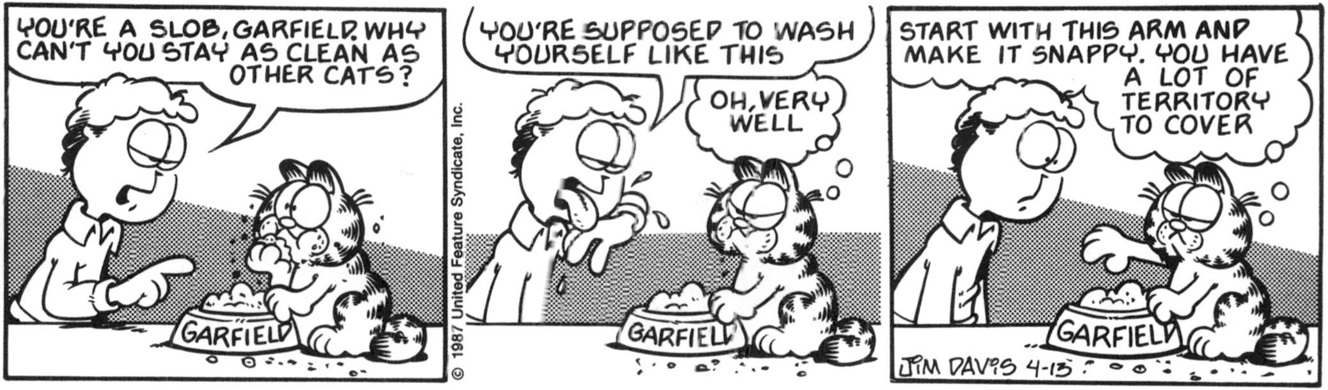
YOU'RE A SLOB, GARFIELD. WHY CAN'T YOU STAY AS CLEAN AS OTHER CATS?
GARFIELD
© 1987 United Feature Syndicate, Inc.
YOU'RE SUPPOSED TO WASH YOURSELF LIKE THIS
OH, VERY WELL
GARFIELD
START WITH THIS ARM AND MAKE IT SNAPPY. YOU HAVE A LOT OF TERRITORY TO COVER
GARFIELD
JIM DAVIS 4-13

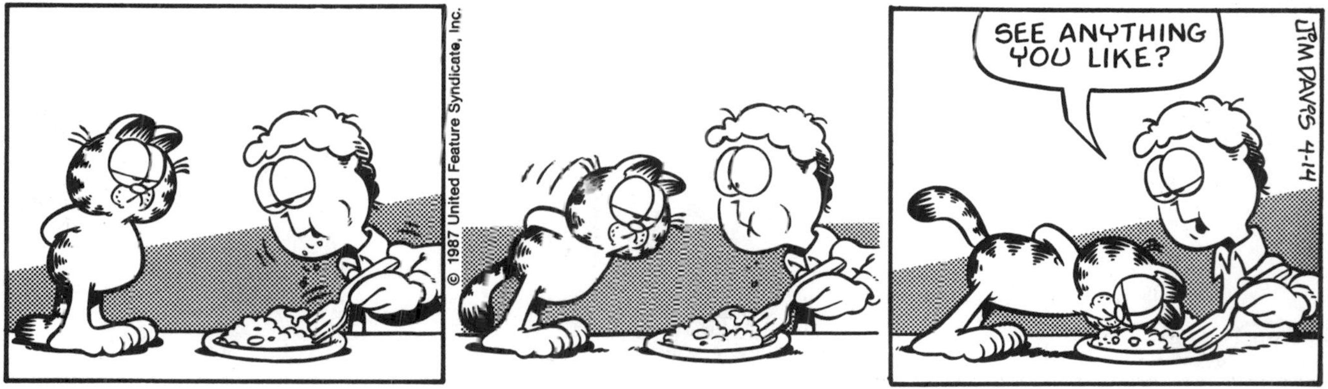
© 1987 United Feature Syndicate, Inc.
SEE ANYTHING YOU LIKE?
JIM DAVIS 4-14

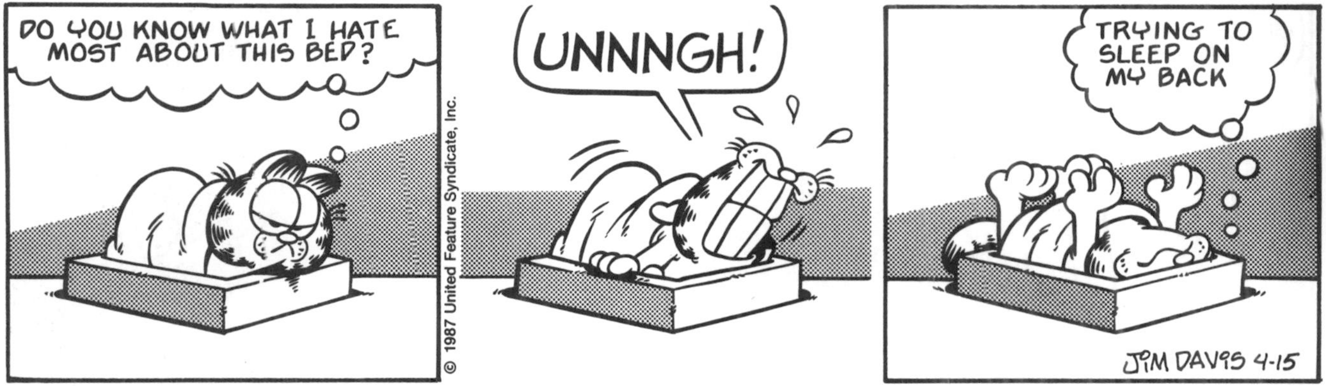
DO YOU KNOW WHAT I HATE MOST ABOUT THIS BED?
© 1987 United Feature Syndicate, Inc.
UNNNGH!
TRYING TO SLEEP ON MY BACK
JIM DAVIS 4-15

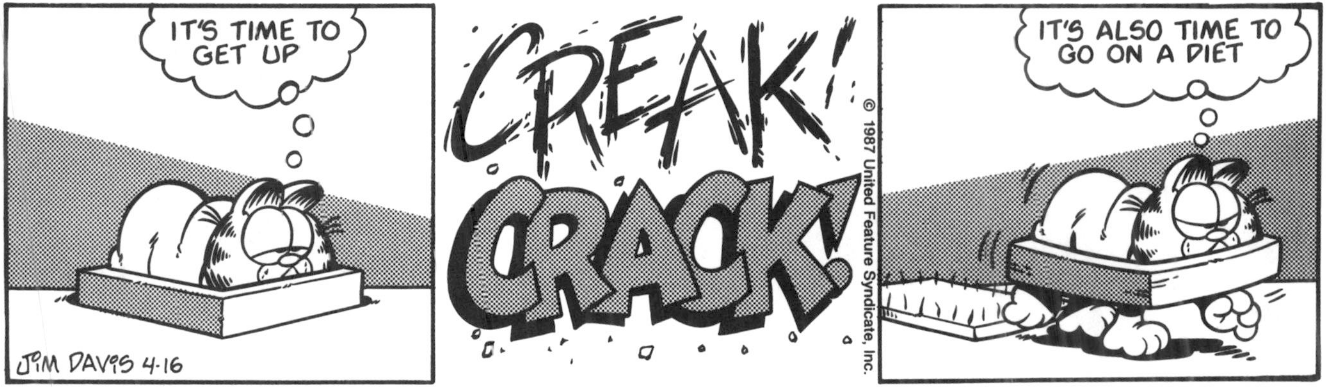
IT'S TIME TO GET UP
JIM DAVIS 4-16
CREAK!
CRACK!
© 1987 United Feature Syndicate, Inc.
IT'S ALSO TIME TO GO ON A DIET

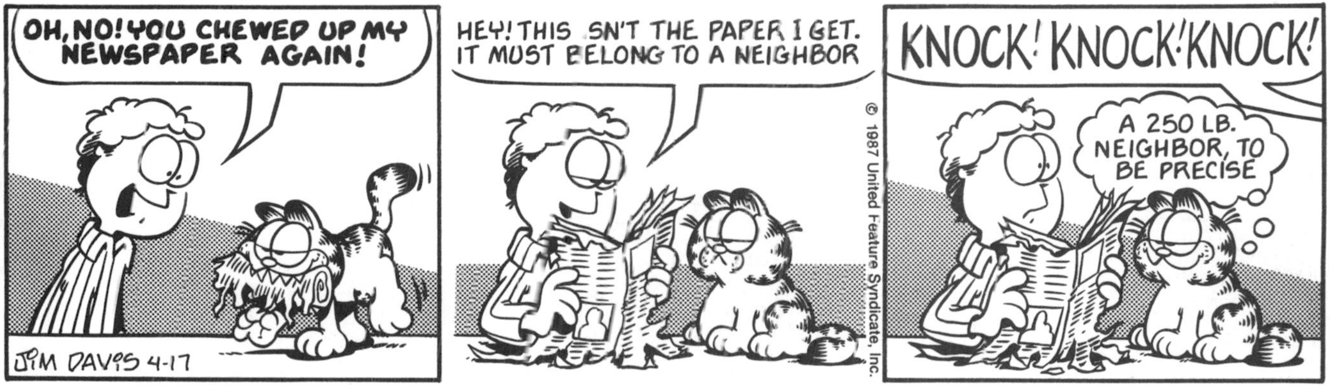
OH, NO! YOU CHEWED UP MY NEWSPAPER AGAIN!
JIM DAVIS 4-17
HEY! THIS ISN'T THE PAPER I GET. IT MUST BELONG TO A NEIGHBOR
© 1987 United Feature Syndicate, Inc.
KNOCK! KNOCK! KNOCK!
A 250 LB. NEIGHBOR, TO BE PRECISE

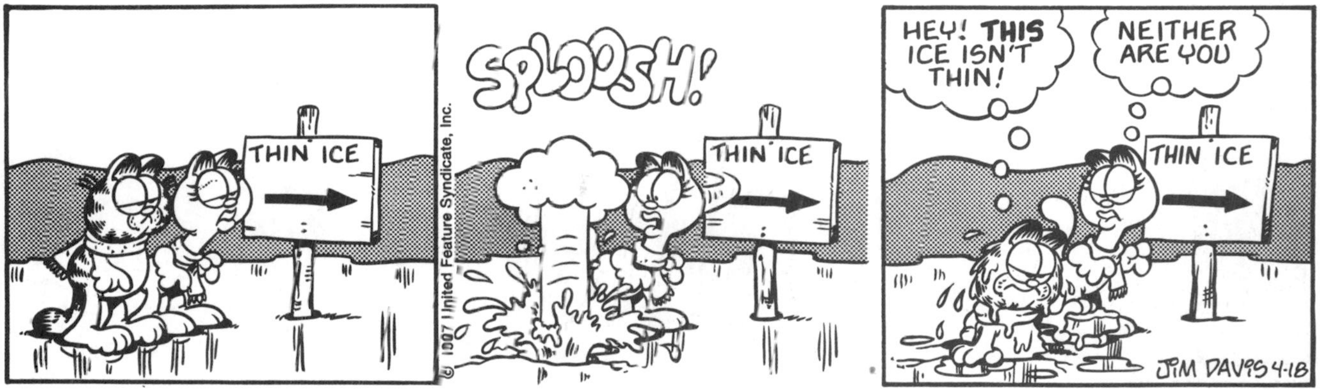
THIN ICE
© 1987 United Feature Syndicate, Inc.
SPLOOSH!
THIN ICE
HEY! THIS ICE ISN'T THIN!
NEITHER ARE YOU
THIN ICE
JIM DAVIS 4-18

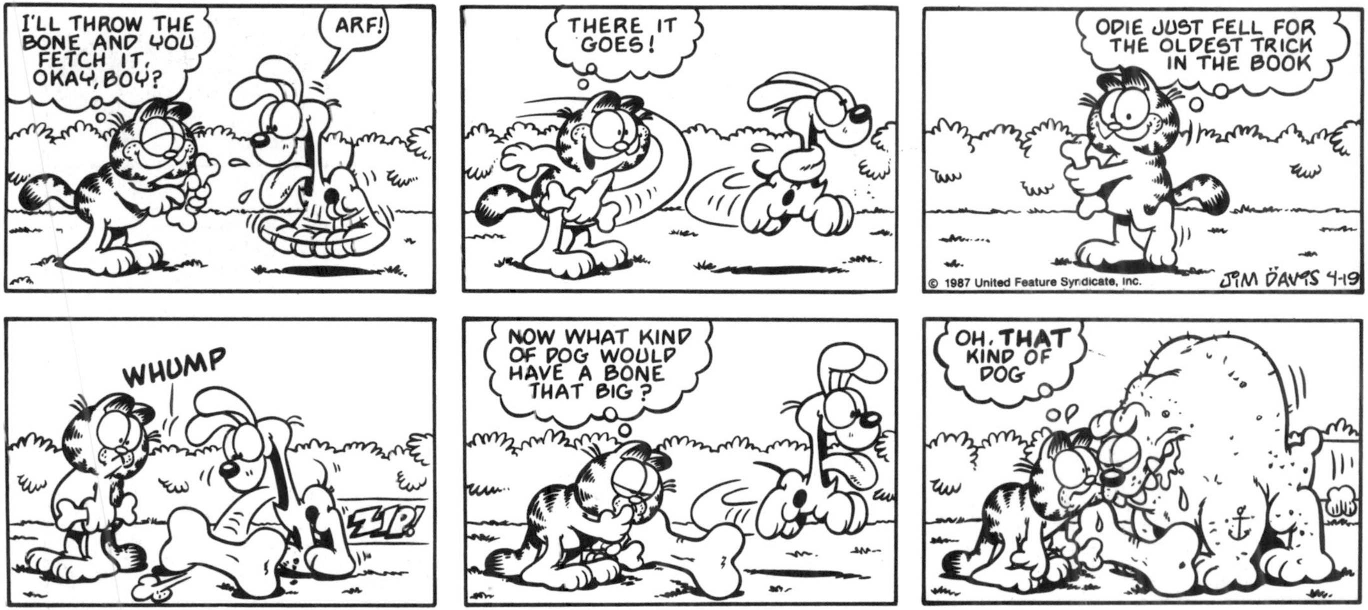
I'LL THROW THE BONE AND YOU FETCH IT, OKAY, BOY?
ARF!
THERE IT GOES!
ODIE JUST FELL FOR THE OLDEST TRICK IN THE BOOK
© 1987 United Feature Syndicate, Inc.
JIM DAVIS 4-19
WHUMP
ZIP!
NOW WHAT KIND OF DOG WOULD HAVE A BONE THAT BIG?
OH, THAT KIND OF DOG

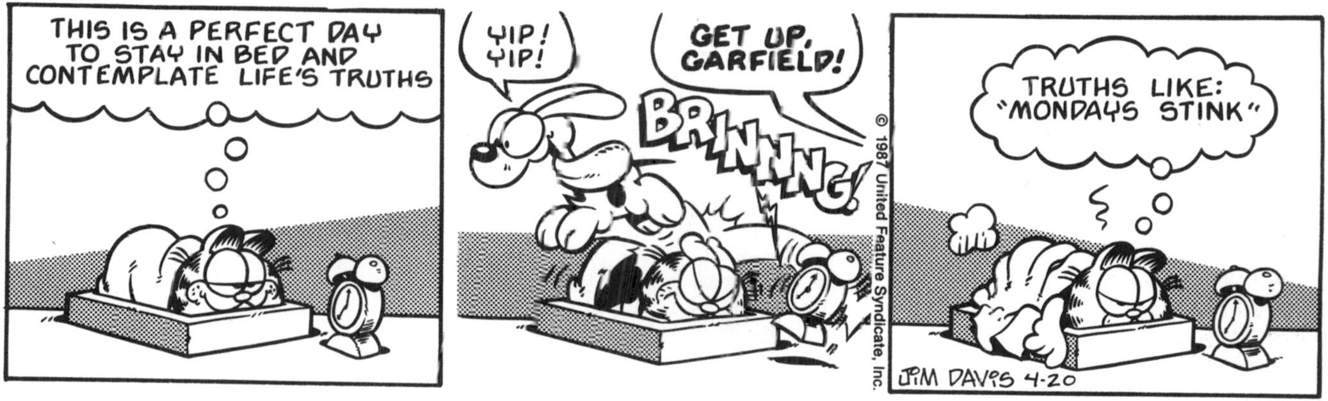
THIS IS A PERFECT DAY TO STAY IN BED AND CONTEMPLATE LIFE'S TRUTHS
YIP! YIP!
GET UP, GARFIELD!
BRINNNG!
© 1987 United Feature Syndicate, Inc.
TRUTHS LIKE: "MONDAYS STINK"
JIM DAVIS 4-20

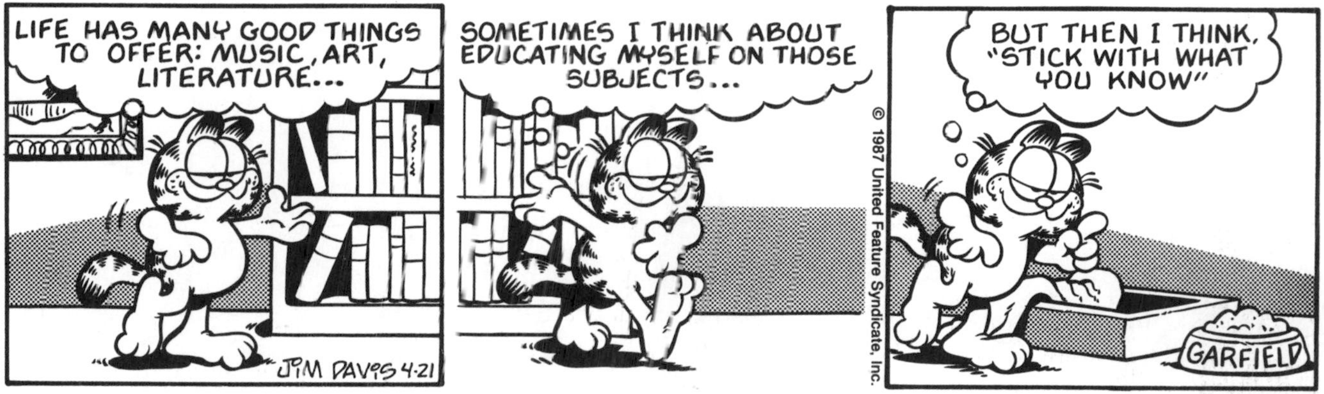
LIFE HAS MANY GOOD THINGS TO OFFER: MUSIC, ART, LITERATURE...
JIM DAVIS 4-21
SOMETIMES I THINK ABOUT EDUCATING MYSELF ON THOSE SUBJECTS...
© 1987 United Feature Syndicate, Inc.
BUT THEN I THINK, "STICK WITH WHAT YOU KNOW"
GARFIELD

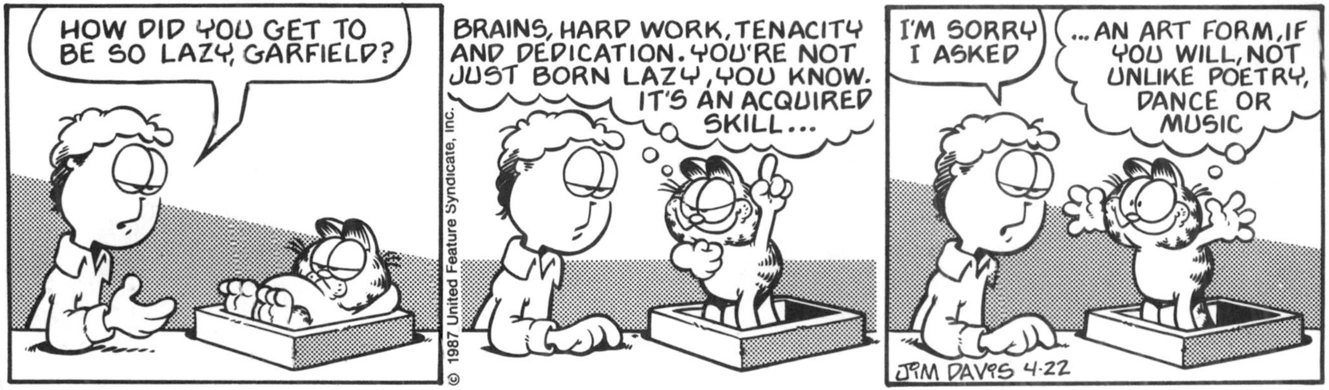
HOW DID YOU GET TO BE SO LAZY, GARFIELD?
BRAINS, HARD WORK, TENACITY AND DEDICATION. YOU'RE NOT JUST BORN LAZY, YOU KNOW. IT'S AN ACQUIRED SKILL...
I'M SORRY I ASKED
...AN ART FORM, IF YOU WILL, NOT UNLIKE POETRY, DANCE OR MUSIC
© 1987 United Feature Syndicate, Inc.
JIM DAVIS 4-22

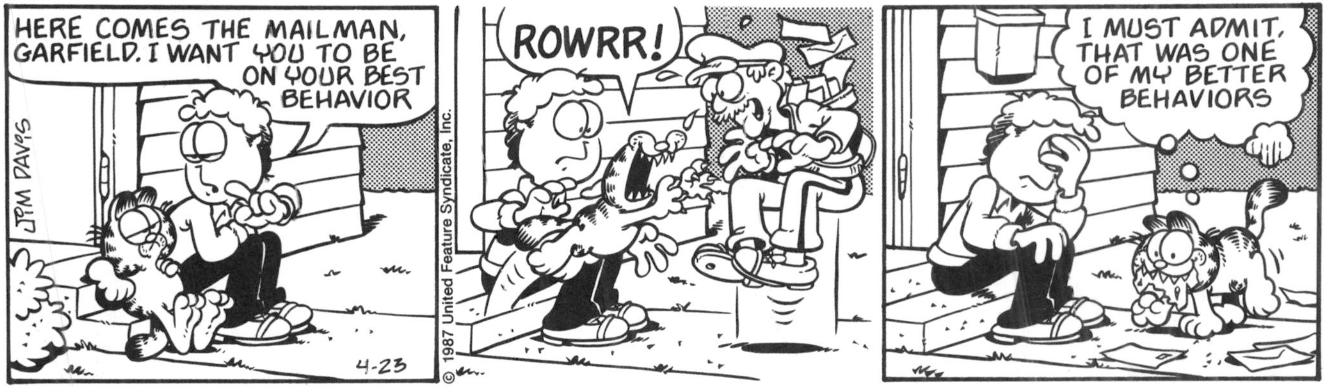
HERE COMES THE MAILMAN, GARFIELD. I WANT YOU TO BE ON YOUR BEST BEHAVIOR
JIM DAVIS
4-23
ROWRR!
© 1987 United Feature Syndicate, Inc.
I MUST ADMIT, THAT WAS ONE OF MY BETTER BEHAVIORS

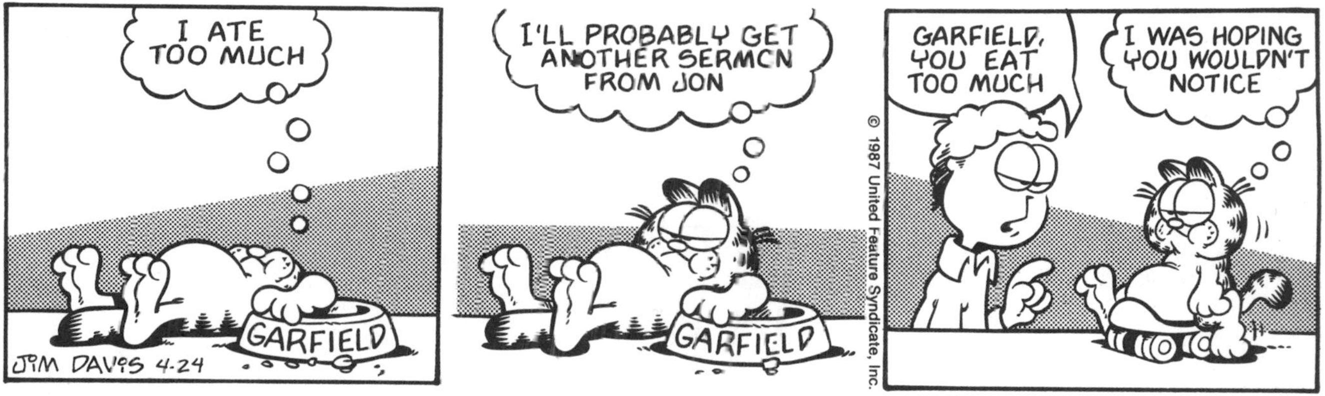
I ATE TOO MUCH
JIM DAVIS 4-24
GARFIELD
I'LL PROBABLY GET ANOTHER SERMON FROM JON
GARFIELD
© 1987 United Feature Syndicate, Inc.
GARFIELD, YOU EAT TOO MUCH
I WAS HOPING YOU WOULDN'T NOTICE

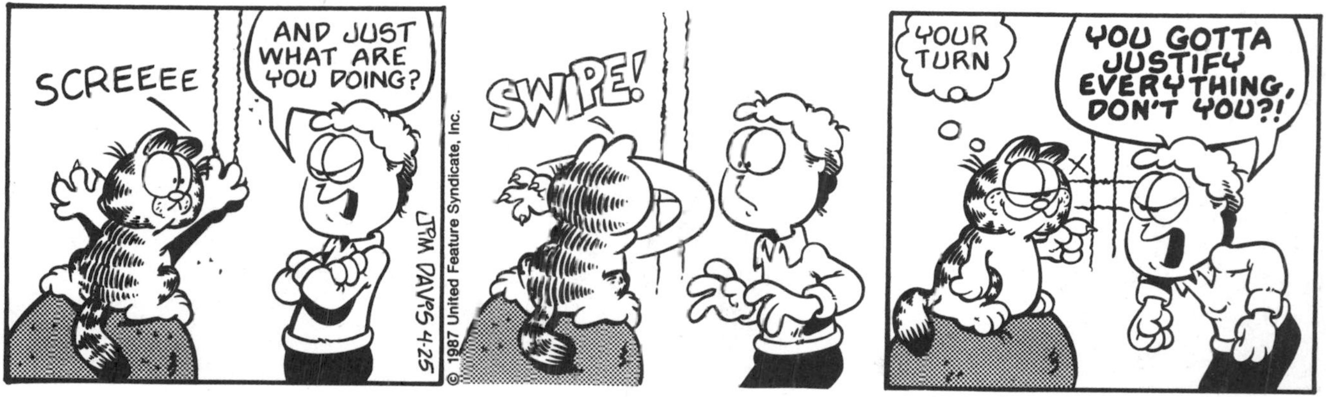
SCREEEE
AND JUST WHAT ARE YOU DOING?
JIM DAVIS 4-25
© 1987 United Feature Syndicate, Inc.
SWIPE!
YOUR TURN
YOU GOTTA JUSTIFY EVERYTHING, DON'T YOU?!

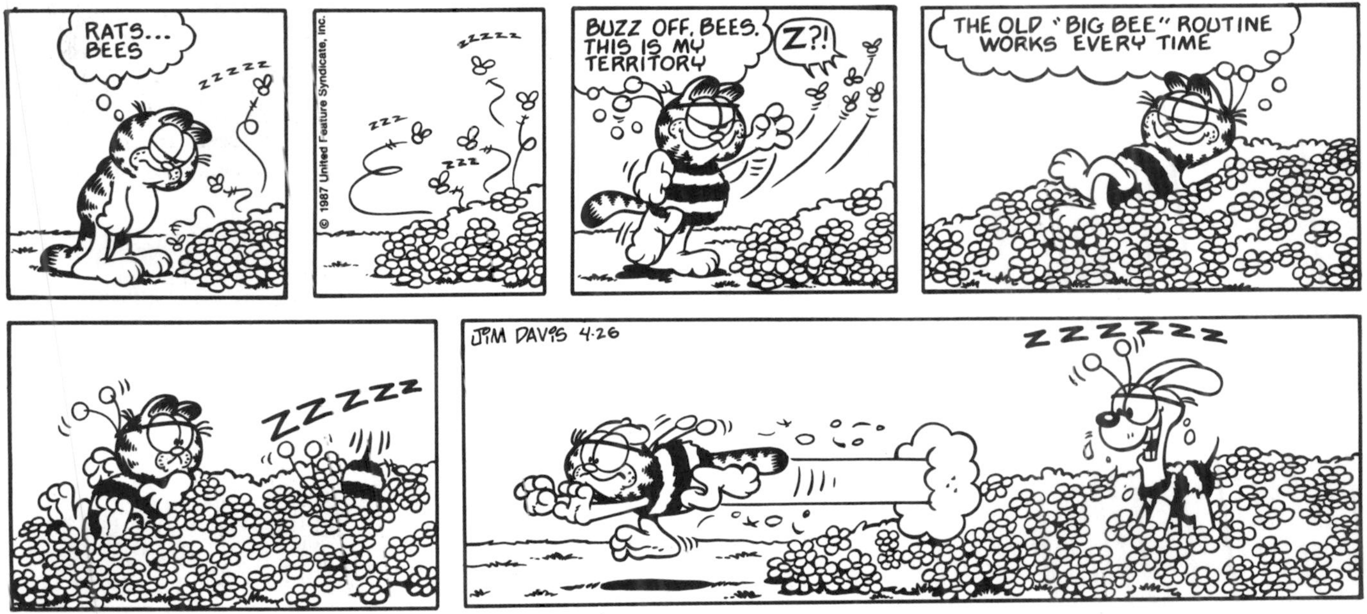
RATS... BEES
ZZZZZ
ZZZZZ
ZZZ
ZZZ
© 1987 United Feature Syndicate, Inc.
BUZZ OFF, BEES. THIS IS MY TERRITORY
Z?!
THE OLD "BIG BEE" ROUTINE WORKS EVERY TIME
ZZZZZ
JIM DAVIS 4·26
ZZZZZZZ

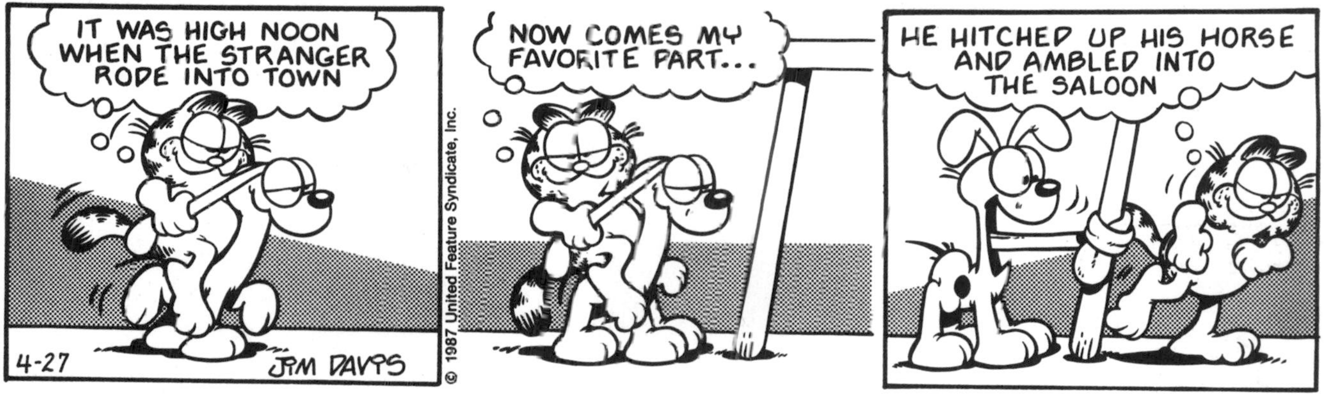
IT WAS HIGH NOON WHEN THE STRANGER RODE INTO TOWN
4-27
JIM DAVIS
© 1987 United Feature Syndicate, Inc.
NOW COMES MY FAVORITE PART...
HE HITCHED UP HIS HORSE AND AMBLED INTO THE SALOON

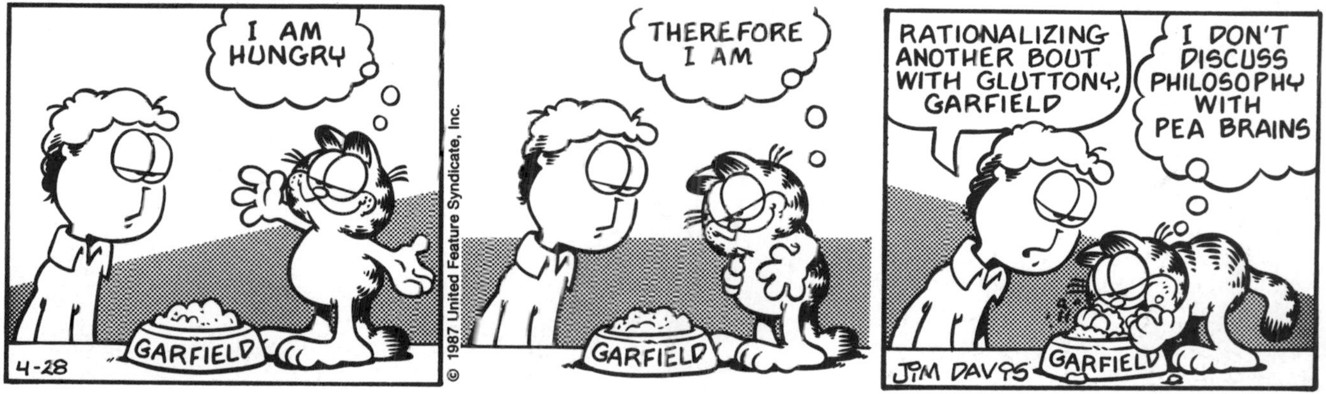
I AM HUNGRY
GARFIELD
4-28
© 1987 United Feature Syndicate, Inc.
THEREFORE I AM
GARFIELD
RATIONALIZING ANOTHER BOUT WITH GLUTTONY, GARFIELD
I DON'T DISCUSS PHILOSOPHY WITH PEA BRAINS
JIM DAVIS
GARFIELD

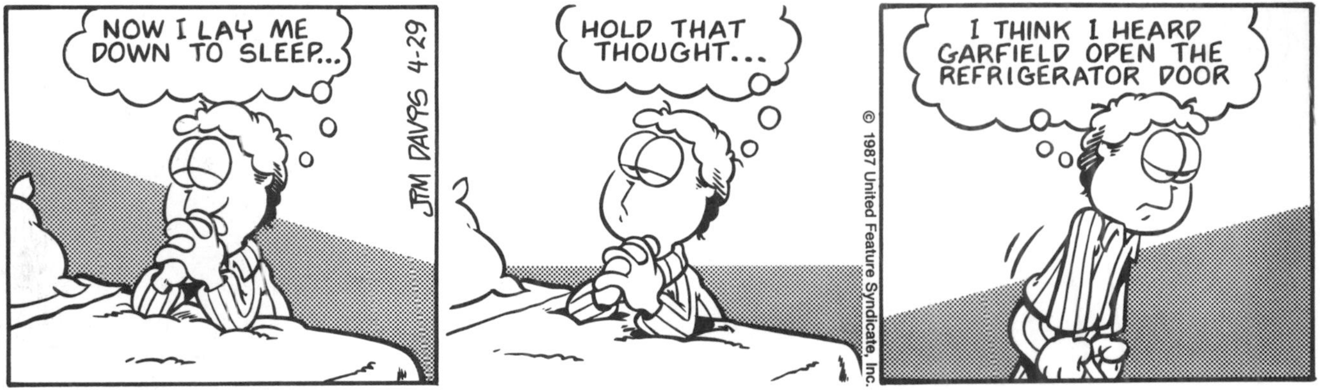
NOW I LAY ME DOWN TO SLEEP...
HOLD THAT THOUGHT...
I THINK I HEARD GARFIELD OPEN THE REFRIGERATOR DOOR
JIM DAVIS 4-29
© 1987 United Feature Syndicate, Inc.

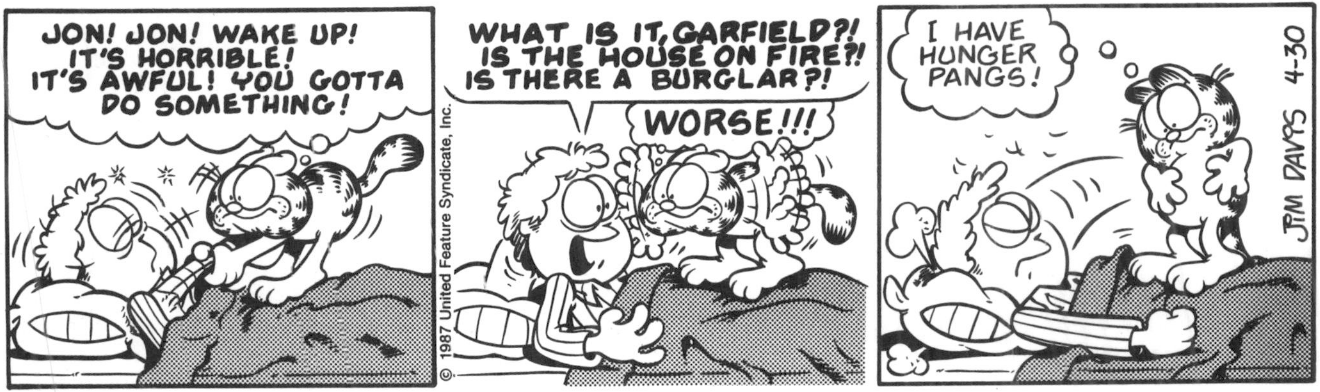
JON! JON! WAKE UP! IT'S HORRIBLE! IT'S AWFUL! YOU GOTTA DO SOMETHING!
WHAT IS IT, GARFIELD?! IS THE HOUSE ON FIRE?! IS THERE A BURGLAR?!
WORSE!!!
I HAVE HUNGER PANGS!
JIM DAVIS 4-30
© 1987 United Feature Syndicate, Inc.

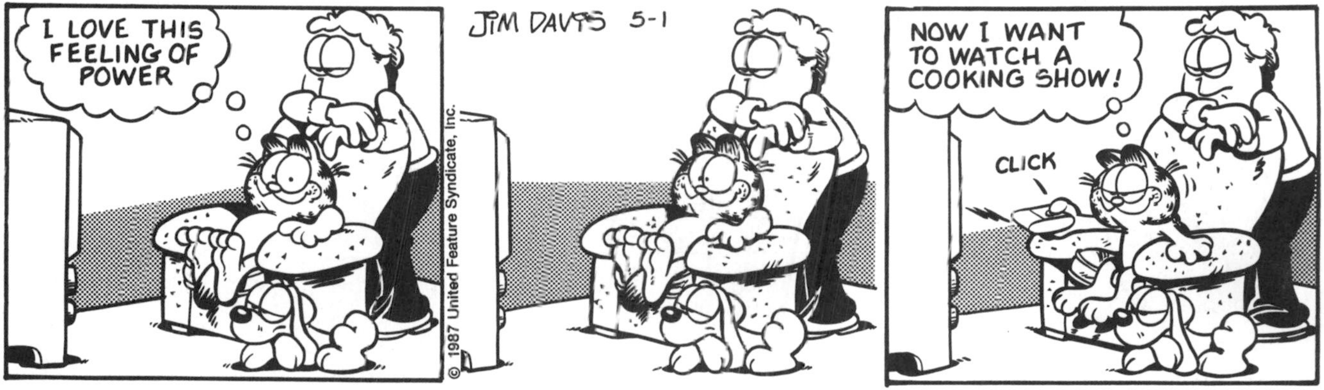
JIM DAVIS 5-1
I LOVE THIS FEELING OF POWER
NOW I WANT TO WATCH A COOKING SHOW!
CLICK
© 1987 United Feature Syndicate, Inc.

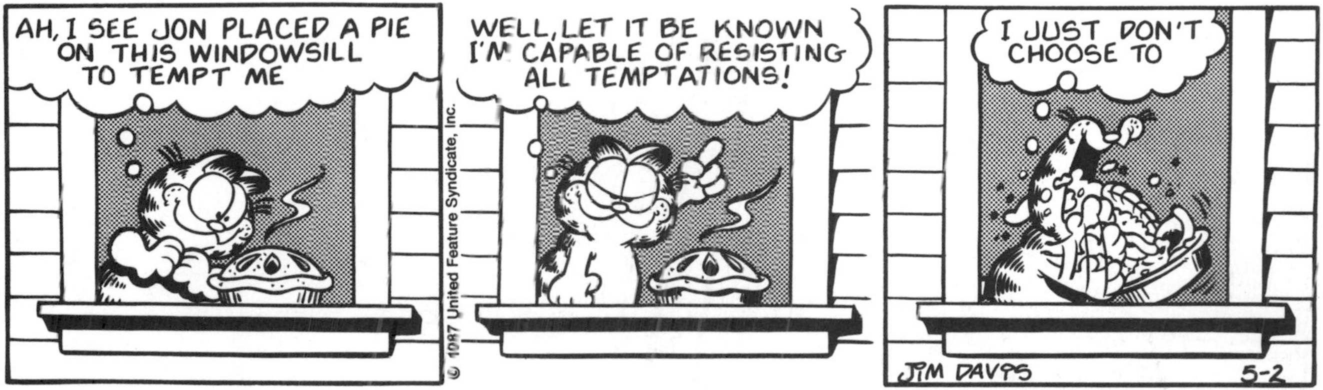
AH, I SEE JON PLACED A PIE ON THIS WINDOWSILL TO TEMPT ME
WELL, LET IT BE KNOWN I'M CAPABLE OF RESISTING ALL TEMPTATIONS!
I JUST DON'T CHOOSE TO
© 1987 United Feature Syndicate, Inc.
JIM DAVIS 5-2

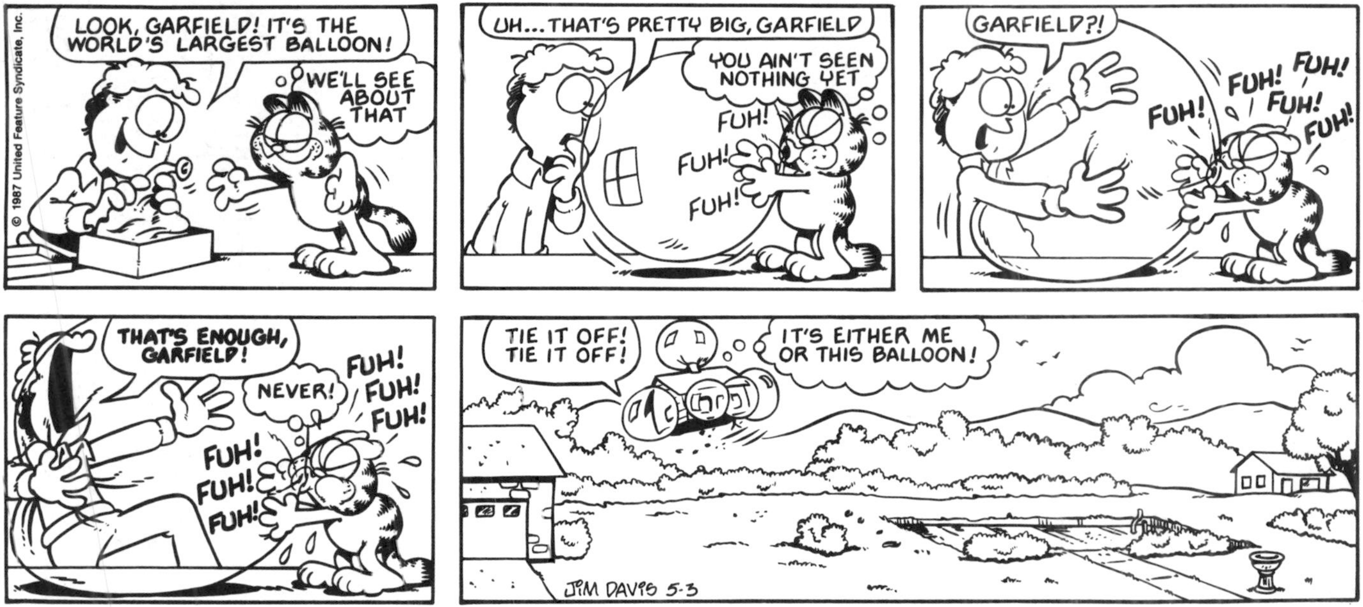
© 1987 United Feature Syndicate, Inc.
LOOK, GARFIELD! IT'S THE WORLD'S LARGEST BALLOON!
WE'LL SEE ABOUT THAT
UH... THAT'S PRETTY BIG, GARFIELD
YOU AIN'T SEEN NOTHING YET
FUH!
FUH!
FUH!
GARFIELD?!
FUH!
FUH!
FUH!
FUH!
FUH!
THAT'S ENOUGH, GARFIELD!
NEVER!
FUH!
FUH!
FUH!
FUH!
FUH!
FUH!
TIE IT OFF! TIE IT OFF!
IT'S EITHER ME OR THIS BALLOON!
JIM DAVIS 5-3

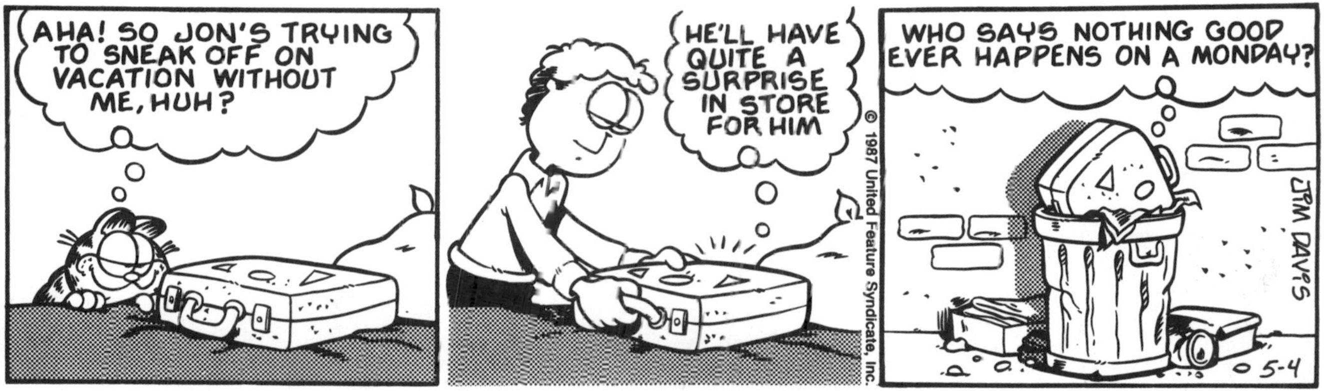
AHA! SO JON'S TRYING TO SNEAK OFF ON VACATION WITHOUT ME, HUH?
HE'LL HAVE QUITE A SURPRISE IN STORE FOR HIM
© 1987 United Feature Syndicate, Inc.
WHO SAYS NOTHING GOOD EVER HAPPENS ON A MONDAY?
JIM DAVIS
5-4

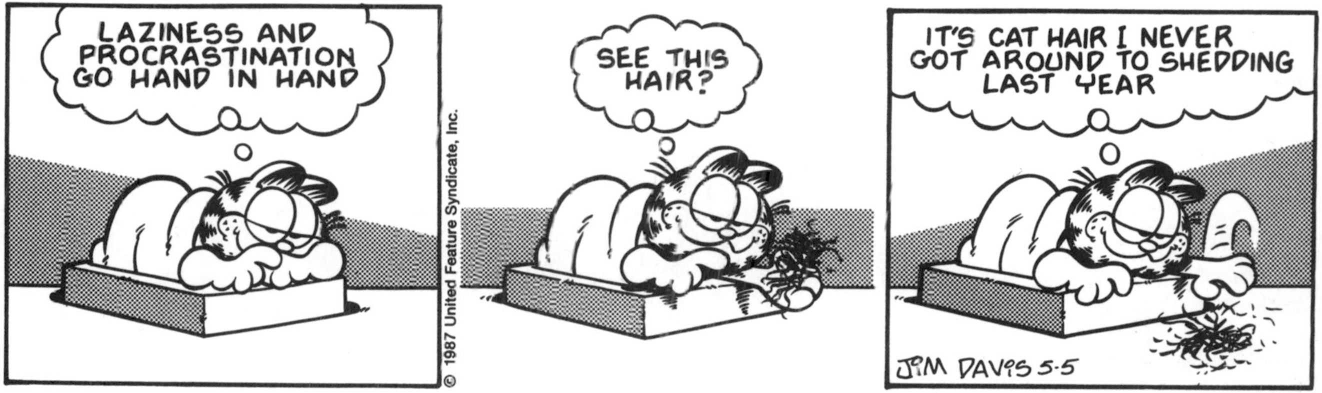
LAZINESS AND PROCRASTINATION GO HAND IN HAND
© 1987 United Feature Syndicate, Inc.
SEE THIS HAIR?
IT'S CAT HAIR I NEVER GOT AROUND TO SHEDDING LAST YEAR
JIM DAVIS 5-5

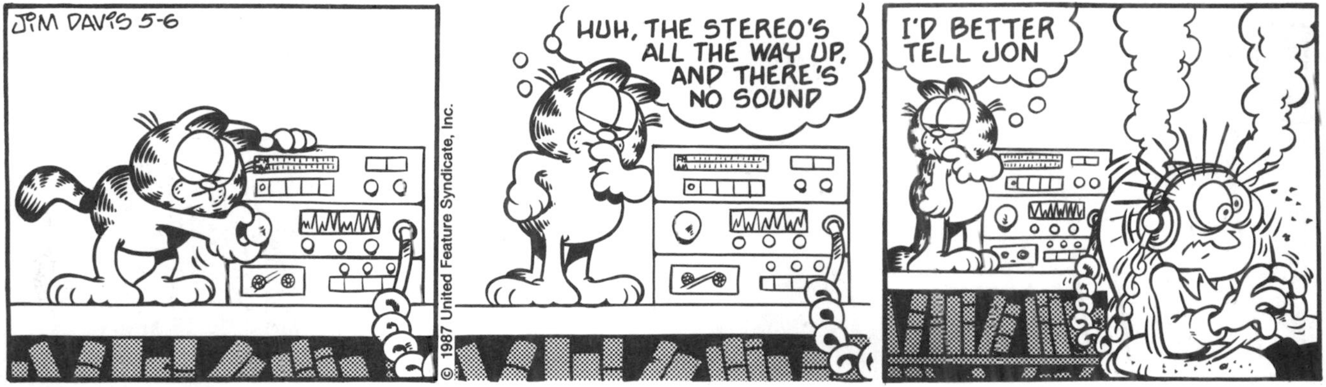
JIM DAVIS 5-6
© 1987 United Feature Syndicate, Inc.
HUH, THE STEREO'S ALL THE WAY UP, AND THERE'S NO SOUND
I'D BETTER TELL JON

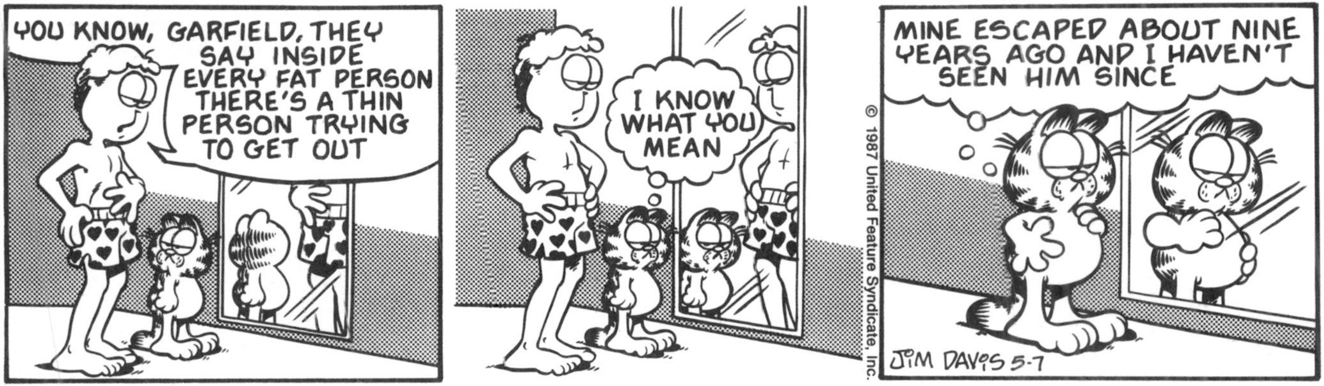
YOU KNOW, GARFIELD, THEY SAY INSIDE EVERY FAT PERSON THERE'S A THIN PERSON TRYING TO GET OUT
I KNOW WHAT YOU MEAN
© 1987 United Feature Syndicate, Inc.
MINE ESCAPED ABOUT NINE YEARS AGO AND I HAVEN'T SEEN HIM SINCE
JIM DAVIS 5-7

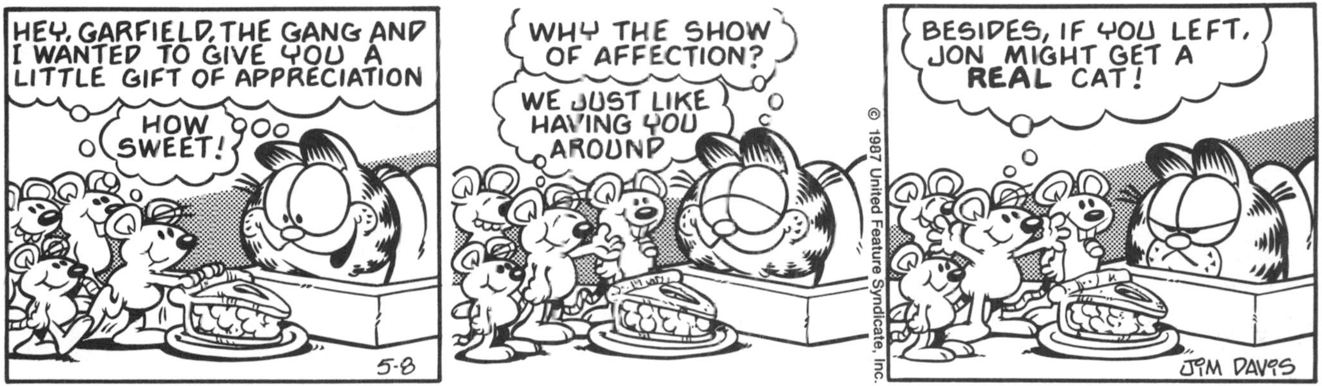
HEY, GARFIELD, THE GANG AND I WANTED TO GIVE YOU A LITTLE GIFT OF APPRECIATION
HOW SWEET!
5-8
WHY THE SHOW OF AFFECTION?
WE JUST LIKE HAVING YOU AROUND
© 1987 United Feature Syndicate, Inc.
BESIDES, IF YOU LEFT, JON MIGHT GET A **REAL** CAT!
JIM DAVIS

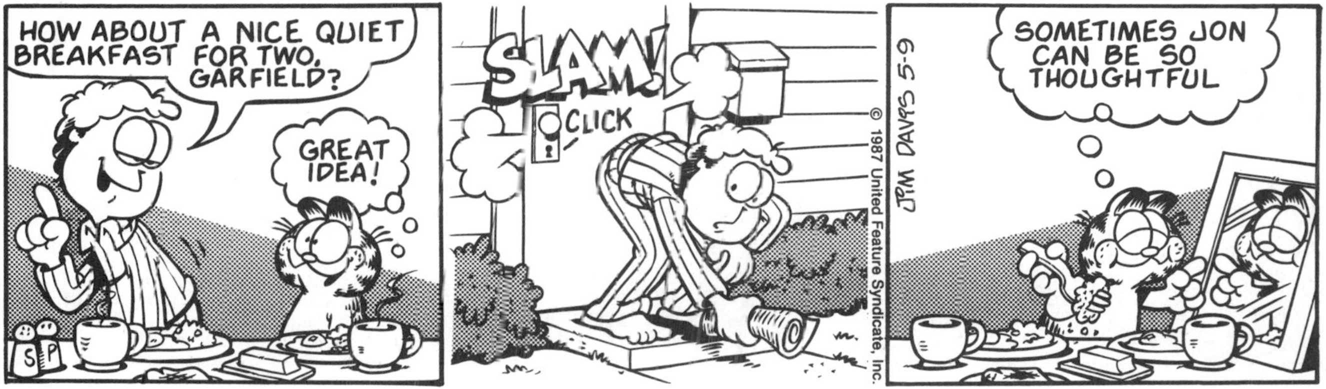
HOW ABOUT A NICE QUIET BREAKFAST FOR TWO, GARFIELD?
GREAT IDEA!
S
P
SLAM!
CLICK
© 1987 United Feature Syndicate, Inc.
JIM DAVIS 5-9
SOMETIMES JON CAN BE SO THOUGHTFUL

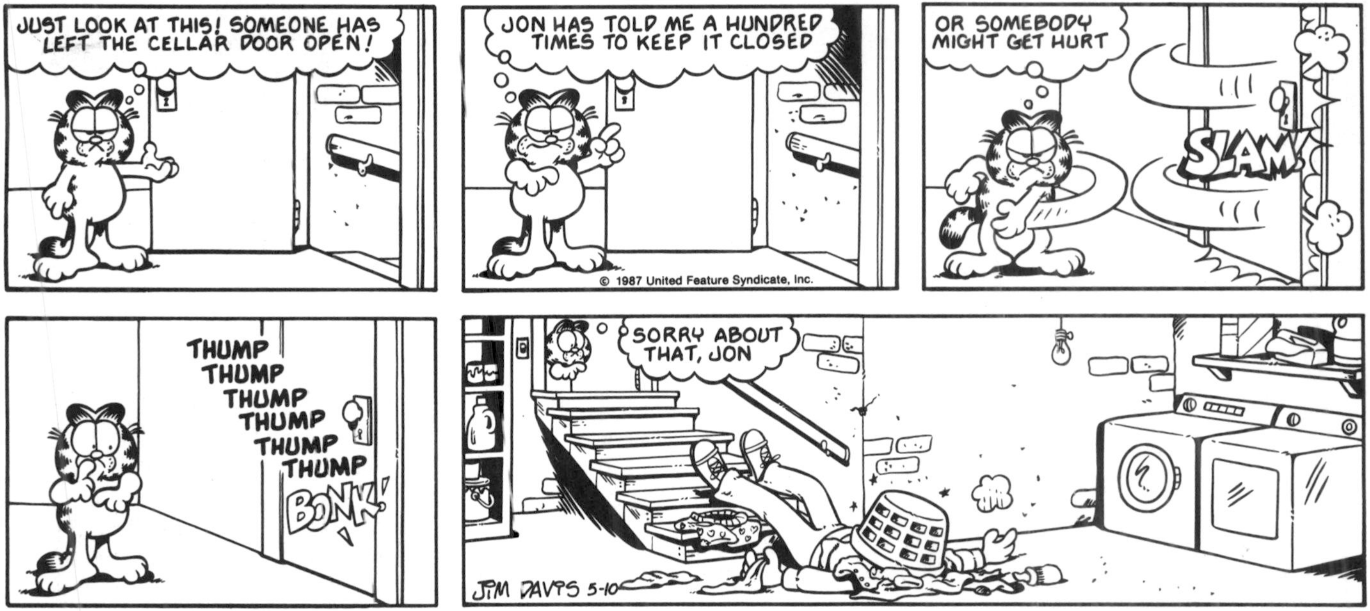

JUST LOOK AT THIS! SOMEONE HAS LEFT THE CELLAR DOOR OPEN!
JON HAS TOLD ME A HUNDRED TIMES TO KEEP IT CLOSED
© 1987 United Feature Syndicate, Inc.
OR SOMEBODY MIGHT GET HURT
SLAM!
THUMP
THUMP
THUMP
THUMP
THUMP
THUMP
BONK!
SORRY ABOUT THAT, JON
JIM DAVIS 5-10

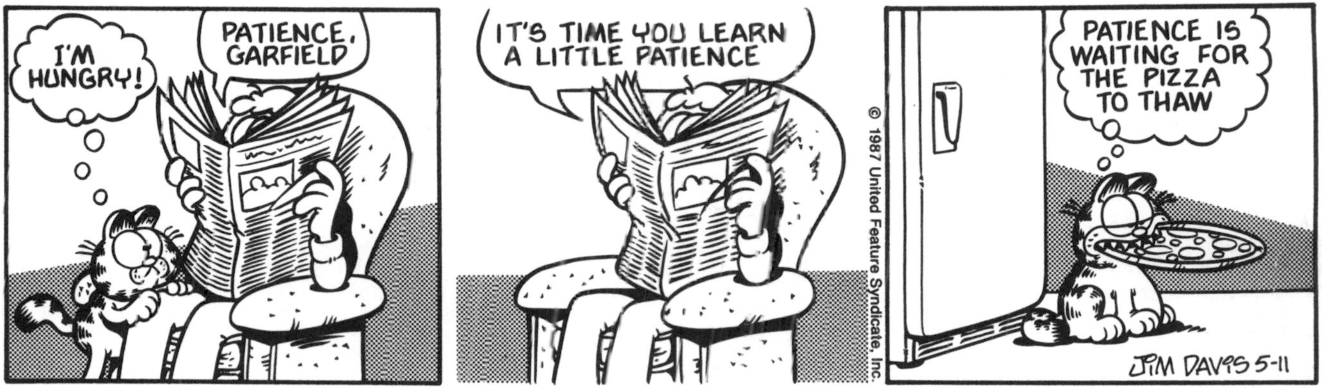
I'M HUNGRY!
PATIENCE, GARFIELD
IT'S TIME YOU LEARN A LITTLE PATIENCE
© 1987 United Feature Syndicate, Inc.
PATIENCE IS WAITING FOR THE PIZZA TO THAW
JIM DAVIS 5-11

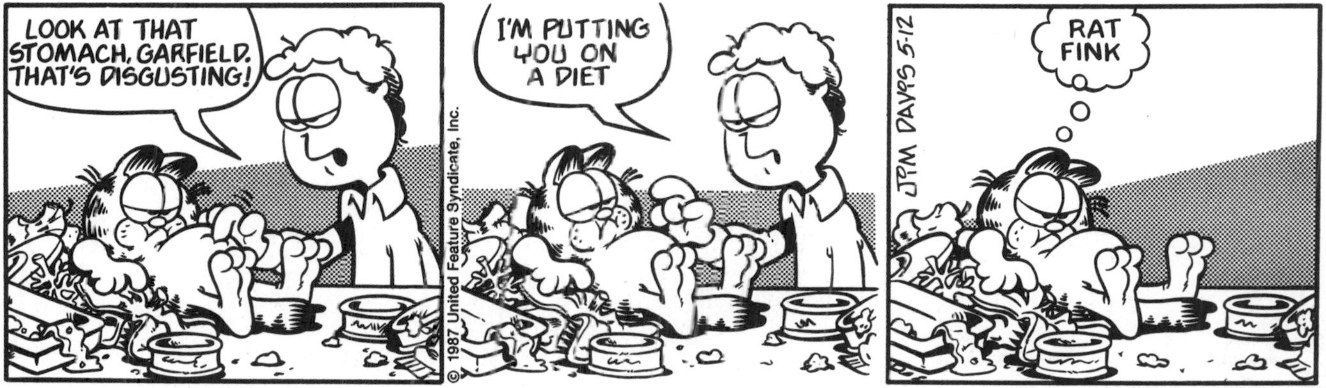
LOOK AT THAT STOMACH, GARFIELD. THAT'S DISGUSTING!
© 1987 United Feature Syndicate, Inc.
I'M PUTTING YOU ON A DIET
JIM DAVIS 5-12
RAT FINK

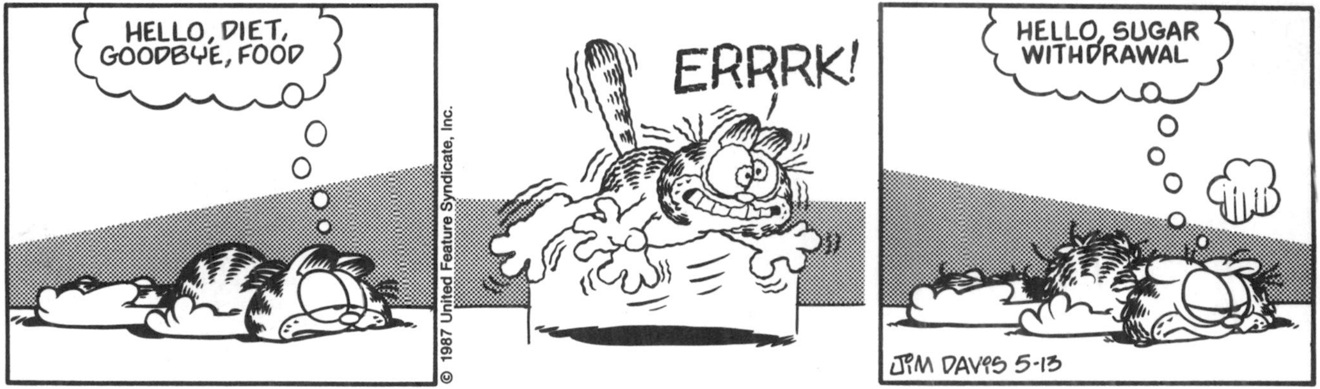
HELLO, DIET, GOODBYE, FOOD
ERRRK!
HELLO, SUGAR WITHDRAWAL
JIM DAVIS 5-13
© 1987 United Feature Syndicate, Inc.

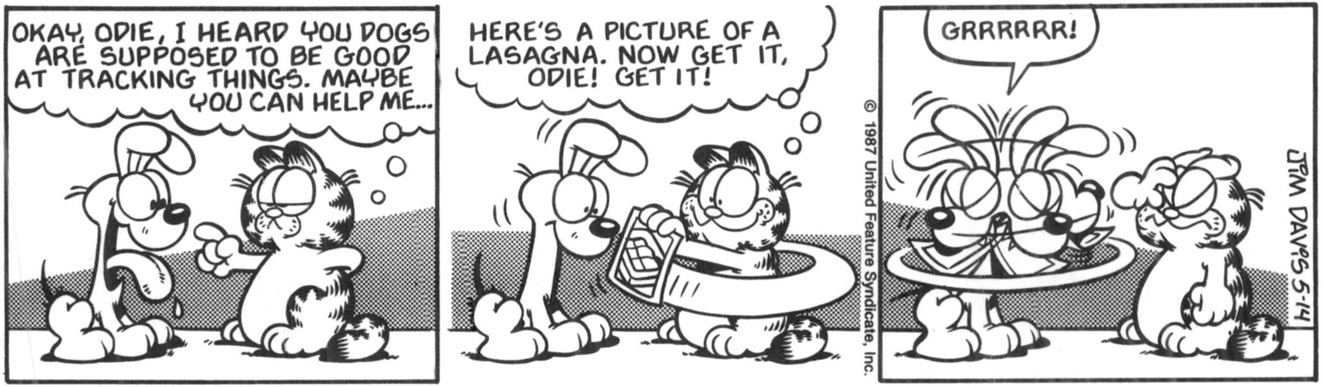
OKAY, ODIE, I HEARD YOU DOGS ARE SUPPOSED TO BE GOOD AT TRACKING THINGS. MAYBE YOU CAN HELP ME...
HERE'S A PICTURE OF A LASAGNA. NOW GET IT, ODIE! GET IT!
GRRRRRR!
JIM DAVIS 5-14
© 1987 United Feature Syndicate, Inc.

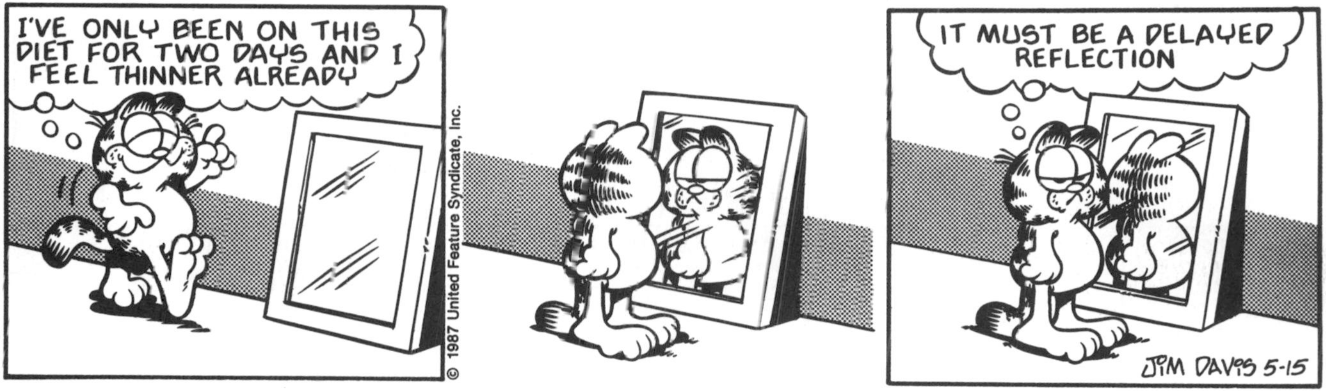
I'VE ONLY BEEN ON THIS DIET FOR TWO DAYS AND I FEEL THINNER ALREADY
IT MUST BE A DELAYED REFLECTION
© 1987 United Feature Syndicate, Inc.
JIM DAVIS 5-15

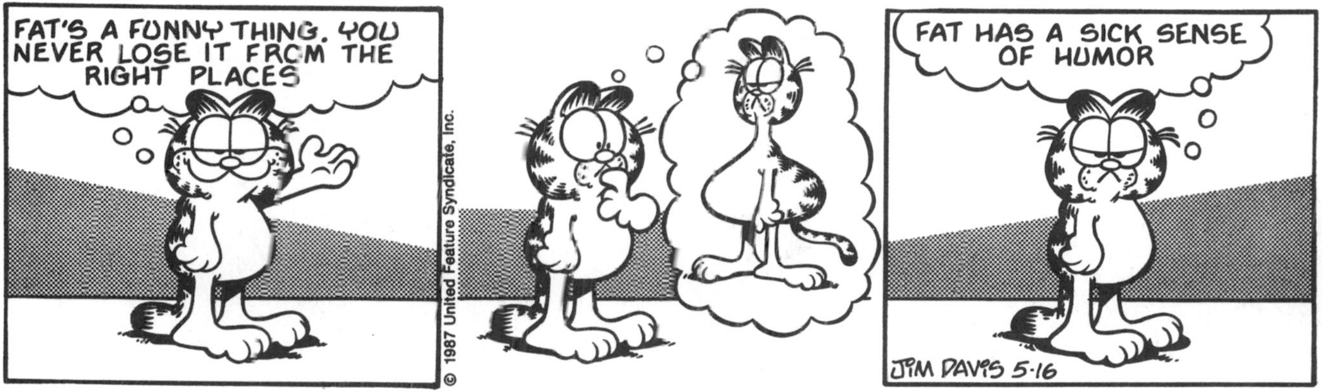
FAT'S A FUNNY THING. YOU NEVER LOSE IT FROM THE RIGHT PLACES
FAT HAS A SICK SENSE OF HUMOR
© 1987 United Feature Syndicate, Inc.
JIM DAVIS 5-16

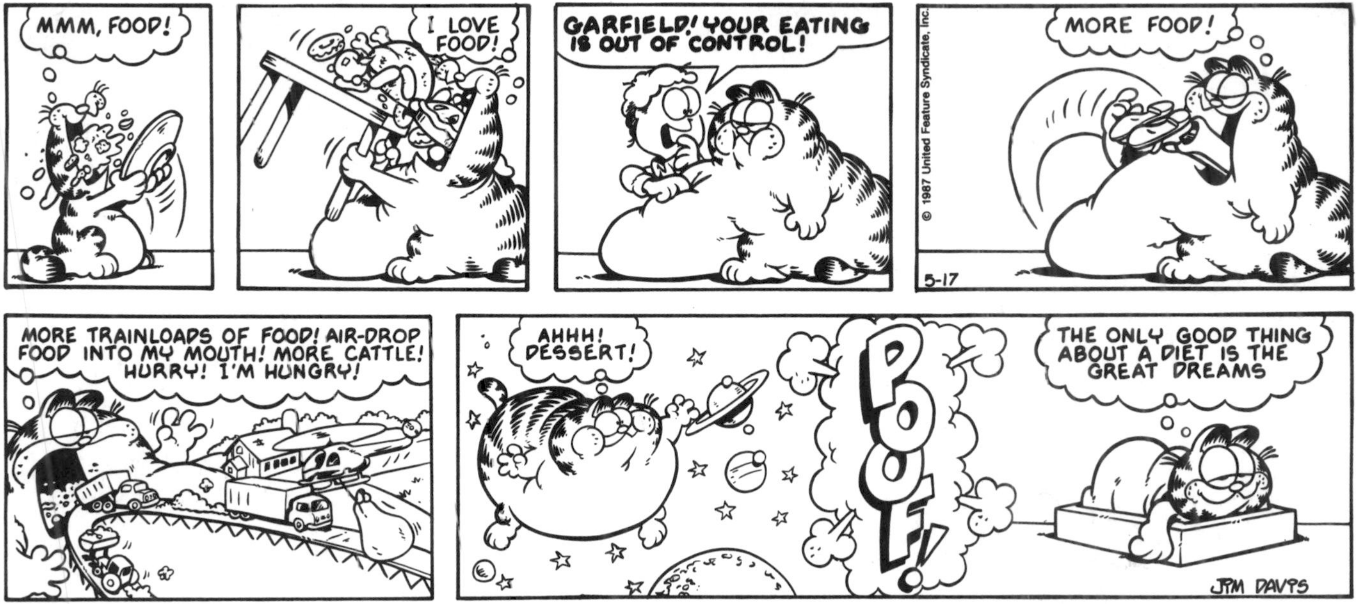
MMM, FOOD!
I LOVE FOOD!
GARFIELD! YOUR EATING IS OUT OF CONTROL!
MORE FOOD!
© 1987 United Feature Syndicate, Inc.
5-17
MORE TRAINLOADS OF FOOD! AIR-DROP FOOD INTO MY MOUTH! MORE CATTLE! HURRY! I'M HUNGRY!
AHHH! DESSERT!
POOF!
THE ONLY GOOD THING ABOUT A DIET IS THE GREAT DREAMS
JIM DAVIS

# HOW TO DRAW GARFIELD

RIGHT

WRONG

JIM DAVIS

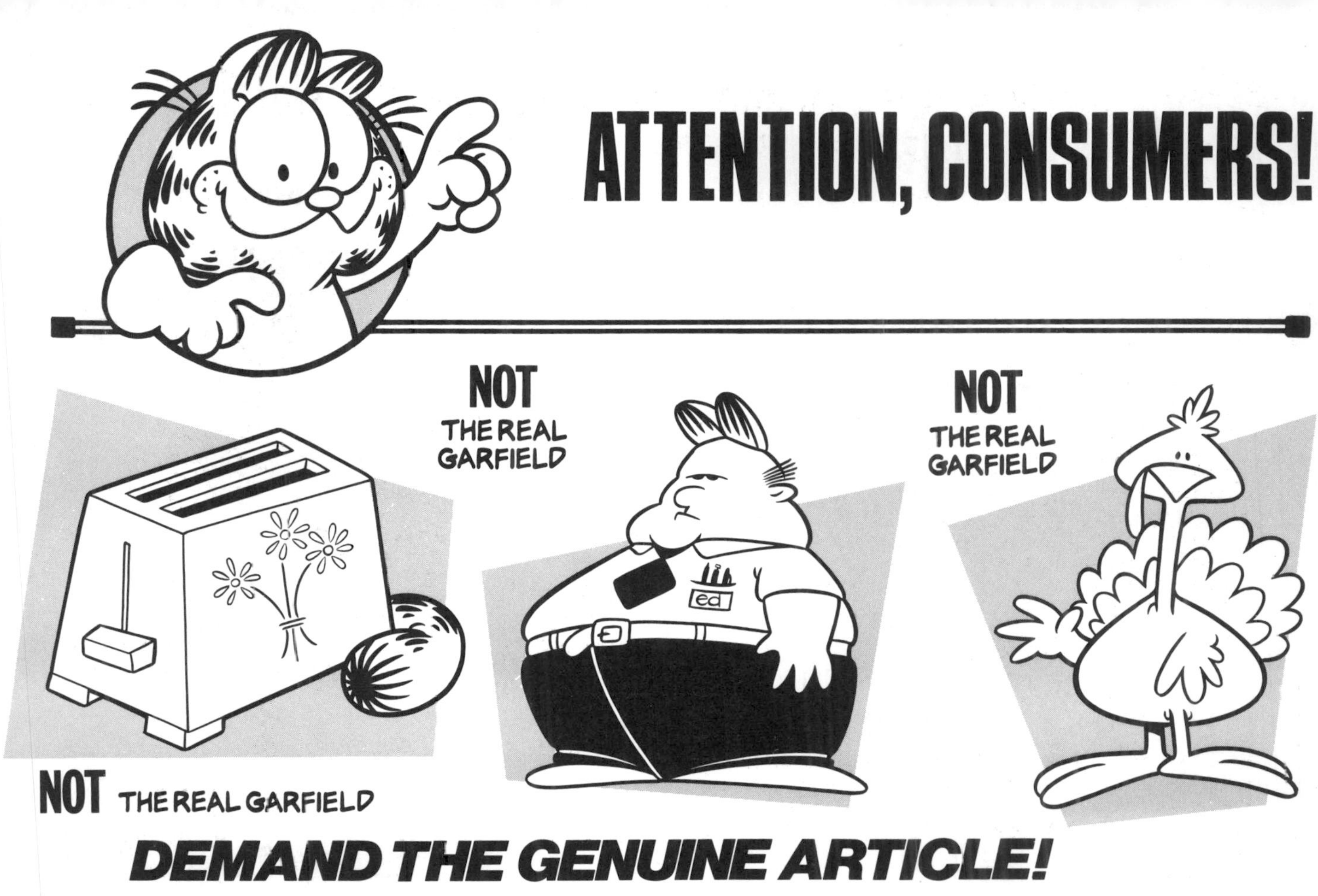
ATTENTION, CONSUMERS!
NOT THE REAL GARFIELD
ed
NOT THE REAL GARFIELD
NOT THE REAL GARFIELD
DEMAND THE GENUINE ARTICLE!

# HOW TO DRAW GARFIELD

RIGHT

WRONG

JIM DAVIS

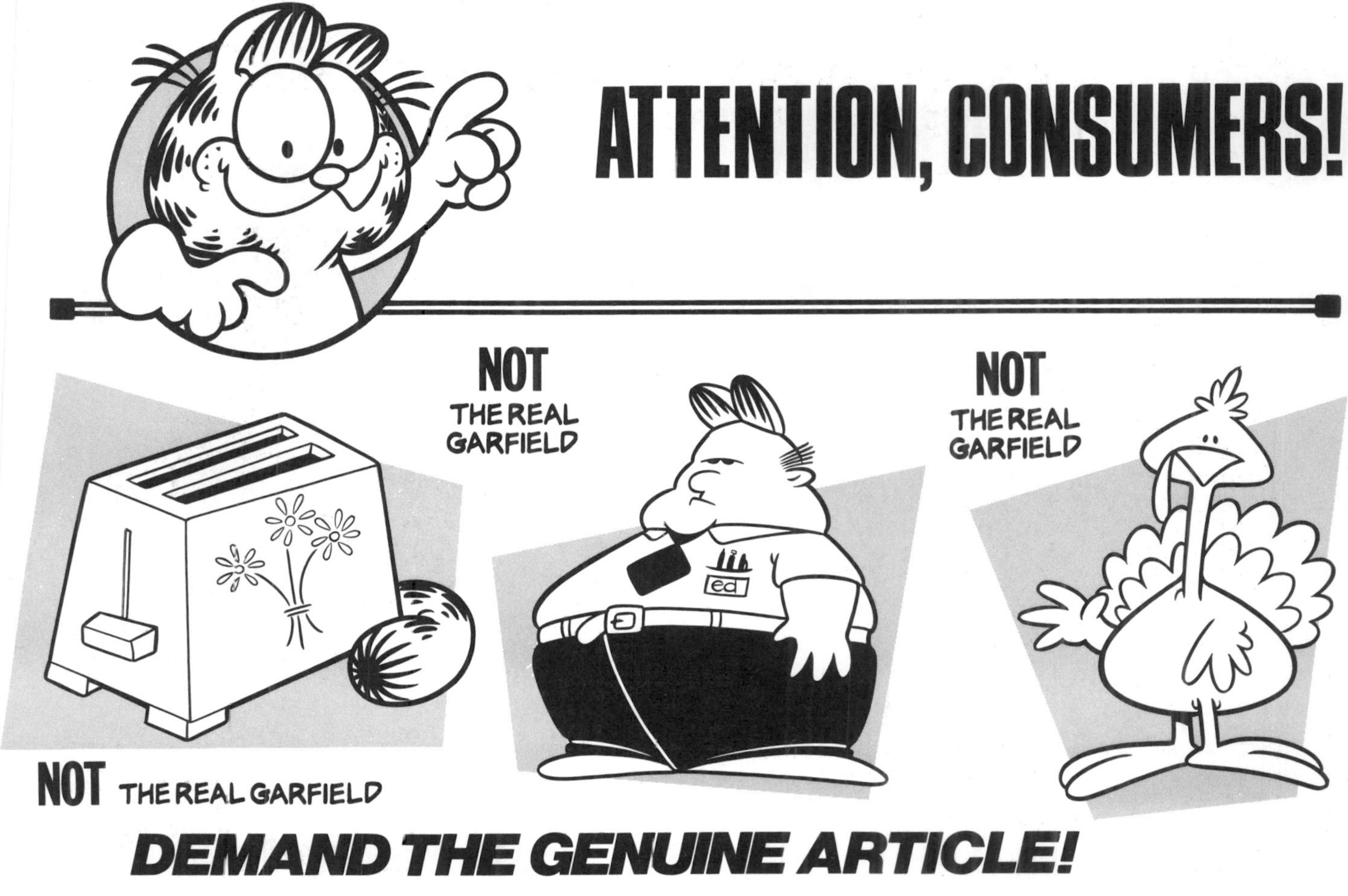
ATTENTION, CONSUMERS!
NOT THE REAL GARFIELD
NOT THE REAL GARFIELD
ed
NOT THE REAL GARFIELD
DEMAND THE GENUINE ARTICLE!